WORLD BANK WORKING PAPER NO. 188

The Education System in Swaziland

Training and Skills Development for Shared Growth and Competitiveness

Mmantsetsa Marope

Africa Region Human Development Department

THE WORLD BANK
Washington, D.C.

Copyright © 2010
The International Bank for Reconstruction and Development / The World Bank
1818 H Street, N.W.
Washington, D.C. 20433, U.S.A.
All rights reserved
Manufactured in the United States of America
First Printing: April 2010

 Printed on recycled paper

1 2 3 4   13 12 11 10

World Bank Working Papers are published to communicate the results of the Bank's work to the development community with the least possible delay. The manuscript of this paper therefore has not been prepared in accordance with the procedures appropriate to formally-edited texts. Some sources cited in this paper may be informal documents that are not readily available.

The findings, interpretations, and conclusions expressed herein are those of the author(s) and do not necessarily reflect the views of the International Bank for Reconstruction and Development/The World Bank and its affiliated organizations, or those of the Executive Directors of The World Bank or the governments they represent.

The World Bank does not guarantee the accuracy of the data included in this work. The boundaries, colors, denominations, and other information shown on any map in this work do not imply any judgment on the part of The World Bank of the legal status of any territory or the endorsement or acceptance of such boundaries.

The material in this publication is copyrighted. Copying and/or transmitting portions or all of this work without permission may be a violation of applicable law. The International Bank for Reconstruction and Development/The World Bank encourages dissemination of its work and will normally grant permission promptly to reproduce portions of the work.

For permission to photocopy or reprint any part of this work, please send a request with complete information to the Copyright Clearance Center, Inc., 222 Rosewood Drive, Danvers, MA 01923, USA, Tel: 978-750-8400, Fax: 978-750-4470, www.copyright.com.

All other queries on rights and licenses, including subsidiary rights, should be addressed to the Office of the Publisher, The World Bank, 1818 H Street NW, Washington, DC 20433, USA, Fax: 202-522-2422, email: pubrights@worldbank.org.

ISBN: 978-0-8213-8324-7
eISBN: 978-0-8213-8361-2
ISSN: 1726-5878   DOI: 10.1596/978-0-8213-8324-7

Library of Congress Cataloging-in-Publication Data has been requested.

Contents

Foreword ix
Acknowledgments xi
Acronyms and Abbreviations xii
Executive Summary xv
    Introduction xv
    Strategic Orientation xv
    Coverage xvi
    Key Conclusions and Recommendations xvii

1. Swaziland's Growth and Competitiveness in a Global Context 1
    Introduction 1
    Current Performance against Vision 2022 and PRSAP Goals 2

2. Early Childhood Care and Development (ECCD) 14
    Introduction 14
    Why Should Swaziland Invest in ECCD? 15
    Policy Orientation of ECCD 17
    Structure and Nature of ECCD Provision 17
    Access and Equity 18
    Quality and Equity 19
    Efficiency 23
    Conclusion 24

3. General Education and Training 25
    Introduction 25
    Rationale for Improving GET 25
    Policy Orientation and Recent Subsector Developments 26
    Equity of Access and Attainment 26
    Education Quality and Equity 35
    Internal Efficiency 50
    Conclusion 53

4. Technical and Vocational Education, Training, and Skills Development ... 55
    Introduction 55
    Policy Orientation 55
    Legal Framework 56
    Organizational and Management Framework 56
    Access and Equity 58

    Range and Levels of Provision 58
    Access and equity 66
    Quality of TVETSD 67
    Relevance 75
    System Efficiency 79
    Conclusion 81

5. Higher Education 83
    Introduction 83
    Historical Overview 84
    Policy Orientation 84
    Institutional and Management Framework 85
    Accountability 87
    Equity and Access 87
    Quality and Equity 92
    Relevance 100
    Efficiency 102
    Conclusion 105

6. Cost and Financing of Education, Training, and Skills Development 107
    Introduction 107
    Government Finances 107
    Public Spending on the ETSDS 108
    Public Spending on the Sector in a Subregional Perspective 110
    Private Spending on ETSDS 110
    External Financing of the Sector 112
    Share of Public Spending by Subsector 112
    Unit Cost 114
    Intra-Subsector Allocation and Unit Cost 114
    Equity of Public Spending 124
    Conclusion 125

7. Conclusions and Recommendations 128
    Introduction 128
    Strategic Orientation 128
    Conclusions 129

References 140

Appendix: Applicable Practices and Lessons from the Republic of Korea and Singapore 146

Tables

Table 1: Hierarchy of Challenges by Subsector xviii
Table 1.1: Proxy Indicators of Quality of Life for Swazis Relative to other AMICs 6
Table 1.2: Swaziland's Relative Knowledge Economy Readiness 11
Table 2.1: The State of Swaziland's Children and Implications for ECCD 15
Table 2.2: Perceived Needs to be Addressed by ECCD Programs...................................... 17
Table 2.3: Number of Pre-School Inspections by MoE 23
Table 3.1: Recent Trends in Primary and Secondary Education Enrollment by Gender 27
Table 3.2: Sebenta Enrollment.. 28
Table 3.3: Enrollment by Level and Year 28
Table 3.4: Enrollment Rates in Selected Countries (2006) 30
Table 3.5: OLS Regressions on Enrollment (ages 6-20), Attainment (ages 20-24) 34
Table 3.6: Distribution of Primary School Teachers by Qualification and Region (%).. 36
Table 3.7: Proportion of Secondary School Teachers by Qualification and Region (%).. 37
Table 3.8: Employer Ranking Importance of Employee Basic Skills 40
Table 3.9: Primary Certification Examination Pass Rates by Level (%) 43
Table 3.10: Junior Secondary Examination Pass Rates by Level (%) 44
Table 3.11: Distribution of Learning Outcomes by Region.. 44
Table 3.12: Average Pupil Performance on SACMEQII Reading and Mathematics Tests 45
Table 3.13: OLS Regression on SACMEQ Reading and Mathematics Scores.................. 50
Table 3.14: Repetition Rates 2006 and 2007 (%).. 50
Table 3.15 Percentage of Pupils who are Repeaters in the Region.................................... 51
Table 4.1: Examples of Programs Offered by Line Ministries 58
Table 4.2: Overview of Publicly Funded TVETSD Provision (2006 or most recent year) 59
Table 4.3: Summary of Public Provision by Duration 59
Table 4.4: Examined Trainees as Indicative Enrollment in Prevocational Programs 60
Table 4.5: SCOT Enrollment by Year of Study, 2000–2006.. 62
Table 4.6: Prevalence of Firm-based Training as a Percentage of Trained Workers 64
Table 4.7: Instructor Qualifications for Selected Institutions... 68
Table 4.8: SCOT Percentage Pass Rates by Year and Faculty 72
Table 4.9: VOCTIM Percentage Pass by Year 72
Table 4.10: Participation and Pass Rates in Trade Tests 2004–2006 73
Table 4.11: Examination Pass Rates in Prevocational Programs 2004–2007 (%) 73
Table 4.12: Trade Testing—Participation and Estimated Fee Income, 2006 80
Table 5.1: Tertiary Education Enrollment SADC MICs and in Selected Regions for Selected Years... 87
Table 5.2: Enrollment by Faculty, 2000–2007 88
Table 5.3: Share of Private Tertiary Education 2004 92
Table 5.4: Research Allocations in SZL Million 98
Table 5.5: Research Activities Not Financed by UNISWA Research Board, 2006/07 99
Table 5.6: Students per Staff by Faculty, 2002/03 to 2007/08...103

Table 6.1: Government Revenue 2000/01 to 2009/10 107
Table 6.2: Total Government Expenditure 2000/01 to 2009/10 108
Table 6.3: Public Spending on Education as a Share of GDP and TGE (2000–2009) 109
Table 6.4: Capital Spending on ETSDS (2000–2009) 110
Table 6.5: Public and Private Financing of ETSDS (2007) 111
Table 6.6: Public Recurrent Unit Cost by Level of ETSDS (2007) 112
Table 6.7: Financing Details for Primary Education (2007) 115
Table 6.8: Financing Details for Secondary Schools (2007) 118
Table 6.9: Financing Details for TVETSD—SCOT and VOCTIM (2007) 120
Table 6.10: Financing Details for Public Teacher Education (2007) 121
Table 6.11: Financing Details for the University (2007) 122
Table 7.1: Key Recommendations in Sequential Order 134

Figures

Figure 1.1: Swaziland's Annual Real GDP Growth Rate in Perspective 1
Figure 1.2: Swaziland's HDI in Regional Perspective 4
Figure 1.3: Swaziland's HDI Relative to GDP Per Capita PPP in US$ 4
Figure 1.4: HIV Prevalence by Age Group 7
Figure 1.5: Impact of HIV/AIDS on Human Capital 8
Figure 1.6: Skills, Technology Absorption and Growth 12
Figure 2.1: Rates of Return to Human Capital Investment Across all Ages 14
Figure 2.2: Institutional Landscape of ECCD Providers 18
Figure 3.1: Comparative Long Range Educational Attainment 27
Figure 3.2: Entry and Exit Points within the National Education and Training
    System 29
Figure 3.3: School Enrollment Rate by Gender 31
Figure 3.4: Enrollment Rate by Grade and Location 31
Figure 3.5: Educational Attainment of 15 to 19 Year Olds by Location 32
Figure 3.6: Enrollment Rate by Region 32
Figure 3.7: Enrollment Rates by Income Groups by SES 33
Figure 3.8: Attainment Profile of Individuals Aged 15-19 by SES 34
Figure 3.9: Kernel Density Curve for Swaziland, Lesotho and South Africa,
    SACMEQII Reading Scores 45
Figure 3.10: Kernel Density Curve for Swaziland, Lesotho and South Africa,
    SACMEQII Mathematics Scores 46
Figure 3.11: Kernel Density Curve for Reading Scores of Urban and Rural
    Learners 46
Figure 3.12: Kernel Density Curve for Mathematics Scores of Urban and Rural
    Learners 47
Figure 3.13: Kernel Density Curve for Reading Scores by Region 47
Figure 3.14: Kernel Density Curve for Mathematics Scores by Region 48
Figure 3.15: Kernel Density Curve for Reading Scores by SES Group 48
Figure 3.16: Kernel Density Curve for Mathematics Scores by SES Group 49
Figure 3.17: Retention and Dropping Out by Age 52
Figure 3.18: Enrollment and Attainment Patterns by Age 52

Figure 4.1: Structure of Swaziland's TVETSD Sector 57
Figure 4.2: VOCTIM Total Enrollment 1995–2007 61
Figure 4.3: VOCTIM Enrollment by Department 2000–2007 61
Figure 4.4: SCOT Total Enrollment 2000–2006 62
Figure 4.5: Enrollment in Rural Education Centers 63
Figure 4.6: Intake, Enrollment and Completion in Apprenticeship Training 1997 to 2007 65
Figure 4.7: Trade Test Results in Selected Occupations 2004–2006 73
Figure 5.1: UNISWA Organizational and Management Structure 86
Figure 5.2: Admission Rates as a % of Qualified Applicants 88
Figure 5.3: Total Enrollment by Faculty 2000/01–2007/08 89
Figure 5.4: Total Enrollment by Gender, and Degrees Awarded 1992–2007 90
Figure 5.5: Percent of Female of Total Enrollment by Faculty, 2007/08 90
Figure 5.6: Income Quintiles of UNISWA Student's Households, 2007 91
Figure 5.7: Staff Qualifications by Citizenship, 2006/07 93
Figure 5.8: Academic Staff by Rank and Gender, 2007/08 94
Figure 5.9: Female Teachers in Percentage of Total 2007/08 94
Figure 5.10: Percentage of Swazi Staff by Rank, 2006/07 95
Figure 5.11: Average Space per Student by Campus (1999–2005) 95
Figure 5.12: Use Factor of Teaching Spaces by Type 96
Figure 5.13: Average Completion Index by Faculty, 2000–2007 97
Figure 5.14: Number and Amount of Funded Research Projects 2003/4 to 2006/7 98
Figure 5.15: Total Enrollment by Faculty 2000/01–2007/08 100
Figure 5.16: IDE Enrollment by Field 2007/08 101
Figure 5.17: Repetition Rates by Faculty and Year, 1999–2006 102
Figure 5.18: Actual Class Sizes at the Kwaluseni Campus, 2008 103
Figure 5.19: Nonacademic to Academic Staff Ratios for Selected African Countries .. 104
Figure 6.1: Education Spending in Real Terms in the National Context 109
Figure 6.2: Subregional Proportions of GDP over GDP per capita PPP Allocated to Education 111
Figure 6.3: Fees Charged by ECCD Centers 113
Figure 6.4: Swaziland's Primary Education Unit Cost in a Regional Perspective 116
Figure 6.5: Secondary Education Unit Cost in a Regional Context 119
Figure 6.6: UNISWA Unit Within a Sub-regional Context 123
Figure 6.7: Higher Education Unit Cost by Population Size 123
Figure 6.8: Fiscal Incidence of Education Spending 2006–2007 125

Boxes

Box 1.1: The role of ETSD in Growth Acceleration, Social Equity, and
    Competitiveness 9
Box 2.1: Benefits of ECCD Programs 16
Box 3.1: Labor Market and Workplace Changes already Evident in Swaziland 39
Box 3.2: Skills and Competencies for Consideration in Curricula 39
Box 4.1: Scotland—Occupational Standards for TVETSD Instructor 69
Box 4.2: Purchaser Provider Financing Model for TVETSD 70
Box 4.3: Training Through Production 71

Foreword

In 1999, Swaziland articulated a long-term and broad development reform framework in the form of Vision 2022. Since then, several instruments have been developed to give effect to the Vision. The latest of these is the Poverty Reduction Strategy and Action Plan (PRSAP) of 2007. Its overarching goal is to accelerate shared growth and its ultimate outcome is improved quality of life for all Swazis. This goal and, the outcome are to be pursued against formidable challenges of endemic poverty and the highest HIV/AIDS prevalence rate in the world. Among others, the Government has underscored the critical role of the Education, Training and Skills Development Sector (ETSDS) in contributing to the attainment of shared growth and enhanced quality of life for all. However, the adequacy of the ETSDS in playing this expected role had hitherto not been fully analyzed.

We are pleased to jointly present in this report, key findings and recommendations of an analysis of the adequacy of the current ETSDS to effectively make its expected development contribution. The analysis was jointly undertaken by the Government of The Kingdom of Swaziland and the World Bank. It comprehensively covers all levels of the sector, from early child care and development to higher education, including its cost and financing issues.

In addition to the national development reform framework, this analysis derives its strategic orientation from two premises that further point to the central role of the ETSDS in Swaziland's development. The first premise is that because Swaziland is not natural resource-rich, the acceleration of its growth and global competitiveness will most likely be knowledge and technology-driven. The second premise is that because Swaziland currently has limited internal growth poles, its immediate growth strategy needs to focus on harvesting both national and regional opportunities. Among these regional opportunities is the reality that notwithstanding the global economic downturn, Swaziland is surrounded by fast growing natural resource-rich countries— Botswana, Namibia, South Africa, Angola, Mozambique—with acute skills shortages. Swaziland may therefore consider as its niche area, the export of skilled labor first to its neighbors and ultimately to the world. Along similar lines as the Irish development experience, Swaziland's immediate to intermediate gains would be remittances and the refinement of technical capacities of its exported labor. Its long-term benefit would be the development impact of the brain circulation which will provide the technical leadership required to spearhead knowledge and technology-driven growth.

The analysis concludes that the current ETSDS is inadequate to supply the quality, mix and threshold of skills required to effectively spearhead knowledge and technology driven shared growth. Key weaknesses pertain to poor strategic grounding, low access especially beyond primary education, inequity of access and outcomes in favor of the nonpoor, acute resource inefficiencies, doubtful development relevance and insufficient delivery capacity, including capacity to respond to HIV/AIDS.

The report proposes prioritized actions for redressing identified weaknesses. It acknowledges that the financing of proposed reforms will be a challenge, especially in the context of global financial crisis and the limited external financial support for the sector. It is expected that the sector reform program emanating from this analysis may be used to leverage some of the much-needed external financing. These constraints notwithstanding, diligent implementation of recommended sector reforms would put Swaziland on track toward using its ETSDS as an effective tool for supporting the national development reform agenda.

Honorable Wilson Ntshangase
Minister of Education
The Kingdom of Swaziland

Yaw Ansu
Director: Human Development Department
Africa Region

Acknowledgments

This synthesis report was written by Mmantsetsa Marope. It is based on background reports produced by a joint Government of Swaziland and World Bank technical team comprising Mmantsetsa Marope (Team Leader), Gwendolyn Simelane, Zethu Ntuli, Dudu Hlophe, Thulie Sihlongonyane, Alzinah Khumalo, Israel Simelane, Mboni Dlamini, Peterson Dlamini, Comfort Mndeble, Thembinkosi Mambe, Bernadetta Ndunguru, Tonic Maruatona, Richard Johanson, Robert Stowell, Erik Thulstrup, Ibrahim Dione, Sanjay Argawal, Martin Gustafsson, Cristina Romero, and Servaas van der Berg.

The team acknowledges with gratitude, the unwavering support and enduring guidance of the former Minister of Education Honorable Titus Msibi, the current Minister of Education, Honorable Wilson Ntshangase, the Minister of Finance Honorable Majozi V. Sithole, the Minister of Economic Planning and Development Honorable Prince Hlangusemphi, the Minister of Health Honorable Benedict Xaba, the former Principal Secretary of Education Goodman Kunene, the current Principal Secretary Patrick N. Muir and the Vice Chancellor of the University of Swaziland Professor Cisco Magagula. Special thanks to Mr. Mboni Dlamini, Director of Planning, Ministry of Education, who tirelessly co-managed this work with Mmantsetsa Marope.

The work presented in this report would not have been possible without the joint financial support of the Government of Swaziland, the World Bank, and the Norwegian Government EPDF, which is administered by the World Bank. The European Commission also financed the national consultative fora, which were critical in building national consensus on the conduct, methodology, scope, coverage, and final outputs of this analysis. Mr. Derek von Wissell, (Director of the National Emergency Response Council on HIV/AIDS (NERCHA), also made invaluable contributions.

This report also benefited from reviews and comments by colleagues at the World Bank's Human Development Department of the Africa Region, particularly Luis Benveniste and Eugenia Marinova. Invaluable comments and inputs were also received from the broader World Bank's Swaziland Country Team particularly Phindile Ngwenya. Special thanks go to the peer reviewers of this report, Mr. Robin Horn, Mr. Arvil Van Adams, and Mr. Pablo Gonzalez. Their technical comments were vital in shaping this report and in enhancing its quality. Ms. Cristina Romero provided invaluable support throughout the analysis, including the formatting and copy editing of this report.

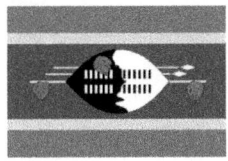

Acronyms and Abbreviations

ABET	Adult Basic Education and Training
ACCA	Association of Chartered Accountants
ADEA	Association for the Development of Education in Africa
AGOA	Africa Growth Opportunity Act
AMICs	Africa Middle Income Countries
ARV	Antiretroviral
ASER	Age Specific Enrollment Rate
AQTF	Australian Quality Training Framework
BMP	Basic Minimum Package
CBET	Competency Based Education and Training
CCC	Curriculum Coordinating Committee
CCS	Center for Community Services
CODEC	Cooperatives Development Center
COSDECs	Community Skills Development Centers
CPD	Continuing Professional Development
DHS	Demographic and Household Survey
DIVT	Directorate of Industrial and Vocational Training
E	Swaziland Lilangeni
EC	European Commission
ECD	Early Childhood Development
ECCD	Early Childhood Care and Development
EDC	Emlalatini Development Center
ENTO	Employers National Training Organisation
ERC	Economic Recovery Commission
ESRA1	Economic and Social Reform Agenda 1
ESRA2	Economic and Social Reform Agenda 2
ETSD	Education, Training and Skills Development
ETSDS	Education, Training and Skills Development Sector
EU	European Union
FBOs	Faith Based Organizations
FDIs	Foreign Direct Investors
GDP	Gross Domestic Product
GER	Gross Enrollment Ratio
GET	General Education and Training
GoS	Government of the Kingdom of Swaziland
HDI	Human Development Index
HE	Higher Education
HICC	Health Information and Counseling Center
HRDS	Human Resources Development Strategy
HIV/AIDS	Human Immunodeficiency Virus/Acquired Immune Deficiency Syndrome

HTMTP	Head Teacher Management Training Program
ICA	Investment Climate Assessment
ICTs	Information Communication Technologies
IDE	Institute of Distance Education
IGCSE	International General Certification of Secondary Education
INGO	International Nongovernmental Organization
IPGS	Institute of Post Graduate Studies
IRN	Institution Register of Needs
ISCED	International Standard Classification of Education
IT	Information Technology
IVTB	Industrial and Vocational Training Board
JCE	Junior Certificate of Education
KAM	Knowledge Assessment Methodology
KEI	Knowledge Economy Index
KI	Knowledge Index
LLL	Life Long Learning
LLUK	Lifelong Learning United Kingdom
LMICs	Low Middle Income Countries
MDGs	The Millennium Development Goals
MICS	Multiple Indicator Cluster Survey
MICs	Middle Income Countries
MITC	Manzini Industrial Training Center
MoE	Ministry of Education
MoEE	Ministry of Enterprise and Employment
MoPSI	Ministry of Public Service and Information
MRDYA	Ministry of Rural Development and Youth Affairs
MTEF	Medium Term Expenditure Framework
NASTIC	Nhlangano Agricultural Skills Training Center
NCCU	National Children's Coordinating Unit
NCP	Neighborhoods Care Point
NDS	National Development Strategy
NER	Net Enrollment Ratio
NERCHA	National Emergency Response Council on HIV/AIDS
NFE	Nonformal Education
NGO	Nongovernmental Organization
NICI	National Information and Communications Infrastructure
NOAS	National Open Apprenticeship Scheme
NQF	National Qualification Framework
NTA	National Training Authority
NTQA	National Training Qualification Authority
NUPE	Nonformal Universal Primary Education
OECD	Organization for Economic Co-operation and Development
O'Level	Ordinary Level Examination
OVCs	Orphans and Vulnerable Children
PBL	Problem Based Learning
PPP	Purchasing Power Parity

PRSAP	Poverty Reduction Strategy Action Plan
PSCE	Primary School Certificate Examination
PTA	Parent Teacher Association
R&D	Research and Development
RECs	Rural Education Centers
REOs	Regional Education Officers
RPL	Recognition of Prior Learning
SACMEQ	Southern Africa Consortium for Monitoring Education Quality
SACU	Southern Africa Customs Union
SAQA	South African Qualifications Authority
SCOT	Swaziland College of Technology
SES	Socioeconomic Status
SITC	Sitegi Industrial Training Center
SMCs	School Management Committees
SPCE	Swaziland Primary Certificate Examination
SSA	Sub-Saharan Africa
SSTC	Swaziland Skills Training Centers
STC	Skills Training Centers
STR	Student Teacher Ratio
SVQs	Scottish Vocational Qualifications
SZL	Swaziland Lilangeni
TB	Tuberculosis
TVETSD	Technical and Vocational Education and Training and Skills Development
UK	United Kingdom
UN	United Nations
UNESCO	United Nations Education Science and Culture Organization
UNICEF	United Nations Children's Education Fund
UNISWA	University of Swaziland
UFPE	Universal Free Primary Education
VET	Vocational Education and Training
VOCTIM	Vocational and Commercial Training Institute Matsapa
VTC	Vocational Training Center
WBI	World Bank Institute
WDR	World Development Report
WEF	World Economic Forum
WFP	World Food Program
WHO	World Health Organization
ZAR	South African Rand

Executive Summary

Introduction

In September 2007, the Government of the Kingdom of Swaziland (GoS) approved a broad national development reform agenda in the form of a poverty reduction strategy and action plan (PRSAP). The plan is intended to update and operationalize the National Development Strategy (NDS) of 1999, as well as to begin to actualize Vision 2022; which was also launched in 1999. The ultimate outcome of these instruments is "improved quality of life for all Swazis." Their key goal is "growth acceleration with equity or accelerated and shared growth." A critical intermediate goal expressed in the PRSAP is a 30 percent reduction in poverty by 2015, and ultimate poverty eradication by 2022. It is estimated that reaching these targets will require a 5 percent average annual GDP growth over a sustained period of time.

The starting point toward improving the quality of life for all Swazis is substantially low and development challenges are significant. The economic downturn, which Swaziland took since the mid-1990s, limits the resources required to finance development reforms. Average annual growth declined from 8 percent in the 1980s, to 3.5 percent in 2007. The country is at the epicenter of HIV/AIDS, which, among others, drains the already limited resources and threatens to deplete the current human capital base. Prevalence rates are 19 percent nationally, 26 percent for 15 to 49 year olds and 59 percent for women between 25 and 29 years of age. Poverty is endemic. Nearly 70 percent of the population is below the poverty datum line and close to 50 percent lives on less than US$1 per day (2005 est.). Both income and social inequalities are acute. Swaziland's Gini coefficient is .61 (2005 est.) and among the world's highest. The top income quintile claims 56 percent of total consumption relative to only 4 percent for the lowest quintile. Broad social inequalities are evident in a human development index (HDI) of .547 (2005 est.).

This report presents an analysis of the adequacy of Swaziland's education, training and skills development sector (ETSDS) to effectively contribute toward addressing the above outlined challenges and toward achieving national development goals presented in the PRSAP. Key sector weaknesses are identified and recommendations for their redress are made.

Strategic Orientation

Two premises provide a strategic orientation for this analysis. The first premise is that because Swaziland is not natural resource-rich, the acceleration of its growth and global competitiveness will most likely be knowledge driven and technology-driven. Even if Swaziland were rich in natural resources, global economic growth is becoming progressively knowledge-driven and technology-driven. Successful natural resource rich countries are those that have been able to transform their natural resource-based industries into knowledge- and technology-intensive, natural resource–based industries.[1] Knowledge and technology are also among key factors of global competitiveness. Developing capacity for knowledge and technology driven growth is therefore necessary for Swaziland to steadily integrate into the global economy and to be competitive. This capacity will require, at least in part, expanded access to post-basic education and training opportunities.[2] Other than enhancing growth and competitiveness, broadening access to higher levels of education could have the redistributive effects required for sharing the benefits of growth in line with the PRSAP.

The second premise is that because Swaziland currently has limited internal growth poles, its immediate growth strategy needs to focus on harvesting both national and regional opportunities. One of the regional opportunities is the reality that, notwithstanding the global economic downturn, Swaziland is surrounded by fast-growing natural resource-rich countries most of which have acute skills shortages, as elaborated in the report. These countries include—Botswana, Namibia, South Africa, Angola, and Mozambique. In the immediate run, Swaziland may consider the export of skilled labor with expected benefits being remittances and the deepening of the technical capacity of the exported skill base through practice. In the long run, Swaziland may expect to benefit from the brain circulation which will provide the technical leadership required to spearhead knowledge and technology-driven growth.

If adopted, this strategy may require an alignment of Swaziland's ETSD programs with those of its neighbors. Such alignment may be facilitated by the Southern Africa Development Community's (SADC) protocol on education and training and by existing national qualification frameworks (NQFs). Swaziland may also want to better exploit sub-regional human resource development capacities and joint human resource development programs, if any.

Assuming they hold, the above-outlined premises place human capital at the core of Swaziland's growth acceleration and social equity strategies. Indeed human capital development is a cornerstone of the PRSAP, not only because it is one of its key pillars but also because success in strengthening other pillars hinges on the adequacy of Swaziland's human capital.

Swaziland's recognition of human capital as a key driver of growth is consistent with modern economic growth theory, which purports that human capital/skills, technology-absorptive capacity/innovation, and investment climate are among critical determinants of productivity and self-sustaining growth. This report also presents an analysis of the adequacy of Swaziland's education, training and skills development sector (ETSDS) to supply the human capital required to enable technology-absorptive capacity/innovation, and to complement the investment climate in spurring value-added productivity and sustainable growth.

Coverage

In terms of scope, the report focuses on the analysis of the supply of human capital, even then, in the limited sense of knowledge and skills. For an understanding of the state of other determinants of growth, it relies on recent findings of the World Bank Investment Climate Assessment (ICA), the World Bank Institute's (WBI) annual analysis of countries' knowledge and technology readiness, and the World Economic Forums' (WEF) annual analysis of countries' global competitiveness. These analyses point to the need to substantially improve Swaziland's investment climate, technology-absorptive capacity, and global competitiveness. Key indices requiring improvement pertain to: macroeconomic stability, governance, Information Communication Technologies (ICTs), innovation, education and knowledge readiness.

The report covers all levels of the ETSDS, from early childhood care and development (ECCD) to higher education (HE). However, given the recency (2006) of the World Bank-supported analysis of the general education subsector—grades 1 to 12—this report provides an update and not another in-depth analysis of this subsector. Because of data limitations across the whole sector, the reader may find the analytical rigor of this report a bit varied across the covered subsectors. Data limitations were particularly acute for the ECCD and for the nonformal education (NFE) subsectors.

These weaknesses notwithstanding, this report adopts an integrated approach to the ETSDS, and views it as a seamless life-long learning (LLL) system. Levels of the system are assessed on the basis of the adequacy of their access, quality, equity, relevance, efficiency, and delivery capacity, including capacity to respond to HIV/AIDS.

Key Conclusions and Recommendations

The current ETSDS is not sufficient to support national development aspirations and goals, accelerated and shared growth, and global competitiveness. Key weaknesses pertain to low access, uneven and inequitable quality, acute inequalities, resource inefficiency, poor relevance and weak strategic direction and delivery capacity. In addition, poor data and information management also permeates the sector. Without intervention, this limitation may adversely affect planning for future sector development, any required future sector analysis, effective monitoring of sector reforms, and, effective assessment of the impact of future sector reforms.

Although quite pervasive, the intensity of each of the above-outlined key weaknesses differs across subsectors. At the point of designing the sector reform program, this will demand a different prioritization and sequencing of interventions at each level of the sector. Table 1 summarizes the intensity of each challenge within each subsector and implies the prioritization of interventions to be instituted.

Access is limited across all levels of the ETSDS

Current levels of access are inadequate to supply the right threshold and mix of skills required to meet national and regional labor market demands, to support accelerated and shared growth, and to make Swaziland globally competitive. Access is particularly low from the secondary level upwards, the very levels which are proven to be essential for the supply of knowledge workers required to attract foreign direct investors (FDIs), as Swaziland intends, to create knowledge—and technology-absorption capacity, which FDIs demand, to facilitate innovation, higher value—added productivity and growth, and to create employment opportunities for lower-level skills, and for the unskilled. An estimated 74 percent of children of eligible age are not enrolled in junior secondary education, and 88 percent are not enrolled in senior secondary education. The higher education net enrollment ratio (NER) is estimated at only 2.6 percent (2007 est.). Access is also very low for the ECCD level, where 65 percent of children of eligible age are not enrolled. The situation is somewhat better for the primary level where only 16 percent of children of eligible age are not enrolled. However, it is noteworthy that without intervention, the current level of access to primary education may risk Swaziland's attainment of the "millennium development goal (MDG)" pertaining to access by 2015.

Table 1: Hierarchy of Challenges by Subsector

Subsector	Challenge 1	Challenge 2	Challenge 3	Challenge 4	Challenge 5	Challenge 6
ECCD	Weak strategic direction and delivery capacity	Poor access	Systemic inequities	Poor quality	Low internal, market and development relevance	Low resource efficiency and poor resource mobilization and utilization
Primary Education	Poor quality	Low resource efficiency and poor resource mobilization and utilization	Systemic inequities	Poor internal, market and development relevance	Poor access	Weak strategic direction and delivery capacity
Junior secondary education	Weak strategic direction and delivery capacity	Poor access	Systemic inequities	Poor quality	Low resource efficiency and poor resource mobilization and utilization	Low internal, market and development relevance
Senior secondary education	Weak strategic direction and delivery capacity	Poor access	Systemic inequities	Poor quality	Low internal, market and development relevance	Low resource efficiency and poor resource mobilization and utilization
TVETSD	Low internal, market and development relevance	Weak strategic direction and delivery capacity	Poor quality	Expand access	Eradicate sources of inequities	Low resource efficiency
Tertiary Education	Low internal, market and development relevance	Poor quality	Weak strategic direction and delivery capacity	Poor access	Systemic inequities	Low resource efficiency and poor resource mobilization and utilization
Higher Education	Low resource efficiency and poor resource mobilization and utilization	Low internal, market and development relevance	Systemic inequities	Poor access	Weak strategic direction and delivery capacity	Improve quality
Adult nonformal Education	Low internal, market and development relevance	Weak strategic direction and delivery capacity	Poor access	Systemic inequities	Poor quality	Low resource efficiency and poor resource mobilization and utilization

Source: Data compiled by author.

The cost of education and training services to both households and to the government is a binding constraint to expanding access. General education fees are too high for most households and this leads to the low participation of children of low socioeconomic status (SES). Households contribute about 14 percent and 30 percent of primary and secondary school expenditure respectively. Primary education fees account for about 22 percent of the income of poor households. Because of financial barriers, the poorest region of Shiselweni, rural areas, and poor households tend to have lower access. Unit costs for post-secondary education are prohibitive and this limits the number of learners the GoS may sponsor. Other barriers to access are: (i) the low physical capacity of the system, especially, for ECCD and secondary education; (ii) enormous distances some learners walk to school, averaging 17 kilometers per day and (iii) the lack of facilities for learners with disabilities.

Adopt a balanced expansion of access across all levels of the ETSDS

In order to build the threshold and mix of skills required to support growth acceleration, social equity and global competitiveness, Swaziland needs to adopt a balanced expansion of access to all levels of the ETSDS. The expansion plan should balance immediate needs to catalyze growth with long-term needs to sustain shared growth. Meeting immediate needs will entail a pro-poor expansion of access to tertiary education and training whose outputs can immediately take up jobs nationally and regionally as well as create jobs for the lower levels. For the ETSDS in particular, tertiary level outputs create the regenerative capacity for building the lower levels of the system. Meeting long-term needs will require strengthening the ETSDS at the base—ECCD to senior secondary levels—and broadening access; thus giving the new generations a chance to break the cycle of intergenerational poverty through education. The extent and nature of the balance should be based on development considerations and should be guided by cost simulations that enable decision-makers to debate trade-offs and to select sustainable options.

Recommended actions for expanding access are presented below in order of priority and are considered both viable and feasible only when complemented by recommendations to improve equity and resource efficiency.

- Attain full operational capacity for UNISWA and SCOT: With effect from academic year 2011/2012, the annual intake to the University of Swaziland (UNISWA) and to the Swaziland College of Technology (SCOT) should be dissociated from the number of available government scholarships and should be based on the capacity of these two institutions and the availability of qualified candidates.
- By academic year 2012/2013, UNISWA and SCOT should be operating at their full capacity. For SCOT, this would mean using its currently unused 79 percent physical capacity. For UNISWA it would entail the admission of 80 percent of qualified applicants. Both these action would re-instate the institutions back to their operating capacity before the decline in government scholarships.
- Expand access to general education and training (GET or grades 1 to 12 equivalent) to reach '100' percent NER for primary education by 2015, using both the formal and the nonformal channels. Concurrently, expand the system's physical capacity for 100 percent progression from primary to junior secondary education by 2015. For the senior secondary level, ensure a 50 percent NER to formal senior secondary education by 2015, and 60 percent by 2022. In parallel, build capacity for 15 percent progression from junior secondary school to vocational education and training (VET) by 2015, and 30 percent progression by 2022. For the remaining 10 percent of junior secondary school completers, build adequate absorptive capacity in nonformal education centers. This expansion program should include the regularization of the

currently so-called "illegal schools" and their formal registration by the Ministry of Education (MoE) by 2012.
- Minimize financial barriers to access to all levels of the ETSDS: The GoS should institute the universal free primary education (UFPE) policy at the beginning of the 2010 academic year. Direct and indirect primary school costs to households should be abolished. An operational plan should be developed and adopted to ensure a 100 primary NER by 2015; in line with MDGs Junior secondary education should be substantially subsidized to reach a ratio of 10:90, households to GoS contributions to the subsector expenditures, by 2022. The ratio for senior secondary education should be 20:80 by the same year. Orphans and Vulnerable Children (OVCs) grants should be sustained to ensure their effective participation in GET; and should be made conditional on their successful completion. Tertiary education and training unit costs should be restructured and aligned to those of other low middle income countries (LMICs) by 2012.
- Minimize other barriers to access to general education and strengthen alternative delivery modes: By 2015, a catchment area system that enables grade 1 to 12 learners to be within a 3-kilometer radius, or 30 minute walking distance of their school, should be in place. Where the density of learner population does not warrant it, alternatives like learner transport or hostels should be adopted. In addition, all schools must be accessible to learners with disability by 2015. Nonformal education centers should be expanded and strengthened to provide a viable alternative mode as well as a second chance opportunity for general education.
- Create capacity for 80 percent progression rate from senior secondary to tertiary education and training by 2022: The distribution of the progression should be about 40 percent to technical and vocational education, and training, and skills development (TVETSD), inclusive of nursing education and other health sciences, 20 percent to HE, and 20 percent to educator training of diverse forms.
- Pro-poor expansion of access to ECCD: Access to early childhood development (ECD 0-3) programs should be expanded to reach 60 percent of eligible children by 2015, and 80 percent by 2022. The first 60 percent of new ECD places should be allocated to children from poor households. This will demand the articulation of clear criteria on what constitutes poor households. In order to facilitate access, the GoS should provide per-capita grant support to private service providers in day care centers, as well as to neighborhood care points (NCPs) and to KaGogo centers (grandma's centers) that provide ECD services. The GoS grants should be steadily phased in to account for a quarter of ECD expenditures by 2015 and half by 2022.
- Pro-poor expansion of access to preprimary education: Access to preprimary education should be expanded to reach 80 percent of eligible children (four and five year olds) by 2015, and 100 percent by 2022. As with ECD, the GoS should provide per capita grant support to private service providers, NCPs, and KaGogo centers that run preprimary classes. To the fullest extent possible,

preprimary classes should be integrated into primary schools where there is adequate demand.

Quality is uneven and inequitable

Quality is uneven across levels of the ETSDS but tends to be better for a select minority from high income households. For general education, quality is better than for other Southern Africa Customs Union (SACU) countries[3], but this advantage disappears once Swaziland is compared with countries beyond its immediate neighbor. Education quality also seems to be reasonable at the higher levels of the system, where children of the poor are substantially under-represented. All the same, there seems to be adequate elements of quality upon which Swaziland can build its sector improvement program.

Core issues and sources of doubt with education quality are the lack of standards and the lack of clear operational definitions of outputs at each level in terms of key competencies and skills to be acquired. For instance, at the ECD level, the indicators or markers of a 'holistically developed Swazi child' remain unclear. At preprimary level, it is not clear what constitutes child development and school readiness. For the rest of the GET and TVETSD levels, it is not clear what competencies and skills learners should acquire at each level.

Lack of standards and unclear outputs make it difficult to benchmark the system in absolute and in relative terms. In absolute terms, Swazi learners tend to do fairly well on continuous assessments. However, as suggested, the quality implied by those passes remains unclear when there are no standards. In relative terms, Swazi learners perform fairly well on international examinations and this serves as some form of benchmarking. For instance, student performance on the 2000 SACMEQ tests was better than for other SACU countries, but lower than for some low income countries—Kenya for instance. The Junior Secondary Certificate Examination (JCE) and the International General Certificate of Secondary Education (IGCSE) provide the relative quality of general education. In addition, Swazi VET trainees write the Pitman and the City and Guilds tests which is another relative indicator of quality.

For general education a great source of ambivalence about the quality is the high repetition rates which signal poor quality and the stringent selectivity of the system owing to shortage of places at higher levels. This leads to a conclusion that the relatively good performance on international examinations is most likely indicative of the stringent selectivity of the system and not so much its quality. This conclusion is backed by the strong association between SES and learning outcomes including educational attainment. It is also backed by the virtual absence of children from low-income quintiles in HE. A safe conclusion, therefore, seems to be that the system is of reasonable quality for a select few learners who tend to be of high SES. For the majority of learners, who tend to be disproportionately under-represented, the system is not of a quality that enables them a successful completion or a fair competition in the national, regional, and global labor markets.

The quality of the system is also varied across subjects with students' performance being particularly low for mathematics, science and siSwati. In addition, there is almost a total absence of students who take ICTs as a subject or for basic e-literacy.

Improve the quality of ETSD

To improve student learning, and to be able to benchmark that improvement within and across countries, Swaziland needs to adopt a competency-based approach to all levels of learning and to use this approach as a base for systemic quality improvement. Sequenced actions to improve the quality of the ETSDS are:

- Clearly define standards in terms of skills and competencies to be acquired at each level: For ECD, there should be an operational definition of holistic child development within the context of Swaziland. Such a definition should be benchmarked against international indicators and even an international holistic child development index. A clear and operational definition of school readiness should be developed and formally adopted. Skills and competencies to be acquired at each level of GET and TVETSD should be defined and formally adopted. Such definitions should reflect contextual relevance as well as what is progressively being recognized as skills and competencies required for effective functioning in post-industrial or knowledge economies. SCOT and UNISWA should adopt more rigorous quality assurance mechanisms that allow them to be benchmarked against other tertiary education and training institutions.
- Revise curricula and assessment: By 2012, curricula should be revised to reflect agreed skills and competencies. In addition a periodic curricula review—3 to 5 yearly suggested—should be instituted to ensure currency and relevance of programs. Student/trainee assessments and systemic evaluations should also be revised to focus on agreed skills and competencies. Student report cards and other instruments for communicating progress in student learning, such as the MoE annual reports and citizen score cards, should also be redesigned to reflect set skills and competencies.
- Define teacher/instructor competencies and institute time-bound licenses: By 2012, the skills and competencies that teachers/instructors require to effectively teach at each level should be clearly defined and used to guide the revision of pre-and in-service training programs. For TVETSD instructors particularly, competencies must include technical and pedagogical qualification, as well as current—no more than 3 years old—industry experience. A teacher/instructor skills audit should be undertaken by 2013 to determine the extent of required in-service training. All practicing teachers/instructors who need in-service training should receive it by 2014. During 2014, a time-bound teacher/instructor license should be designed and adopted. The application of the license system should commence by 2016 as a key measure to ensure teacher/instructor quality and currency.
- Strengthen the teaching of mathematics, science, and ICTs: As immediate measures, Swaziland must develop an incentive package to attract teachers of these subjects to rural areas. It should also recruit qualified expatriate teachers for mathematics, science, and ICTs ensuring adequacy by 2011. In the case of expatriate teachers, a localization plan for all expatriate teachers should be developed and implemented with a view to have full localization by 2022. A teacher-upgrading course should be designed to allow practicing teachers

with aptitude to qualify for the teaching of these three subjects, starting with teachers in rural areas. The current UNISWA program should be adapted to distance delivery mode through the Institute of Distance Education (IDE) to enable teachers to upgrade while in service. Distance education delivery should be strengthened through face-to-face programs at the IDE during school holidays. The long-term solution of offering Education degree courses in these subjects at UNISWA should be sustained.

- Define competencies for school/VET institution heads and place them on performance contracts: Skills and competencies required to qualify as a school/institution head should be defined by 2012 and used to elaborate the current head teacher management training program (HTMTP) into a modularized professional qualification program by 2014. The program should be implemented with a view to have all school heads qualified by 2018. Thereafter, learner/trainee competencies should be used to set performance standards for school/institution heads and to hold them accountable for results. By 2020, all school/institution heads should be on renewable performance contracts. An annual school/institution performance league should be created and publicized to communicate performance to the general public.
- Based on leaner and educator skills and competencies, a National Qualification Framework (NQF) should be developed to formalize standards and adopt them by 2015. All GET and VET institutions should be in compliance with the NQF and re-registered by 2020.
- The NQF should be used as a primary vehicle for transforming the current ETSDS into a seamless life-long learning (LLL) system. As stated, the NQF should take into account sub-regional "equivalencies" and relevant international NQFs. Key features of the LLL system should be clear standards and equivalencies across subsectors and across modes of delivery, portability of credits, and flexible pathways.
- Develop input norms and define a Basic Minimum Package (BMP) for GET and TEVET institutions. In order to hold school/institution heads accountable for results, they should first be provided the inputs required to facilitate their delivery. Inputs norms and standards that constitute a BMP deemed necessary to enable set performance levels should be articulated and adopted by 2014. The BMP should highlight key inputs like qualified teachers, books and instructional materials, library stocks, laboratory equipment, ICTs, etc. The latter should be fast tracked to ensure that all schools are equipped with ICTs and with connectivity by 2012 as stated in the PRSAP; BUT following a pro-poor approach.

The system is inequitable

Overall, learners from high income households have higher levels of access and better quality of ETSD services. This is ultimately evident in patterns of learning outcomes, educational attainment and in the disproportionately high enrollment (70%) of student from the highest quintile at UNISWA. Students in rural areas also tend to have lower access and lower education inputs, especially with regard to qualified teachers.

Reportedly, some of the key disincentives for teachers to stay in rural areas include: poor amenities especially lack of housing, electricity and health facilities; difficult access to amenities due more to poor roads and poor transport rather than to long distances from such amenities; limited opportunities for self-improvement, such as part-time further studies, alternative employment and investment opportunities; professional isolation including limited visits by school inspectors and other cadres that are supposed to professionally support and mentor teachers.

Inequities of education access, inputs, and outcomes make it difficult for Swaziland to use the ETSDS as one of the powerful 'equalizers' it ought to be. Instead of the expected redistributive effects, current inequities in the sector may reproduce or even cement existing social inequalities. This current situation is contrary to the PRSAP goals of "shared growth" and of "improving the quality of life for all Swazis." In order of priority, recommendations to improve equity follow.

Eradicate sources of inequalities

- Notably, all measures to remove barriers to access outlined above will have a positive impact on equity. To better ensure this, a pro-poor approach should be adopted in the phasing of all recommended actions. In addition, a quota system should be instituted to allow learners from disadvantaged areas and household's entry into senior secondary and tertiary institutions. Academic support programs should be instituted to enable such students to catch up with their counterparts.
- Eradicate inequality of inputs: Guided by the BMP, a school/VET institution input survey should be undertaken and completed by 2013. The results should be used to establish an institution register of needs (IRN), and maintain it in order to capture provisioning real-time. The IRN should be used as a base for a pro-poor provisioning plan, which should be completed by 2014. A provisioning module should be developed and integrated into the annual EMIS report, starting with the 2015 EMIS report. The results should also be used to de-register and re-register schools in compliance with inputs norms. By 2015, all operating schools should be in compliance with input norms and duly registered.
- Adopt a per capita financing of GET and VET in order to enable resources to follow learners and to enable schools to afford resource inputs commensurate with their enrollment levels. This funding approach should cover all formal and nonformal government and government-aided institutions. Where per capita financing alone does not equalize resource provision, conditional grants should be considered to enable under-resourced schools/VET institutions to catch up with the rest.
- Redeploy qualified teachers to rural areas: An incentive package—including housing, hardship allowance and promotion criterion—should be instituted to attract qualified teachers to remote rural schools.

The system is inefficient at resource mobilization and utilization

Key factors of resource inefficiency include: low utilization of existing physical capacity, broad curricula, and the consequent low student to teacher ratios (STRs), mismanagement of funds, high unit costs, extended duration of study programs and high repetition rates. The current physical capacity for ECCD, TVETSD and HE is underutilized. For the latter two subsectors, underutilization is mostly due to the linking of intake to the GoS scholarships, which are markedly insufficient for all the qualified candidates and available spaces. GET, repetition rates are too high. GET curricula are too broad and therefore expensive. Moreover, the prevocational subjects offered in 16 senior secondary schools seem unsustainable. Schools are reputed for their mismanagement of funds from school fees and the MoE offers little to no control. STRs are low for GET—mainly because of prevocational and practical subjects—and for TVETSD. At the tertiary level, unit costs are unjustifiably high and this is another drain on resources. Poor curricula/program articulation and limited pathways within and between subsectors add to the resource inefficiency. For instance, people with 3-year UNISWA diplomas have to re-start their studies at year 1, if they should want to upgrade to a degree level. The same applies to other levels and subsectors of the system.

Improve efficiency of resource mobilization and utilization

- Swaziland will require substantial external and national resources to finance the reforms proposed in this report. However without prior measures to redress current inefficiencies, additional resources may be wasted. Sequential actions to realize efficiency gains, as recommended below, should therefore be among topmost priority reforms.
- As elaborated on elsewhere in the document, optimize the use of existing physical capacity for ECCD and tertiary institutions by defining the optimum class size and STR. For post-basic education and training, de-link intake from the availability of scholarships and allow fee-paying applicants to enroll.
- Optimize STRs: Where student population density allows, STRs should be increased to 40:1 for primary education, 35:1 for secondary education, 15:1 for TEVET and colleges.
- Implement the current repetition policy which allows for no more than 10 percent repetition for each year up to 2015. Support policy implementation with systematized remedial teaching and assessed progression. Then revise the policy to reduce repetition rates to 5 percent of the learners from 2016 onwards; still supported with remedial teaching and assessed progression.
- Integrate financial management into the HTMP and regularize formal audits of school accounts. The new audit program should be operational by 2010.
- Rationalize curricula: Secondary school curricula should be rationalized into a core of 4 subjects—mathematics, English, science and siSwati—and 3 electives. Prevocational subjects should be removed from regular school curriculum and transferred to the VTCs. By 2015, the current prevocational curriculum should be redesigned into a level III qualification that is integrated into the NQF. Senior secondary school learners who wish to take this qualification should concurrently enroll in neighboring VTCs. Regional Education Centers (RECs) and Swaziland Skills Training Centers (SSTCs) should be upgraded to offer level III qualifications, including for learners from neighboring senior secondary schools.

- Reduce the duration of tertiary education and training programs: Given the overall good quality of intake, the duration of university programs should be reduced by one year. For fields of studies where the foundation year may be necessary—mathematics, science, ICTs, etc.—translate the foundation year into a university pre-entry program, which should be outsourced to any qualified entity on a competitive basis. Based on curricula articulation enabled by the NQF, prior tertiary qualifications should be accorded credits and such credits should be counted toward the duration of upgrading programs. Both measures should be instituted by 2012.
- Reduce unit costs to comparable international levels: By 2012, the unit costs of tertiary education and training, including HE, should be aligned to those of other LIMCs.
- Institute full tertiary student loans except for scarce skills: By 2012, the current GoS tertiary scholarship should be redesigned into a fully recoverable student loan scheme and administered through a private entity such as a commercial bank. The GoS involvement should be restricted to the guaranteeing of the loans. At the GoS's discretion, a gradation of levels of scholarships may be instituted as an incentive for students to enroll in programs that address scarce skills.
- Decentralize the management of SCOT and VET institutions and allow them to manage own-source revenues. Progressively increase the proportion of own source revenues for SCOT and UNISWA to reach 10 percent of expenditures by 2022.
- Intensify efforts to broaden partnerships for sector development and to diversify sources of funding.

System relevance is weak on several dimensions

In general the sector is not responsive to its own internal needs. Poor internal relevance is evident in the system's apparent ineffectiveness in preparing learners for entry to subsequent levels. As already noted, this weakness stems from the lack of standards and the lack of a NQF. In many respects, the sector does not function as a system, but is more of a collection of loosely coupled subsectors. This is evident in the lack of pathways that could enable student movement within a "system." Instead, students are confronted by blockades that make progression difficult, are exceedingly expensive, and server as a disincentive, particularly for adult learners.

Due mainly to lack of information and relevant instruments, the sector is not adequately responsive to labor market and development needs. In terms of information, there are limited labor market surveys, and those that exist are not clear on the types and levels of skills required. In addition, there seems to be no clear mechanism for monitoring sub-regional labor markets in which Swazi graduates could compete for jobs. Tertiary institutions tend to not undertake tracer studies which could inform them on how their graduates fare, what life-long learning (LLL) opportunities they should offer them, and what program changes may be required.

In terms of instruments, Swaziland does not have a current human resources development strategy that could guide the supply of skills. It also lacks a current sector strategy that is well-anchored in the national development strategy and which is cognizant of global development trends. Overall, the sector lacks clear pointers on what it ought to respond to. Furthermore, it lacks mechanisms for the periodic review and renewal required to sustain relevance.

Improve internal, labor market, social and development relevance

Recommendations to improve relevance are:

- Implement the NQF: A lean and executive structure should be established to lead the implementation of the NQF and to ensure internal relevance of all levels of the sector.
- By 2010, establish a national training authority (NTA) with employer majority and employee representation on the board to ensure labor market responsiveness of TVETSD programs. The NTA should be autonomous and should be enabled to lead the development of a market responsive TVETSD subsector. It should replace the current TVETSD directorate in the MoE. In collaboration with the Ministry of Enterprise and Employment (MoEE) and the NQF executive structure, the NTA should regularize labor market surveys and maintain current labor market information. The MoEE should establish a sub-regional labor market observatory to augment national labor surveys.
- UNISWA should widen and deepen its current practice of having employers and industry representation on the University Council.
- Regularize tracer studies: Tertiary institutions must regularize tracer studies and use feedback from the studies and labor surveys to update regular programs and to mount just-in-time training programs. Program reviews should be regularized to once every 3 to 5 years and/or as need arises. As noted under the section on quality, curricula/program revisions must include skills and competencies considered critical for effective functioning in post-industrial economies.
- Establish competitive Research and Development (R&D) grants to stimulate university/industry collaboration and reward university professors for significant contributions to R&D.
- Establish a national, regional, and international labor market observatory at the UNISWA Faculty of Social Sciences.
- Strengthen responsiveness to HIV/AIDS: Across all levels, curricula/programs must deepen the mainstreaming of life skills, health and nutrition, and HIV/AIDS. Whenever possible, these elements should be part of the examinable subjects/learning areas. A small HIV/AIDS unit should be established in the MoE and replicated in the regions to coordinate and support programs.

The sector's strategic direction and delivery capacity are weak

Sector development is proceeding without a clear strategic direction that aligns sector developments to the overall national development strategy, and that support's global competitiveness. At a broader level, sector development is guided by a dated 1999 policy, which, though still relevant in several aspects, is no longer suitable to guide service delivery in the current national, regional and global context. The overall sector policy should be updated. In addition, specific policies should be developed for critical subsectors and topical areas that require concerted development effort. These include: TVETSD, adult education and training (AET), ECCD, HE, HIV/AIDS, ICTs, and the development and provisioning of books and instructional materials.

Developments in the sector are also proceeding without the data, information and, analysis that should inform planning, monitoring and evaluation, and impact assessment. Poor data and information management pervade the sector, but are particularly worse for ECCD and NFE.

The weak sector policy translates into weak strategic, legal, institutional, and financing frameworks.

Strengthen policy and strategic direction and delivery capacity

Key recommendations for strengthening sector delivery capacity are:

- Update the sector policy into a development responsive LLL policy by 2010: The 1999 sector policy should be updated and transformed into a LLL policy and not just a current ETSDS policy. Moreover, the LLL policy should be deliberately anchored in the national development strategy, global thinking on human capital development, and the human resources development plan being drafted by the Ministry of Public Service and Information (MoPSI). Subsector/topical policies on ECCD, TVETSD, HE, HIV/AIDS, textbooks, and ICTs should be developed in alignment with the LLL policy by 2012.

- Strengthen the legal, institutional, and strategic frameworks required to enforce and implement policies: Current legal instruments such as the Education Act, the Training Bill, and the HE Act, should be updated in alignment with new policies. A long-term strategic plan should be developed to guide policy implementation. The strategic plan should be operationalized through periodic medium-term sector programs. With the strategic plan in place, the delivery capacity of the GoS structure—particularly the MoE and its decentralized structures—should be assessed and, if necessary, an institutional capacity development program should be articulated and integrated into medium-term sector programs.

- Diversify the financing base for future sector development by raising funds from diverse external sources. Relative to other SACU countries, Swaziland has a striking dearth of international development partner' support for the sector. This situation should be reversed. A fund raising strategy for the sector should be articulated and executed as a matter of urgency. Also, introduce a payroll levy to partially finance TVETSD. Consideration should be given to the re-institution of tax breaks in order to further increase enterprise-based training.

- Ensure financial feasibility and sustainability of proposed reforms: A simulation model should be developed to estimate the cost of proposed-long-term sector reforms. The model should also be used to guide national dialogue on trade-offs and final decisions on investing in the sector. Medium-term sector programs should be periodically costed and, where necessary, the sector simulation model should be periodically updated and decision makers informed of any significant cost changes.

- Clearly plan for the implementation of proposed sector reforms ensuring that the scale of medium-term programs matches the GoS's implementation capacity: Some of the key implementation support instruments that should back the sector programs include: implementation, procurement and disbursement plans, a monitoring and evaluation system results framework and decentralized implementation arrangements.
- Strengthen capacity for data and information management, and the analysis required to inform policy development, planning, implementation, monitoring and evaluation and impact assessment.

Note

[1] Examples include the United States, Australia, Finland, and Sweden.
[2] See World Economic Forum 2008. *Global Competitiveness Report 2008-2009*. pp 6-8.
[3] Botswana, Lesotho, Namibia, and South Africa.

CHAPTER 1

Swaziland's Growth and Competitiveness in a Global Context

Introduction

From the mid 1990s Swaziland's growth took a downturn which is yet to be reversed. Real GDP growth declined from an annual average of 8 percent in the 1980s[1] to 2.4 percent in 2008 and is projected to reach close to 0 percent in 2009. The downward spiral was initially sparked by the relocation of foreign direct investors (FDIs) to South Africa after the collapse of apartheid and Swaziland's diminished attractiveness as an investment destination. Since then, a range of factors has made it difficult to recover growth rates of the 1980s. From a sub-regional and global perspective, Swaziland is not only failing to catch up, but has fallen behind countries which once had much lower growth rates: South Africa, Mauritius, Namibia, Singapore, and Ireland (figure 1.1).

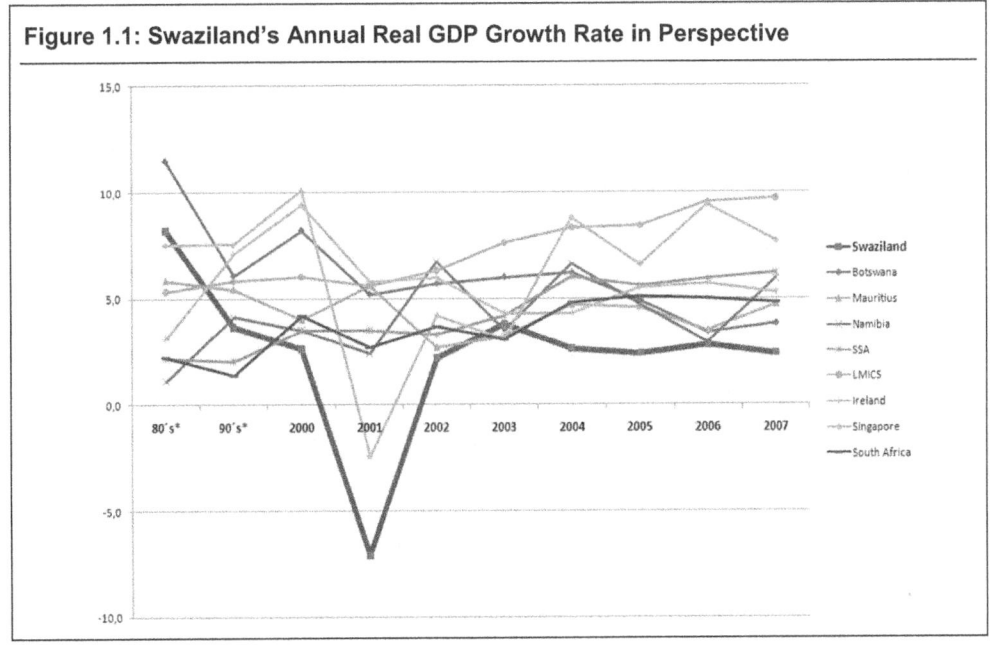

Figure 1.1: Swaziland's Annual Real GDP Growth Rate in Perspective

Source: World Bank. 2009. Development data platform.

The government has developed a range of policy and strategic instruments that are designed to provide a roadmap to economic recovery, all of which are yet to deliver. Key among them are the Economic Recovery Commission Report (ERC) of 1995, the first Economic and Social Reform Agenda (ESRA1) of 1997, and ESRA2 of 1999, Vision 2022 launched in 1999, the National Development Strategy (NDS) adopted in 1999, and the Poverty Reduction and Action Plan (PRSAP) which received Cabinet approval in September 2007.

An aspiration of the national Vision is that "by the year 2022, the Kingdom of Swaziland will be in the top 10 percent of the medium human development group of countries founded on sustainable economic development, social justice and political stability" (pp.2). The Vision laid a foundation for the development of a NDS 1997–2022. Both the Vision and the strategy prioritize the improvement of people's quality of life. Sustainable and shared growth is identified as a fundamental facilitator of the aspired for quality of life. The NDS is to be implemented through the PRSAP "Yingcamu—Toward Shared Growth and Empowerment—A Poverty Reduction Strategy and Action Program." More pragmatic perhaps, the PRSAP aims for a 30 percent poverty reduction by 2015; which is 20 percent below the Millennium Development Goal (MDG) target. It also aims to totally eradicate poverty by 2022. It is estimated that attaining this goal will require an annual average growth rate of 5 percent.

Key pillars of the PRSAP are:

- Macro-economic stability and accelerated growth based on broad participation
- Empowering the poor to generate income and reduce inequalities
- Fair distribution of benefits of growth through fiscal policy
- Human development
- Improving the quality of life of the poor and
- Improving governance and strengthening institutions.

Current Performance against Vision 2022 and PRSAP Goals

Improving governance and strengthening institutions

Swaziland is the last absolute monarchy in Africa, a status sustained even after independence on September 6, 1968. The governance system is complex and somewhat unique in its combination of a "Westminster" bi-cameral Parliament, or Libandla, and a traditional system of Tinkundla. Two thirds of the 30 Parliamentary seats are appointed by the monarch and a third by the House of Assembly. Ten of the 65 House of Assembly seats are appointed by the monarch, and the rest are elected by popular vote. Elections are held on a nonparty basis, with local councils nominating 3 candidates who are elected by their constituents through 2 rounds. The first political election was held in 1972, five years after independence. The first constitution was signed by the King on July 26, 2005, and became effective on February 8, 2008. It is said to allow for political association, leaving the status of political parties[2] very unclear. The constitution undertakes to search for and assert Swaziland's "sustainable and home-grown political order," characterized by a blend of good institutions of traditional law and custom with those of an open democratic society. However, while home-grown institutions are completely legitimate and even more sustainable, Swaziland cannot escape comparisons on a global stage on which it seeks to be an effective competitor. Good governance is one of the key factors of a conducive investment climate, and of competitiveness against which countries are compared. The PRSAP's pillar to improve governance is therefore a step in the right direction.

Global comparisons suggest that a lot is required to strengthen the PRSAP pillar on "improving governance and strengthening institutions." Governance rankings are very low, especially when compared with other African middle income countries (AMICs). The 2008 Mo Ibrahim index of African governance ranked Swaziland 34 out of 48 participating countries. This is relatively low compared to other AMICs like Mauritius (1/48), Seychelles (2/48), Cape Verde (3/48), Botswana (4/48), South Africa (5/48) and Namibia (6/48). The 2007 Transparency International corruption perception index also ranked Swaziland a low (84/179) on the corruption perception index. However, it is noteworthy that this ranking is an improvement from the 2006 rating of 121/163. The actual score increased from 2.5/10 to 3.3/10. Scores are particularly low on indices relating to the upholding of civil freedoms, human rights, freedom of expression, and general press freedom. The latter ranked 138 out of 169.[3] Against the NDS goal of gender parity, a gender related development index placed Swaziland at 146 of 177 developing countries, with Swazi women earning 29 percent of what men earn. Swaziland also ranks below the 50th percentile on all indicators of the World Bank Institute 2008 Governance Matters index. The index presents relative country performance between 1996 and 2007 on political stability and lack of violence (30th), government effectiveness (30th), regulatory quality (40th), rule of law (30th), control of corruption (40th) and voice and accountability (20th). Again, rakings are substantially below those of other AMICs.

Judging by the global ranking of public institutions, an equally strong effort is required to strengthen institutions. The 2009 Doing Business ranks Swaziland 108/181 in terms of the overall ease of doing business. This compares with 24 for Mauritius, 32 for South Africa, 38 for Botswana and 51 for Namibia. Key areas of weakness include the ease of starting a business (153), registering property (153), enforcing contracts (129), and protecting investors (178).

In addition to signaling weaknesses of institutions, these rankings also signal a weak investment climate, and do not bode well for the government-expressed intention to aggressively re-attract FDIs as part of the growth strategy (see PRSAP). An investment climate that deters FDIs (real or perceived), may limit opportunities for technology transfer and diffusion. The combined low technology diffusion and low skills is likely to limit innovation, productivity, and ultimately growth. Anemic growth will impede redistribution and the poverty reduction goals of the PRSAP.

Ascension to the top 10 percent of the medium human development group of countries

A decade after the launch of Vision 2022, Swaziland's human development index (HDI) has substantially deteriorated from the .641 estimate of 1995 to .547 in 2005, placing Swaziland at 141 of 177 countries,[4] and substantially far from realizing the Vision 2022 target of being in the top 10 percent of the medium human development group of countries. As shown in figure 1.2, the HDI value has fallen behind that of East Asia, which Swaziland was nearly equal to in 1990. It has also fallen behind that of South Asia, which was well below Swaziland until 2000, and is getting closer to the Sub-Saharan Africa (SSA) average. The HDI is pulled down by a combined low life expectancy at birth which dropped from 58 in 1993 to 31 in 2008[5] due mainly, but not exclusively, to HIV/AIDS, and to the low combined gross enrollment ratio (GER) for primary, secondary and tertiary education (60%). As shown in figure 1.3, these factors yield a HDI that is well below that of countries that are poorer than Swaziland.

An effective strategy for moving Swaziland toward the "top 10 percent of the medium human development group of countries" will be one that combines the redress of HIV and broad-based expansion of access to quality and development-relevant education and training at all levels.

Figure 1.2: Swaziland's HDI in Regional Perspective

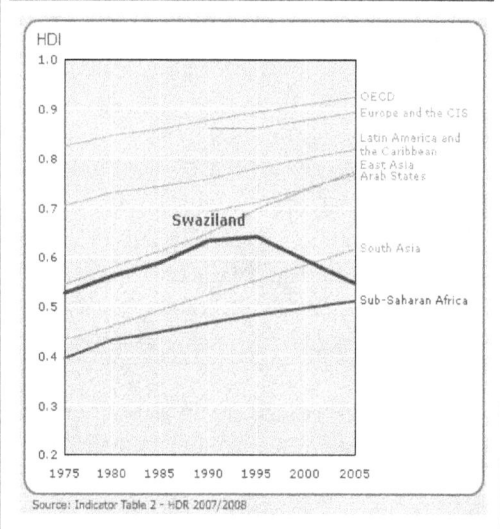

Figure 1.3: Swaziland's HDI Relative to GDP Per Capita PPP in US$

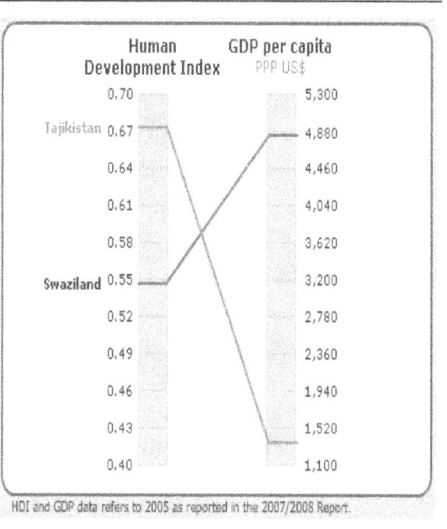

Source: UNDP. 2009. Human Development Report 2007/2008, Country Fact Sheets, Swaziland.

Macroeconomic stability and growth acceleration based on broad participation

Swaziland's macroeconomic performance has been unexpectedly strong over the past 3 years. Recent increase in import growth was offset by a stronger demand for the Swaziland's major exports, including soft drinks concentrate, textiles, which benefited from an extension of the Africa Growth and Opportunity Act (AGOA) to 2015, and increased Southern Africa Customs Union (SACU) receipts. In 2006/2007, SACU receipts rose by 9 percent of the GDP, reaching a remarkable 27.5 percent of the GDP. By 2008, they accounted for 60 percent of government revenues. These favorable terms of trade broke the fiscal deficit, which had been consistent since 2000/2001. The external current account deficit declined to 1.4 percent of the GDP in 2007, and even foreign reserves recovered to an estimated 3.4 months of imports of goods and services.

On the negative side, the SACU windfall facilitated the expansion of the public sector, which may prove unsustainable in future and whose costs may undermine macroeconomic stability. The public wage bill is among the highest in Africa, accounting for about 15 percent of the GDP. In 2007/2008, total public expenditure was about 38 percent of GDP. On the positive side, more efficient future management of government expenditure could release funds for priority development programs, such as in human development.

The exchange rate peg of the Lilangeni (SZL) to the South Africa Rand (ZAR) continues to serve the country well, underpinned by close economic integration with South Africa. However, sustenance of current economic policies may weaken the net external position thus threatening the peg. As such, a medium-term policy for fiscal sustainability needs to be accompanied by strategies to improve competitiveness. Among others, such strategies include the strengthening of Swaziland's skill base/human capital. .

Average annual inflation fell rapidly from nearly 11 percent in 2003 to a little above 3 percent in 2004, but rose again to 8.3 percent in 2007, and is projected to stabilize at about 6 percent by 2012.[6] The rising wage bill, growing government sector, oil prices and persisting high food prices all contribute to increasing inflation rates.

Despite sustained macroeconomic stability, growth acceleration remains elusive. Over the past 3 years, growth averaged a little above 2 percent, allowing a small real increase in per capita income only because of the population growth rate of about zero. In addition to the relocation of firms to post-apartheid South Africa, growth declined because of the erosion of the trade preferences by the European Union (EU) and the United States of America (USA), from the late 1990s to the early 2000s. Over the long-term, growth has also been affected by high public spending, poor management of public expenditure, perceptions of poor governance, weak institutional capacity, and low competitiveness due mainly to the appreciation of the SZL. The appreciation of the SZL in 2006/2007 undermined exports from manufacturing,[7] thus discouraging FDI in the sector. Other contributing factors include drought, and the consequent impact on agricultural outputs, adverse effects of forest fires on the forestry sector, and deceleration in the sugar industry.

Medium-term growth prospects are not encouraging, with growth projected to average 2 percent in the medium term. Key constraints to future growth include a weak investment climate and the consequent low FDI inflows, high costs of doing business, recurring droughts, low productivity, and absenteeism emanating from HIV/AIDS.

In the medium- to long-term, the global economic downturn poses a risk to growth through even more lowered FDI, lower export demand and lower demand from regional exports. The latter two will affect SACU receipts. On the other hand, declines in SACU receipts may make it difficult to contain the deficit. The fiscal risk could be compounded by the mandatory nature of many expenditure programs, which makes them difficult to scale down. Should Swaziland not clearly articulate a medium-term plan for adhering to sustainable fiscal targets, these fiscal risks may undermine poverty reduction and growth acceleration efforts more broadly.

An even greater future risk to growth is for Swaziland to allow a further depletion of its human capital base by failing to reform its ETSDS. This is even more risky given the impact of the HIV/AIDS pandemic and the consequent surge of Tuberculosis (TB), including multi-drug resistant TB (XDR) on human capital. Cross-country comparisons of life expectancy and GDP per capita for low- and middle-income countries show that Swaziland, as do other SACU countries record a life expectancy of about 20 years lower than that of other middle income countries and closer to that of low-income countries.[8]

Empowering the poor to generate income and reduce inequalities. Fair distribution of benefits of growth through fiscal policy

Swaziland's current economy is one of stark inequalities and significant wealth redistribution challenges. With a GDP per capita purchasing power parity (PPP) of US$4,800 (2007 est.) and a Gini coefficient of 0.61 (2005 est.)[9], nearly 70 percent of the population lives below the poverty datum (2005 est.). Poverty is more severe in rural areas (75% vs. 49%), and for female-headed households (63% vs. 53%). Between 1990 and 2005, 48 percent of the population lived on less than US$1 per day while 78 percent lived on less than US$2 per day.[10] The top quintile claimed 56 percent of total consumption while the bottom quintile claimed 4 percent.[11]

The combined levels of poverty and the extent of inequalities, threaten the PRSAP goal for improved quality of life. They also threaten political stability and social integration as aimed for in Vision 2022 and in the PRSAP. Countries with high levels of poverty and inequality have been found to be more prone to political instability than their counterparts.[12] In turn, social instability deters FDIs and stifles associated growths prospects. Unemployment is estimated to be as a high 40 percent using a broad measure, and 30 percent using a strict measure (2006 est.).[13] As noted, poverty is exacerbated by recurring droughts in a country where subsistence farming occupies 80 percent of the population. Between 1980 and 2005, the share of agriculture to the GDP declined from 35 percent to 9 percent.[14]

Improving the quality of life for the poor

Swaziland is not doing well on virtually all indicators that the NDS operationally defines as quality of life, vis. poverty eradication, employment creation, social equity, gender parity, social integration, and environmental protection. In addition to the low HDI, endemic poverty, and food shortages already alluded to, table 1.1 presents further proxy indicators of quality of life.

Table 1.1: Proxy Indicators of Quality of Life for Swazis Relative to other AMICs

AMICs	Life expectancy at birth (2006)	Prevalence of HIV (% of ages 15-49 (2007)	Incidence of Tuberculosis per 100 000 people (2006)	% population with sustained access to improved water source (2006)	% population with sustained access to improved sanitation (2006)	Physicians per 1,000 people (2005)	Maternal mortality ratio modeled estimate per 100 000 live births (2000-06)	% Births attended by skilled health staff
Botswana	49.8	23.9	551	96	47	0.4	380	94
Cape Verde	71	...	168	...	...	...	210	...
Gabon	56.7	5.9	354	87	36	0.3	520	86
Mauritius	73.2	1.7	23	100	94	1.1	15	99
Namibia	52.5	15.3	767	93	35	0.3	210	76
Seychelles	72.2	...	33	...	100	1.5	...	...
South Africa	50.7	18.1	940	93	59	0.8	400	92
Swaziland	40.8	26.1	1155	60	50	0.2	390	74

Source: The World Bank 2009. Africa development indicators: Youth and Employment in Africa: The potential, the problem the promise. Washington, D.C., The World Bank

Human capital development

Swaziland does not fare that well on determinants of quality human capital development as identified in the PRSAP—"access to education, health, safe water, proper sanitation, proper housing, enjoyment of basic freedoms, social security and contentment" (Vol. 1 p. 34). Table 1.1 points to low provision of health services, as well as of water and sanitation. The average educational attainment for Swazis born in the 1980s is 9 years, and is lower than for comparator countries. According to the 2006/2007 Demographic and Health Survey (DHS), completion rates for primary, junior secondary education and senior secondary education are 76 percent, 44 percent, and 24 percent respectively. These are also lower than for other SADC MICs. Refreshingly, adult (15+) literacy rate is high, having averaged 81 percent between 1995 and 2005.

A serious setback to human capital development is that Swaziland is at the epicenter of the HIV/AIDS pandemic. About 19 percent of the population is infected with HIV, 26 percent are between 15 and 49 years old, and the highest percent (59%), are women between the ages of 25 and 29. Figure 1.4 shows HIV prevalence rates by age groups. The highest prevalence is among the most productive age group of people between 20 and 49 years old (figure 1.4).

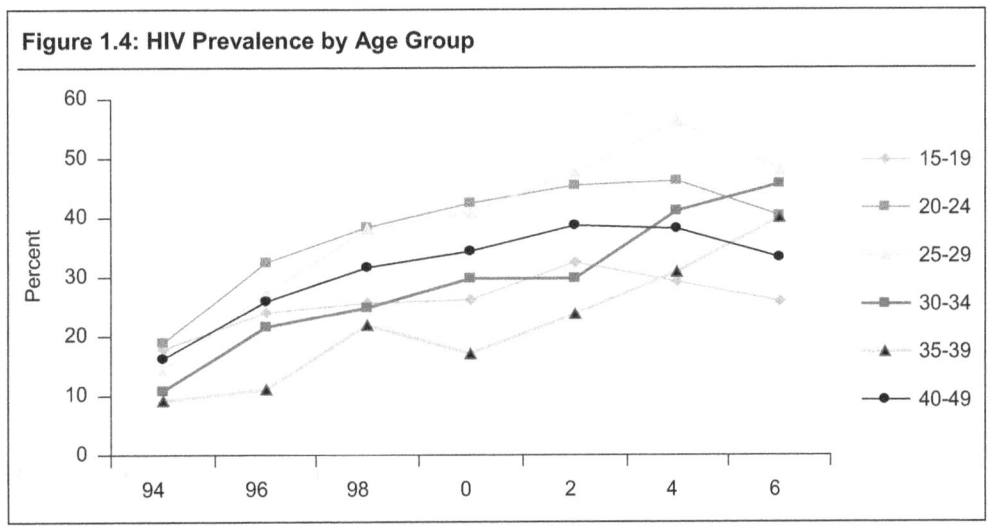

Source: NERCHA 2008.

Without intervention, HIV/AIDS could erode the human capital base built over long periods of time (figure 1.5). As noted, the demographic impact in terms of loss in life expectancy is estimated to be about 20 years, reversing the gains achieved in the 1950s. HIV/AIDS accounts for 31 percent of deaths in the three central Ministries—planning, finance, and labor and enterprise. Crude death rate is estimated at 22 percent. Two thirds of 15 year-olds will die of AIDS.[15] The pandemic is leading to worsening dependency rates, increased poverty and destitution, and increased expectations for government support.

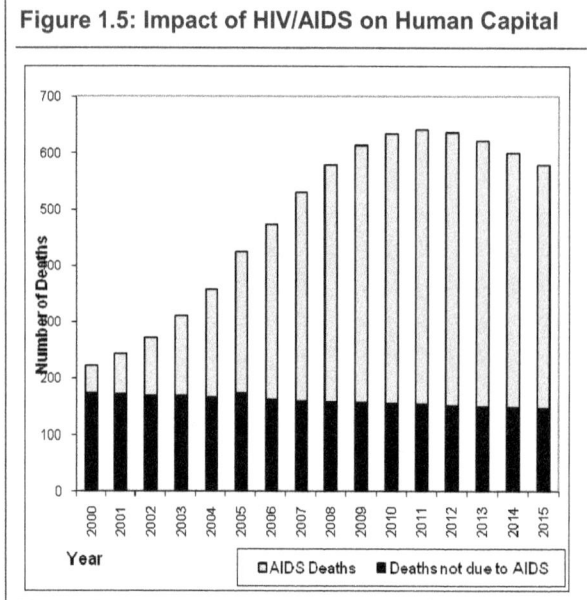

Figure 1.5: Impact of HIV/AIDS on Human Capital

Source: NERCHA 2008.

Part of the direct costs of HIV is that it is overwhelming the health system, accounting for over half of all hospital admissions. It engulfs facilities, and depletes supplies. It increases the costs of health-treatments, and crowds out expenditure and investment on other productivity-enhancing budgetary items, such as education or infrastructure. Even though the introduction of antiretroviral (ARV) has saved many lives, and spared many children from becoming orphans, the peaking of the epidemic has forced governments to dramatically expand costly national treatment programs to provide medication to those in need.

Though hard to quantify, HIV has significant indirect costs to households; including increased poverty, inequality, and child-headed households, with only 22 percent of children growing up in households with two parents. As families lose adult members to the epidemic—bread-winners are often those that succumb to the disease—surviving members are left to face an impoverished and indigent life. Households can hardly recover from the loss of the bread-winner and are often forced to cut expenditure on basic goods. This not only reduces overall consumption but reduces the quality of life, and the capacity to save, and depresses overall investments and aggregate demand, thus lowering economic growth. More importantly, as households see their ability to generate income suddenly decline, investments in human capital—education and training—may fall dramatically, further affecting the country's accumulation of human[16] capital. Again, this lowers overall economic productivity and growth.

In 2008, a third of Swaziland's children were categorized as Orphans and Vulnerable Children (OVCs), with 23 percent of them being orphans. In real terms, there are 130,000 orphans, and the number is expected to reach 200,000 by 2010. It is highly possible that the epidemic affects a larger number of children than orphans. Nonorphaned vulnerable children could include those living with HIV infection themselves, those whose parents are experiencing AIDS-related illness, and more generally, children who are particularly vulnerable due to poverty, discrimination, child labor, or exclusion. Needless to say, orphans are among the most vulnerable social group and are deprived of many services, including ETSD.

Factoring ETSDS into Swaziland's quest for shared growth, and competitiveness

Global knowledge of the role of ETSD in facilitating growth, social equity, and competitiveness is now well documented (see box 1.1).

Box 1.1: The role of ETSD in Growth Acceleration, Social Equity, and Competitiveness

Improved productivity: Higher levels of educational attainment—years of schooling—increases output per worker and may even increase the output of co-workers (OECD. 2005, ILO. 2008). High educational attainment strengthens capacity to apply knowledge and technology to realize higher value-added productivity, which is a key determinant of self-sustaining growth.

Improved GDP growth: Although the estimated impact of education on GDP growth differs across contexts and diverse studies, the overall conclusion is that increased educational attainment is associated with a significant increase in GDP growth (Krueger and Lindhal M. 2001, OECD. 2000. Bloom, Canning, and Chan. 2006, Hanushek and Wößmann. 2007. Global Competitiveness Report. 2007/2008 and the Human Development Report. 2007/08).

Quality of education matters: More recent analyses have established that better quality education is associated with higher annual average increase in GDP per capita (Hanushek and Wößmann. 2007). Due to low quality, the skills acquired in Africa have an overall lower impact on economic growth (Glewwe, Maiga, and Zheng. 2007).

Facilitation of the impact of FDIs on growth: ETSD strengthens the absorptive capacity for new knowledge and technology required to attract FDIs, and to redeploy workers from lower-level to higher-level skills. On the other hand, FDIs are found to have a higher impact on growth in countries that have higher levels of education—secondary education and above (Lumbila, 2005).

Improved competitiveness: A skilled and educated workforce is critical for attaining and sustaining international competitiveness which is shifting from natural resource-based production or basic production factors, toward technological capability and innovation (World Economic Forum. 2008, Dahlman, Zeng and Wang. 2007). This is evident in the declining share of primary products in international trade and the growth in manufactured and high-tech products (Altman and Mayer. 2003, Edwards and Lawrence. 2006, World Bank. 2008). Higher levels of education facilitate the transition from low levels of competitiveness in factor-driven economies to efficiency and innovation-driven economies (World Economic Forum. 2008). Therefore, competitiveness in the modern global economy requires a skilled and technologically advanced labor force.

Social equity: Because labor is the main asset of the poor, improving the quality of labor through education and training has redistributive effects. Higher levels of education and training increase chances of employment (Dias and Posel. 2007) and personal earnings (Bhorat, Lundall and Rospabe. 2002; Burger and Yu. 2007; and Banjerie et al. 2006). Increased productive employment is also associated with higher levels of poverty reduction (ILO. 2008). The share of people in the lowest earning categories declines as overall educational attainment increases (OECD. 2005). In addition, highly skilled workers raise demand for lower level skills and even the unskilled thereby deepening the redistributive effect through broad-based earnings. The education of women facilitates the transformation of gender roles and improves gender equity.

Other benefits of ETSD are better health practices, lower fertility rates, gender equity, higher uptake of social services, including education itself, democratic participation, self-esteem, social skills capacity to respond to adversity, social cohesion, political stability and the attendant positive investment climate. These benefits have an impact on productivity and, therefore, ultimately, growth.

HIV/AIDS infection rates are found to be lower for learners who stay longer in school up to the secondary school level (AIDS Information Center, 2000).

Countries facing development challenges similar to those of Swaziland, but with a sense of urgency and resolve, have developed ETSDS that later contributed to the effective redress of such challenges. Examples include the Republic of Korea, Ireland, and Singapore. However, unlike Swaziland which is struggling to attain and sustain healthy growth, most of these countries (with the exception of Ireland) initially had the fortune of high growth that enabled them to afford required sector reforms. This difference notwithstanding, their experiences bear common principles that are applicable to Swaziland. Key among these principles are:

- a strong and decisive government leadership with the courage to follow through on difficult reforms;
- capable institutions and a civil service that can implement reforms;
- sustained and heightened investment in the sector;
- a clear national development strategic outlook and consensually set development priorities;
- a clear alignment of sector reforms with the overall national development reform agenda;
- the ability and agility to adapt sector programs to emerging labor market demands;
- sustained and sequential sector reforms mostly starting at the base and moving upward, and starting with access and then moving to quality;
- an emphasis on equity of access and quality;
- the alignment of sector budgets with policy and strategic priorities; and
- the adoption of resource-efficient options, especially in the early stages of sector development.

A synopsis of the Korean and the Singaporean case studies is presented in the Appendix. Can Swaziland's current ETSDS support shared growth and competitiveness?

The rest of this report presents an analysis of the adequacy of Swaziland's current ETSDS to effectively support the national development reform agenda and to supply the human capital/skills required to contribute to economic recovery, growth acceleration, and social equity as envisaged in the NDS and the PRSAP. Key weaknesses are identified and remedial actions are proposed.

The analysis proceeded from two premises: The first premise is that since Swaziland is not a natural resource-rich country, growth acceleration and global competitiveness are likely to be knowledge and technology-driven. Yet table 1.2 shows that Swaziland ranks low in its knowledge economy index (KEI) and in its knowledge index (KI); suggesting a low-knowledge economy readiness. Moreover, Swaziland's 2009 relative ranking is much lower than for 1999. Scores are particularly low for indices relating to education, ICTs, and the economic incentive and institutional regime. Improving these indices will get Swaziland on a path towards knowledge and technology-driven growth.

Table 1.2: Swaziland's Relative Knowledge Economy Readiness

Rank	Change from 1995	Country	KEI		KI		Economic Incentive and Institutional Regime		Innovation index		Education Index		ICT Index	
			Recent	1995	recent	1995	Recent	1995	Recent	1995	recent	1995	Recent	1995
AMICs														
103	−19	Swaziland	2.93	4.18	3.05	2.56	5.58	4.55	4.65	1.73	3.14	2.88	3.36	
55	−6	South Africa	5.55	5.92	5.47	5.81	4.19	6.92	7.16	4.51	5.79	4.98	6.52	
64	−2	Mauritius	5.18	5.15	4.58	6.95	6.46	3.70	4.00	4.09	3.72	5.96	6.40	
85	−7	Botswana	3.96	4.51	3.50	5.34	5.69	4.34	4.78	2.58	3.35	3.59	4.21	
81	0	Namibia	4.19	4.28	3.20	7.14	5.29	3.30	4.03	2.57	3.69	3.74	4.10	
Fast Developing Countries														
48	0	Malaysia	6.06	6.03	6.02	6.18	7.21	6.83	6.20	4.14	4.16	7.08	6.57	
24	−4	Singapore	8.24	8.44	7.75	9.71	9.68	9.56	9.04	5.19	6.18	8.50	8.86	
OECD														
3	−1	Finland	9.37	9.56	9.33	9.47	9.43	9.66	9.31	9.78	9.74	8.56	9.75	
5	0	Norway	9.27	9.49	9.27	9.25	9.39	9.06	9.07	9.60	9.71	9.16	9.78	
9	−6	United States	9.08	9.50	9.05	9.16	9.20	9.45	9.56	8.77	9.42	8.93	9.83	
10	1	Australia	9.05	9.23	9.17	8.66	8.75	8.72	8.87	9.64	9.93	9.16	9.35	

Source: World Bank Institute. 2009. Knowledge Assessment Methodology.

The second premise is that since Swaziland has limited internal sources of growth, its effective growth strategy will have to exploit both national and sub-regional potentials. At present, Swaziland is surrounded by fast-growing natural resource rich countries that have acute skills shortages—Mozambique, Angola, Botswana, South Africa, Namibia, and Democratic Republic of Congo. These countries present opportunities for Swaziland to export skilled labor. Immediate benefits would first be remittances, which could boost revenues while improving quality of life and, second, improved capacity of the exported labor. Long-term benefits would include the brain circulation that would spur knowledge and technology-driven growth along similar lines as the Irish and Singaporean growth experiences.

At present, Swaziland seems to have maintained a better ETSD quality than its immediate neighbors—South Africa, Namibia, and Botswana. Strengthening the current foundation of quality should make its graduates attractive to sub-regional markets. However, Swaziland will need to expand access in areas of high regional and even global demand. This will require constant and close monitoring of changing demands in regional and global labor markets using labor market surveys where they exist, periodic reports of the International Labor Organization (ILO), and tracer studies of graduates. Swaziland will also have to benchmark its system to that of neighboring countries in line with "equivalencies" propagated in the SADC protocol on education and training. Some of the specific instruments that give effect to these "equivalencies" are national qualifications frameworks (NQFs), such as those for Botswana, Namibia and South Africa. In order for its graduates to easily fit into sub-regional and global labor markets, Swaziland's NQF would need to be cognizant of those of SADC countries, the SADC NQF, once developed, and those of more advanced systems, such as Australia and Scotland—exemplified later in the report. Swaziland also needs to strategically position itself to benefit from sub-regional human capital development initiatives as and when they arise.

Both these premises have significant implications for the ETSDS as a key supplier of human capital/skills. The export of skills in particular, will require an adequate quantity, quality and market relevance of Swaziland's ETSDS. However, modern economic growth theory highlights that human capital/skills are necessary but not sufficient to support growth acceleration. Other mutually-reinforcing determinants of growth are a conducive investment climate entailing some of the factors discussed above—macroeconomic stability, good governance investment climate, and adequate investment—and technology diffusion/innovation. Figure 1.6 illustrates these factors and how they are interconnected. As discussed above, prior analyses show Swaziland's weak investment climate and technology readiness.

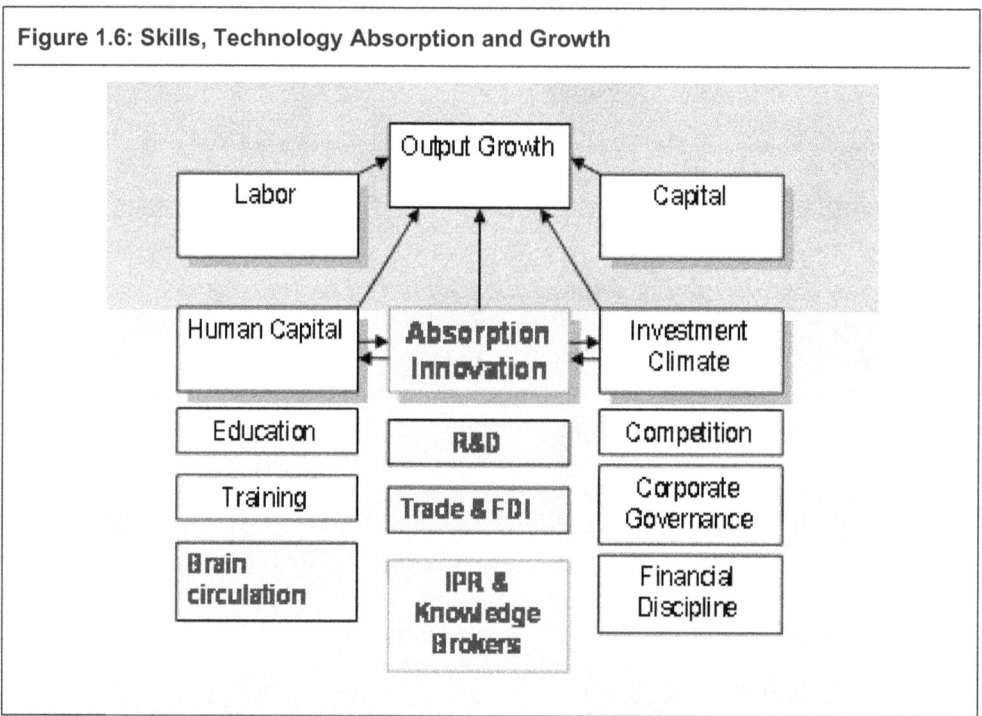

Figure 1.6: Skills, Technology Absorption and Growth

Source: Goldberg et al. 2008.

While recognizing the importance of other factors to growth, the scope of this report is limited to human capital and only from the point of view of knowledge and skills. The report covers all levels of the ETSDS, from ECD to tertiary education and training. Within this broad scope however, it particularly focuses on post-basic education and training.

Notes

[1] Ministry of Economic Planning and Development (MEPD). 2006. Vol 1:42.
[2] Key political associations include the African United Democratic Party (AUDP), Imbokodvo National Movement (INM), Ngwane National Liberatory Congress (NNLC) and People's United Democratic Movement or (PUDEMO).
[3] Reporters Without Borders. 2006 *Annual Report*.
[4] United Nations Development Program. 2009. *Human Development Report*. http://hdrstats.undp.org/countries_fact_sheets/cty_fs_SWZ.html. Accessed Jan 16, 2009.
[5] NERCHA. 2008.
[6] International Monetary Fund. 2008. Staff report for the 2007 Article IV consultations. IMF.
[7] International Monetary Fund. 2006. Staff report for the 2005 Article IV consultations. IMF.
[8] See IMF, World Economic Outlook Database (2008) for GDP per capita, and UN Population Division (2007) for life expectancy.
[9] Economic indicators—Swaziland. Earthtrends Country Profiles. http://earthtrends.wri.org/pdf_library/country_profiles/eco_cou_748.pdf.
[10] The World Bank. 2008. World development indicators. Washington, .DC. The World Bank.
[11] Ibid.
[12] World Bank. 2005. World Development Report (WDR). Washington, D.C. José Luis Machinea. 2004. National visions matter: Lessons of success. Proceedings of a public-private sector development forum. Santiago, Chile.
[13] Physicians for Human Rights. 2007. Epidemic of inequality: Women's rights and HIV/AIDS in Botswana and Swaziland. Cambridge, Massachusetts.
[14] Economic Review and Outlook. 2006.
[15] NERCHA. 2008. Presentation.
[16] Bell, B, Devarajan, S., Gersbach, H. (2003). The long-run economic costs of AIDS: Theory and an application to South Africa.

CHAPTER 2

Early Childhood Care and Development (ECCD)

Introduction

Investment in human capital development has been shown to bear the best dividend in earlier years (figure 2.1). Yet, most African countries—Swaziland inclusive—tend to invest the least in early years only to pay heavily for ineffective remedial actions in later years.

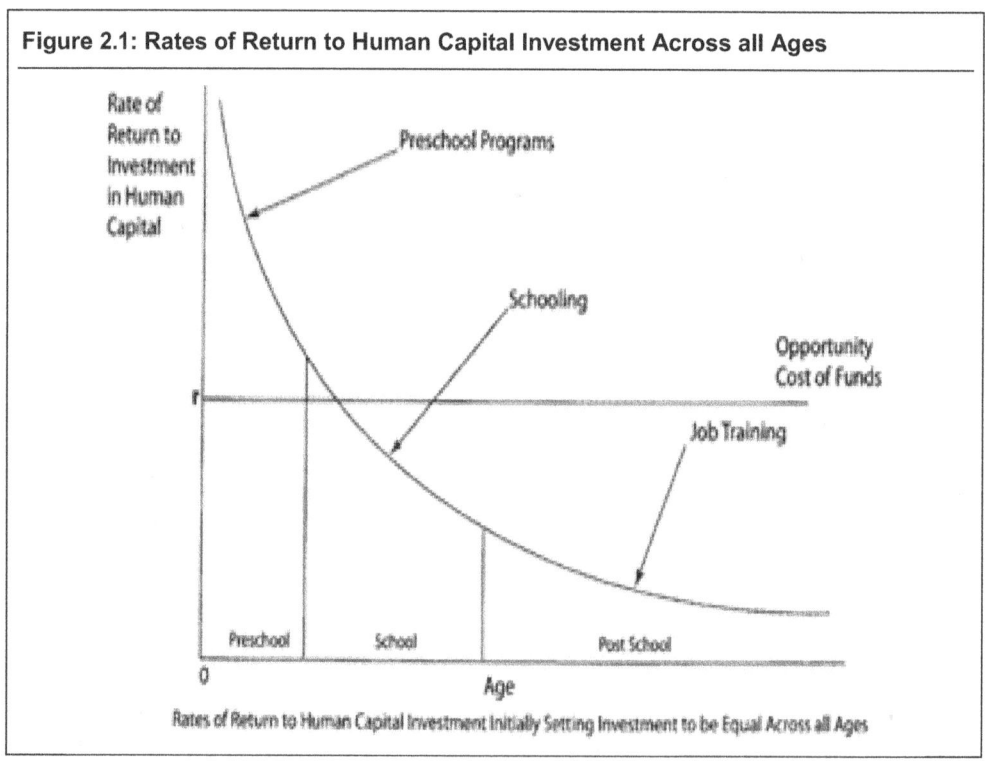

Figure 2.1: Rates of Return to Human Capital Investment Across all Ages

Source: Heckman and Carneiro. 2003.

ECCD provides a structure for the required systematic investment in the early years of life. When well-conceived, it entails a comprehensive set of policies, strategies and programs intended to facilitate holistic development of children from birth to eight years of age. Programs include health, nutrition, education/early stimulation, water and environmental sanitation, legal, social and emotional protection in homes and communities. They also include education and support for parents delivering services to children, the development of capacities of caregivers and teachers, and mass communication for enhancing the knowledge and practices of parents and caregivers.

Why Should Swaziland Invest in ECCD?

For Swaziland specifically, a strong motivation for investment in integrated ECCD is that a significant proportion of children have a poor start in life. As outlined in Chapter 1, they are born into and raised in severe poverty and dire circumstances. Their mortality rate is higher than that of their counterparts in other AMICs. About 40 percent of them do not get basic immunization, nearly 40 percent are stunted and 9 percent are underweight (see table 2.1). In addition, a third of the children—though with a broader age range than in the Table below—are OVCs. Global experience shows that such a poor start as that for Swazi children poses a high risk to the country's human capital development efforts, and to all other efforts whose success is interdependent with well developed human capital/skills (see figure 1.6).

Table 2.1: The State of Swaziland's Children and Implications for ECCD

AMICs	Under 5 mortality rate per 1,000 (2000–06)	Infant mortality per 1,000 live births (2006)	% 12–23 months immunized for measles (2006)	% 12–23 months immunized for DPT (2006)	% under fives stunting (2000–06)	% under fives underweight (2000–06)
Botswana	124	90	90	97	29	11
Cape Verde	34	25	65	72	...	...
Gabon	91	60	55	38	26	8
Mauritius	14	13	99	97	...	...
Namibia	61	45	63	74	30	20
Seychelles	13	12	99	99	...	...
South Africa	69	56	85	99	...	...
Swaziland	164	112	57	58	37	9

Source: World Bank 2009.

Effective ECCD programs have been found to substantially reduce the impact of structural poverty on children's quality of life, including the improvement of their readiness to learn at later stages. Such benefits would bode well for the Vision 2022 and PRSAP goals. Box 2.1 presents some of the evidenced benefits of ECCD that could accrue to Swazi children.

Box 2.1: Benefits of ECCD Programs

International experiences show that ECCD programs lead to:

- Improved nutrition and health: ECCD programs enhance the efficacy of health care and nutrition initiatives. Evidence from the Colombia Community Child Care and Nutrition Project and India's Integrated Child Development Services program also show that the programs can ensure that children receive health care.
- Early brain development and potential to learn: Improved health and nutrition programs associated with well conceived ECCD programs enable children to be more successful in their later schooling, more socially and emotionally competent, and to have higher verbal and cognitive development.
- Improved cognitive development and school achievement: Children participating in ECCD programs score higher in intellectual aptitude tests than nonparticipants as was evident in evaluations of Jamaica's First Home Visiting Program and Turkey's Early Enrichment Project.
- Higher school enrollment: The Colombia Promesa program cited significantly higher enrollment rates (in later schooling) among program children than among nonparticipants. Moreover, various studies show that girls who were enrolled in early childhood programs were better prepared for school and stayed in school longer.
- Better school readiness, attendance, learning, internal efficiency: Studies in Colombia's and Argentina's ECD programs showed that children, on average, had lower rates of repetition. In India's Dalmau program, the only study in which attendance was measured, later school attendance was 16 percent higher for children ages six to eight. In Colombia's Promesa project, third-grade enrollment rates rose by 100 percent, reflecting lower dropout and repetition rates. Overall, ECCD and pre-primary programs facilitate school readiness, lead to better internal efficiency during the basic education cycle, and reduce children's chances of placement in special education and of dropping out. They have a positive impact on the development trajectory of children.
- Improved resource efficiency of the education system and returns to society: Improvements to internal efficiency of education systems accrue better resource efficiency to the society at large. Cost-benefit analyses of early childhood development programs have shown positive results in both developed and developing countries. The High/Scope Perry Preschool Project study in the USA estimated the returns of the program to the public to be as high as US$7.16 for every dollar invested (Young, 2007). Similarly the Jacoby-King study in the Philippines estimated that a dollar invested in an early childhood nutrition program in a developing country could potentially return at least US$3 worth of gains in academic achievement (Glewwe, 2001).
- Help for the disadvantaged and reduced social inequality: ECCD interventions in early childhood benefit the poor and disadvantaged, e.g. in India's Haryana Project, dropout rates fell 46 percent for lower caste children and 80 percent for middle caste children (Chaturvedi et. al, 1987). Similarly a study conducted in Jamaica proved that nutritional supplementation for undernourished children, who are most likely to come from disadvantaged families, improves mental development (Grantham-McGregor et al. 1991).
- Positive effect on female labor force participation and older siblings' schooling: A study in Kenya showed how women's labor force participation and older children's schooling improve due to ECD programs (Lokshin, et al. 2000). Providing safe child care also allows women a chance to continue their education, acquire new skills, and join the formal labor force.

Source: Author.

Nobel Laureate Heckman (1999) argues that investments in children bring a higher rate of return than investments in low-skill adults[1] (figure 2.1).

In essence therefore, ensuring holistic child development is laying a solid foundation for the country's human capital and the attendant development benefits. ECCD is one of the most effective chances that Swaziland has at equitable integration of future generations into the economy and at reducing poverty and inequality[2] in line with Vision 2022 and the PRSAP.

Policy Orientation of ECCD

Despite the benefits of ECCD, its provision in Swaziland is proceeding without a policy or the strategic direction required to optimize associated benefits. Prior efforts at policy formulation have remained in draft since the National Education Review Commission of 1985 (NERCOM, 1985). Recent years have seen renewed efforts to develop a national ECCD policy. However, the draft policy has been at a consultation stage for nearly two years and is expected to be finalized based on the analytical underpinning provided in this report. The draft recognizes diverse children's needs during their ECCD phase as summarized in table 2.2.

Table 2.2: Perceived Needs to be Addressed by ECCD Programs

	Stage	Key Needs
ECD (Pre-natal to 3 years)	Pre-natal and Birth	Maternal and child health; parental support; parenting education
	Infancy (0-18 months)	Health and nutrition
	Toddler and post-toddler (18-36 months)	Health and nutrition; language and social skills; thinking abilities
Pre-school	Pre-Schools (4-5 years)	Pre-schooling; health and nutrition; social skills, protection
Primary Schooling	Lower Primary School (6-8 yrs)	Education, health, nutrition, protection

Source: http://www.iadb.org/sds/soc/eccd/mean.html.

Structure and Nature of ECCD Provision

Swaziland's ECCD services comprise early childhood development (ECD) for 0-3 year olds, preprimary education for 4-5 year olds, and lower primary education for 6-8 year olds An estimated 203,000 children are of eligible age. ECD is provided by daycare centers mainly in urban areas where both parents work. Preprimary education is offered mainly by communities, faith-based organizations (FBOs), Nongovernmental Organizations (NGOs), and private individuals. Lower primary education is part of primary education. In addition, Swaziland has established innovative institutions that offer some elements of ECCD: NCPs and KaGogo centers (see figure 2.2). These centers emerged mainly as a part of the response to the impact of HIV/AIDS. KaGogo centers are modeled after the traditional KaGogo as neutral places of refuge where children can confide. They are now regarded as the coordinating centre of community interventions, such as NCPs, and may in future serve as gateways for decentralized service delivery. Children registered at NCPs must be below 18 years of age, come to the center regularly, and participate in activities. One or both of their parents may be either sick or dead.

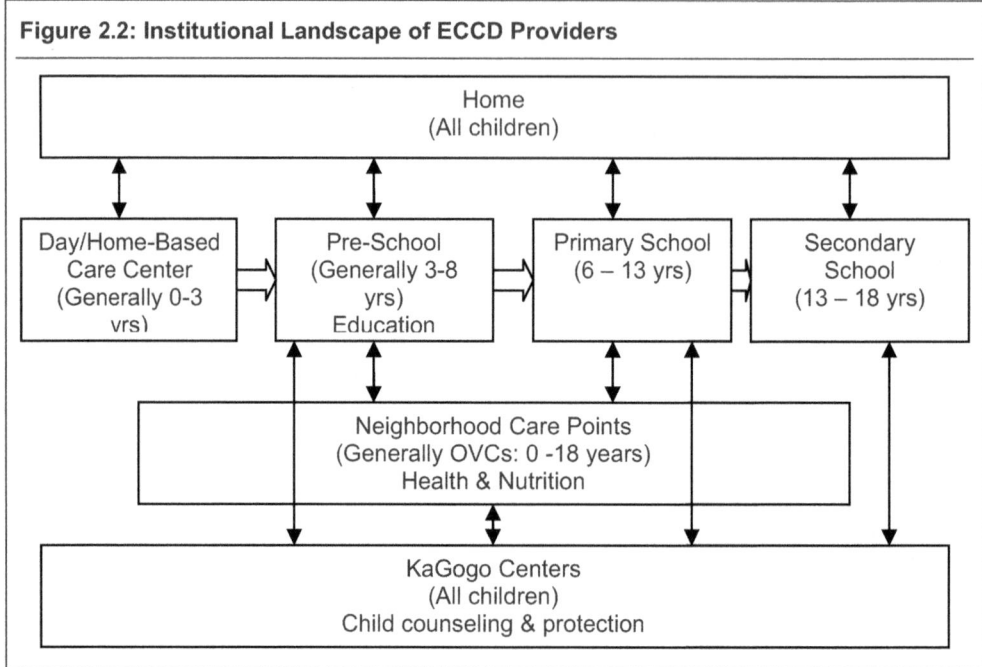

Figure 2.2: Institutional Landscape of ECCD Providers

Source: Data compiled by author.

Access and Equity

Access to ECCD is limited and inequitable by income level, special needs, and being an OVC. Approximately 136,000[3] children are estimated to be eligible for ECCD services. A conservative estimate of the number of children enrolled in 1,000 ECCD institutions is 33,000. An additional 13,200[4] children of 0-8 years were estimated to be enrolled in the 625 NCPs. Therefore the total number of 0-8 year olds covered is around 46,000 leading one to conclude that not more than 34 percent of eligible children[5] have access to some form of ECCD services. The percentage of children with access to formal ECD services 0-3 years would therefore be much lower.[6]

Though dated, the Multiple Indicator Cluster Survey (MICS) of 2000 estimated that children from the richest quintile were 10 times more likely to attend some form of ECCD institution than children from the poorest quintile. A large number of children are deprived of the benefits of ECCD services, especially in a country where 69 percent of the population is below the poverty line.

Only 6.3 percent of children with special needs enrolled in the 478 ECCD centers covered in the 2006 survey. This is much lower than the UN estimate that on average, 10 percent of children have some form of disability. It is even lower than the World Health Organization (WHO) estimate which is that on average, 40 percent of Africa's school-age population has some form of disability.

About half (53%) of surveyed centers indicated that they did not cater to children with special needs, implying that a significant number of the centers are not equipped to enroll such children. Appropriate materials and facilities for their learning were either nonexistent or inadequate across all institutions, reinforcing findings of the 2000 MICS survey. Field visits to ECCD institutions further revealed that a social stigma against disabled children is another reason why only a few of them are enrolled.

OVCs have limited access to ECCD services. In 2006, NPCs covered 33,000 OVCs of 0-18 years of age against an estimated 130,000. The proportion of OVCs who are strictly eligible for ECCD is unknown. However, it can be safely concluded that a significant number of them are not enrolled. OVCs constituted only 2,132 of the 11,029 children covered in the 2006 ECCD survey. ECCD institutions such as pre-schools are less likely to enroll OVCs because of cost implications.

Quality and Equity

Adequacy and equity of quality-enhancing inputs

Mainly because of lack of a policy, regulatory framework and government oversight, the provision of basic and of quality-enhancing inputs vary widely across pre-schools and day care centers. Examples include: qualified teachers, play facilities, books, other educational materials and, health and sanitation facilities. In general, resource inputs are inequitable based on the income level of the children catered for in the institution.

For most rural children, the physical environment in which they are taught is neither safe nor stimulating. Few community based preschools in rural areas had books, play, materials, writing materials, furniture or outside play equipment. The premises are most frequently bare huts, bare grounds, with a pit latrine or no ablution facilities. Some structures are poorly constructed and are hazardous for both children and teachers. 50 of the 478 surveyed centers had structures made of stick and mud. Only 48 percent had dedicated structures used specifically for ECCD services. One fifth could not be accessed by a vehicle, which could be quite dangerous in times of emergencies. One quarter did not have an improved water source. They get water from nearby rivers or springs, which is even more hazardous. Only 25 percent of the centers had electricity.

Most centers are ill-equipped to facilitate and care for children. Only 34 percent had play space or fields, 13 percent had gardens, 5.6 had computers, 20.1 had library books, and only 19.7 percent had first-aid kits. About 40 percent of the centers had sand pits, 13 percent had merry-go-rounds; 20 percent had slides, and 24 percent had climbers. Slightly more than half had tires with which children could play.

Resource inputs—infrastructure, furniture, equipment, play facilities, learning materials, qualified facilitators, and health-compliant facilities—are inadequate because ECCD is under-funded. The proportion of the sector budget allocated to ECCD declined from 0.08 percent in 2000/2001 to 0.05 in 2006/2007. Moreover, the actual expenditure ranged from 47 percent to 68 percent of the allocated budget. ECCD is virtually funded by parents. The GoS contributes an estimated SZ4 per child per year relative to an estimated annual per capita expenditure of SZ500.

Program standards and relevance

Swaziland does not have an operational definition of ECCD outputs such as what constitutes holistic child development or school readiness. There are no common standards that should be used to guide the development of programs. Consequently, there are no benchmarks against which diverse service providers can be monitored. It is also difficult to track a trajectory of improvement, or lack thereof, in the quality of provided services. At present, broad areas that should be covered in pre-primary education include creative arts, language and literacy; movement and music; numeracy; life skills and exploring science.

Without a standard to guide curricula, pre-primary teachers and care givers tend to teach children what they can. Some ECCD centers repeat content to children year after year[7]. This is not the case in ECCD centers that cater to affluent communities, since these have a well-designed curriculum for children of different age groups. For example, at the Pilot International Pre-School in Mbabane, children received even hands-on computer lessons.[8] In contrast, children in the Ematjeni Pre-School in Egundwini Village barely had any educational materials. The ECCD Unit is currently in the process of designing a curriculum for pre-schools and other ECCD centers. However, this effort is proceeding without a clear policy and strategic direction, and clear definitions of what constitutes holistic child development and school readiness.

Other than the weak content, children's ECCD experiences are reduced by the limited time they spend on relevant activities. On average children spend 4 hours in pre-schools and NCPs, which is lower than the 6 hours spent in pre-schools in other countries such as Ghana or Namibia. Half of the children's time is spent on class-room education, 25 percent on play, 10 percent on feeding and the remaining time goes unsupervised[9]. In NCPs, children spent half their time on play, 25 percent on class-room education, and the remaining on feeding or unsupervised.

Health, nutrition, and HIV/AIDS aspects of ECCD are weak. In fact, most ECCD centers do not provide any health and nutrition inputs, nor do they teach children about HIV/AIDS. The latter is a critical loss of opportunity to instill knowledge about this scourge at an early age, and to hopefully instill behavior- modifying habits. The Ministry of Health and Social Welfare is supposed to deliver the School Referral Program in pre-schools, NCPs, and schools to ensure healthy practices and safe learning environments. However, the program was only able to reach out to 3 pre-schools in 2006.[10] Reportedly, key constraints include a lack of dedicated staff, transport and funds. Only 27 percent of the pre-schools surveyed in 2006 had feeding programs, all financed by parents through fees. On the contrary, most NCPs had feeding programs, However, meals were not provided all the year round due to food shortages.

Most programs do not cover relevant aspects of children's psychosocial and emotional development. Again these inputs are supposed to come from the Ministry of Health and Social Welfare but are mostly not been forthcoming.

The protection aspects of ECCD are also weak but are likely to benefit from the recent creation of the National Children's Coordinating Unit (NCCU), which will be the nodal agency for child protection. The NCCU is not yet operational but its Secretariat will coordinate the implementation of a draft National Policy on Children including OVCs. The policy seeks to create a conducive environment within which children can be adequately supported and cared for to grow and develop their full potential. The NCCU will coordinate the implementation of all activities of government Ministries and NGOs pertaining to children's social protection. These will include: supporting and protecting children from all forms of abuse; assisting communities in establishing safety nets for children; reviewing and formulating policies pertaining to children's issues; establishing programs that develop children's life skills; and monitoring programs and developing databases for all vulnerable children.

Human resources

There are no minimum qualifications or competencies for preschool teachers or NPC caregivers. Consequently pre-school teachers and caregivers could be highly qualified or be school dropouts. Many caregivers had not received education beyond grade 5. Both teachers and caregivers often do not have the skills and knowledge required to teach, or care for young children or facilitate their development. Often they resort to rote learning methods which are ill-suited (Litchfield, 2007) and a bit far from the desirable pedagogy which includes approaches that are:

- child-centered;
- activity-oriented;
- focuses on learning through play;
- focused on stimulation; and
- encouraging of experimentation.

The quality of teachers and caregivers is low partly because the government allocation for training is highly insufficient. Training programs have to rely on volunteers and donor support, and this makes them irregular and infrequent. The little in-service training there is, is provided by the ECCD Unit of the MoE. Moreover the absence of a demonstration center and a fixed facility where educational demonstration materials can be developed and stored makes it difficult to deliver quality training. MoE training efforts are augmented by those of FBOs and NGOs: (i) Baha'i National Center; (ii) Free Evangelical Association; and (iii) Likusasa. The programs differ broadly in terms of content and duration.

Despite inadequate resources, the MoE ECCD Unit endeavors to improve the quality of ECCD practitioners. Efforts to standardize teacher/care-giver training curriculum are advanced. The Unit, in collaboration with the Center for Community Training and Development at the Faculty of Education in UNISWA is currently developing a standard certificate program for practitioners in ECCD. The modules of this program include:

- orientation to teaching the young child;
- creative arts;
- language and literacy;
- movement and music;
- numeracy;
- life skills and exploring science;
- planning for health and safety;
- management issues including assessment and reporting;
- identification and accommodation of children with learning and development barriers; and
- practical teaching.

Another strength is the training for NCP caregivers—funded by United Nations Children's Education Fund (UNICEF)—which is relatively well-structured and organized. Caregivers are trained in general management of the facilities, identifying and responding to psychosocial needs of children, improved home-care practices, treatment of illnesses, good hygiene and sanitation practices, and basic information on HIV/AIDS prevention. In collaboration with the National Emergency Response Council on HIV/AIDS (NERCHA) and UNICEF partners' training manuals have been developed in siSwati and English. About 1,500 caregivers in NCPs have been trained using these manuals. In addition, it would be beneficial if parents and communities could receive the basic HIV and TB information, to allow for consistency in messages delivered to children from a very early age. Basic knowledge and proper understanding of how HIV is transmitted is critical for prevention and to fend off stigmatization which can be witnessed in ECCD centers among the youngest. Efforts should be made to contain stigma of all kinds (including stigma against disabled children). The home and ECCD centers are a good starting point.

Teacher/caregivers compensation and incentives

Incentives and compensation for preschool teachers vary widely depending on the location and fee structure of the ECCD centers. Since there is no government support, most pre-schools and day care centers pay teachers out of their own revenues. In a number of pre-schools, fees are paid irregularly and are not sufficient to cover 'teachers' salaries, let alone materials, equipment or maintenance. For example, in Ematjeni Pre-School, Egundvwini Village the monthly fee of E50 per child of the 13 enrolled children was barely sufficient to pay the caregiver's monthly salary of E650. Moreover since most parents do not pay on time, caregivers tend to not receive their salaries on time. At the other extreme, in large private urban ECCD centers, fees could be as high as E2,000 per term, and the most senior qualified teachers could earn as much as E10,000 per term.

Salaries of caregivers and teachers do not conform to regulations. The Regulation of Wages for Pre-Schools and Day Care Centers Order, 2006 passed by the Ministry of Enterprise and Employment (MoEE) stipulates hours of work, annual, sick, compassionate and maternity leave criteria, severance allowances, and minimum wages for all teachers and caregivers in pre-schools and day care centers. However, the order is not enforced and the wages of several caregivers/teachers are below the stipulated wage. In all likelihood, a faithful the implementation of the order would close down several pre-schools and day care centers; as most of them barely manage to break even.

A poor incentive structure threatens the sustainability of services of caregivers in NCPs. Caregivers in NCPs are hired on a voluntary basis from the neighborhoods in which the NCP is located and they have no explicit incentive for working in NCPs. In some regions, caregivers are partially compensated by a food-for-work program supported by WFP. Under this program, a caregiver is provided monthly rations for a household of five (approximately 70 kilograms of maize). NPCs are not supposed to charge fees but the lack of funding for caregivers' compensation allegedly causes some to do so.

Efficiency

Enrollment levels in most ECCD centers are too low to facilitate resource efficiency. About 16 percent (53 of 323) of the centers enrolled less than 20 children. Enrollment in ECCD centers surveyed in 2006 varied from 450 (Thembela Pre-School, Manzini) to 8 (Zamokuhle Pre-School in Mvembili Village, Hhohho District). Given that access to ECCD services is low, the low enrollment suggests unutilized capacity and resource wastage.

The management of most centers is also inefficient. From the 2006 survey, 86 percent of the pre-schools had constituted school management committees (SMCs), while only 17 percent had parent teacher associations (PTAs). Oddly enough only 38 percent of preschools had bank accounts demonstrating poor financial management.

Out of the 404 pre-schools which had SMCs most (186) met only once in a term, despite the stipulation of the pre-school education regulations that they should meet monthly (Section 11.9 of the Pre-School Education Regulations). Only 17 percent of the pre-schools had PTAs. Thirty-five of the 80 PTAs seemed to be active and met two or more times in a term. There were 4 pre-schools in which PTAs were dysfunctional, while in 10 pre-schools PTAs met once a year.

The delivery of ECCD services is an inter-ministerial task. Yet there is no inter-ministerial coordination mechanism to ensure integrated delivery of diverse aspects of ECCD services. Preschools and daycare centers are under the supervision of the MoE. NCPs are under the supervision of the Ministry of Rural Development and Youth Affairs (MRDYA). Health services are delivered by the Ministry of Health and Social Welfare. The lack of coordination has often led to a costly duplication of efforts. Invariably all Ministerial Units that are supposed to deliver ECCD services are short staffed and weak. This translates into poor service delivery. Moreover, the ECCD Unit under the MoE often appears to work in isolation. As earlier noted, the recently created NCCU may address this gap, once it is fully staffed and operational.

The monitoring and evaluation of ECCD service providers is weak. According to the 2006 survey, approximately half of pre-schools covered in the survey had never been visited by an inspector. Approximately a third had been inspected once a year (table 2.3).

Table 2.3: Number of Pre-School Inspections by MoE

Region	More than once	Never visited	Once a term	Once a year	Grand total
Hhohho	31	76	20	64	191
Lubombo	14	51	6	27	98
Manzini	3	61	3	37	104
Shiselweni	1	19	6	15	41
Total	49	207	35	143	434

Source: Data compiled by author.

The monitoring and evaluation of ECCD service providers is weak mainly because the MoE ECCD unit is short-staffed and under-funded. A team of 5—a Senior Inspector and 4 Teacher Leaders—is expected to supervise and monitor approximately 1,000

ECCD centers spread throughout the country. Moreover, the team has multiple functions including curriculum design, in-service pre-school training, policy development, the monitoring of policy implementation and routine administrative functions.

Conclusion

Most Swazi children have a hard start in life. Effective ECCD services could provide them with a gateway out of their circumstance. ECCD services could also prevent unaffordable internal inefficiency and inequity of ETSD services at the higher levels. Yet, ECCD provision is proceeding without a policy and strategic direction necessary to transform it into an effective contributor to the PRSAP poverty reduction and improvement of quality of life goals. Financial allocations for ECCD suggest that it is not a GoS priority. Poor households bear the exclusive burden of financing this subsector. Access to ECCD services is limited and inequitable in favor of high income households and urban dwellers. About 66 percent of Swazi children who are eligible for ECCD services are without access. For the estimated 34 percent who have access, the quality of the services is highly variable and overall not comprehensive in scope. There are no standards to guide provision or regulations to guide providers. Because of lack of standards, ECCD services lack internal relevance to the ETSD system. Except for children of the affluent, it is doubtful if the limited services facilitate holistic child development or if pre-primary education equips children with primary school readiness. Given the deep floor from which the majority of Swazi children start ECCD services are crucial. They are crucial also to lay a foundation for sustainable and pro-poor human capital development. A pro-poor approach could be a powerful gateway for children from poor households to break the cycle of poverty. Current capacity to manage the delivery of ECCD services is weak. Overall, most of the issues in this subsector results from a near total neglect by the GoS when it comes to financing. While other subsectors require improvement, ECCD will require a re-founding.

Notes

[1] Source: Heckman & Carneiro (2003) Human Capital Policy
http://web.worldbank.org/WBSITE/EXTERNAL/TOPICS/EXTCY/EXTECD/0,,contentMDK:20207747~menuPK:527098~pagePK:148956~piPK:216618~theSitePK:344939,00.html.
[2] Press Release, Consulta, San Jose Costa Rica, October 25, 2007 (http://www.iadb.org/res/ConsultaSanJose/).
[3] Of an estimated 203,000 of eligible children—0-8 years—67,000 were enrolled in primary school in 2005, leaving an estimated 136,000 clients for ECCD services.
[4] 40% of the total reported enrollment of 33,000 children in Neighborhood Care Points was estimated to be in the 0-8 year age group.
[5] 46,000 of 136,000 children.
[6] The lack of data makes it impossible to segregate enrollments on the basis of age.
[7] Observations based on field visits to ECCD institutions.
[8] Source: field visits and observations.
[9] This assessment was based on observations in two pre-schools and confirmed in discussions with two regional leaders.
[10] As per the 2006 School Referral Program Implementation Report.

CHAPTER 3

General Education and Training

Introduction

General education and training (GET) comprises 7-3-2 years of primary, junior secondary and senior secondary education respectively. In 2007, there were 556 formally recognized primary schools enrolling 232572 learners of whom 48 percent were females. Some 43 junior secondary schools enrolled 60002 students of whom 47 percent were female and 157 senior secondary schools enrolled 22834 students of whom 48 percent were females. These figures call for effort to close the remaining gender gap. Due to unmet demand for secondary education, an additional 3084 (2007 est.) students were enrolled in the so called "illegal schools" which are registered with the MoEE as businesses but not with the MoE as schools. These schools are not monitored by the MoE and are not recognized as examination centers. Their students register for examinations as private candidates in registered schools or upgrading centers. Nothing about them is captured in the MoE records or in the EMIS.

The formal GET is complemented by nonformal education and training centers that provide adult basic education and training (ABET) programs as well as second chance opportunities for primary and secondary education. In 2008, they enrolled 2408 learners in ABET programs and 700 in secondary education programs.

This chapter presents an analytical **update** of the GET subsector since 2005. It does not repeat the detailed subsector analysis published by the World Bank in 2006.

Rationale for Improving GET

Good quality and broad based GET has the potential to contribute toward the strengthening of several of the PRSAP pillars. The development impact of education, especially women's education on reduced fertility, family health and nutrition, participatory democracy, the absorptive capacity for other social services, including education itself are consistent with Vision 2022, NDS and PRSAP orientation towards improved quality of life for Swazis. Supported by health, nutrition, HIV/AIDS prevention, and protection programs, quality GET equips the population with basic, behavioral and generic skills that are part of the fundamentals of the human capital development pillar of the PRSAP. It also develops labor market entry skills, employability, trainability and self-educability that could contribute to the PRSAP pillar on empowering the poor to generate income and to reduce inequalities. Complimented by employment creation initiatives, quality and labor market responsive GET could contribute to Swaziland's goals to reduce unemployment, especially the 60 percent youth unemployment.

Improved employability, trainability, and adaptability of the labor force are critical for Swaziland's success in attracting FDIs; which is part of the PRSAP's strategic actions for growth acceleration. At the secondary level, quality GET increases the absorptive capacity for knowledge and technology. Because of improved capacity, FDIs are found to have a higher impact on growth in countries that have secondary education enrollment rates of more than 25 percent and where the average secondary school attainment exceeds 0.45 years.[1]

Given its broad coverage, GET has the most compelling social equity and redistribution imperative. Therefore, it has the best potential to meet Swaziland's social equity goal than any other level of the system. A recent review of 28 studies in SSA shows that a mean Mincerian private return to education is 5 percent at the primary level but 14 percent at the secondary level.[2] Similar findings were recorded in Namibia where private returns to primary education were almost zero but 28 percent for senior secondary education[3]. Social returns to secondary education are also significant. Other studies have shown that the gap between urban and rural household incomes tends to narrow as the level of education gets higher.

Even more critical to Swaziland, sustained access to GET can significantly contribute to the national goal to curb the spread of HIV/AIDS. Children who stay longer in school have been found to be less likely to contract the HIV virus than their counterparts. In addition, educated people overall and, women in particular have been found to be less likely to contract the virus.[4] On a whole, children become sexually active during secondary school going age. It is estimated that people between15 and 24 years of old comprise a third of the 38 million people living with HIV/AIDS. More than half of the 5 million newly infected people are in this age bracket. Sustained and broad-based participation in good quality education is therefore a critical tool for redressing the spread of HIV among youth.

Policy Orientation and Recent Subsector Developments

GET is guided by the National Education Policy of 1999. Though dated, the policy identified key sector challenges as: low and inequitable access, limited pathways, poor quality, inadequate student assessment, low relevance, inefficiency, unaffordable costs, poor management and inattentiveness to morals, values and attitudes. In recent years 2005-2008, performance of the GET subsector is assessed against these parameters and, against the demands of the PRSAP, HIV/AIDS, and changing national and global skills requirements.

Equity of Access and Attainment

Historic trends in access and attainment

Access to GET has steadily increased over the years but overall attainment is still lower than for neighboring countries with which Swaziland competes for FDIs and for regional labor markets. Average educational attainment has increased from 3 years for Swazis born in the 1940s to about 9 years for those born in the 1980s (figure 3.1).

Figure 3.1: Comparative Long Range Educational Attainment

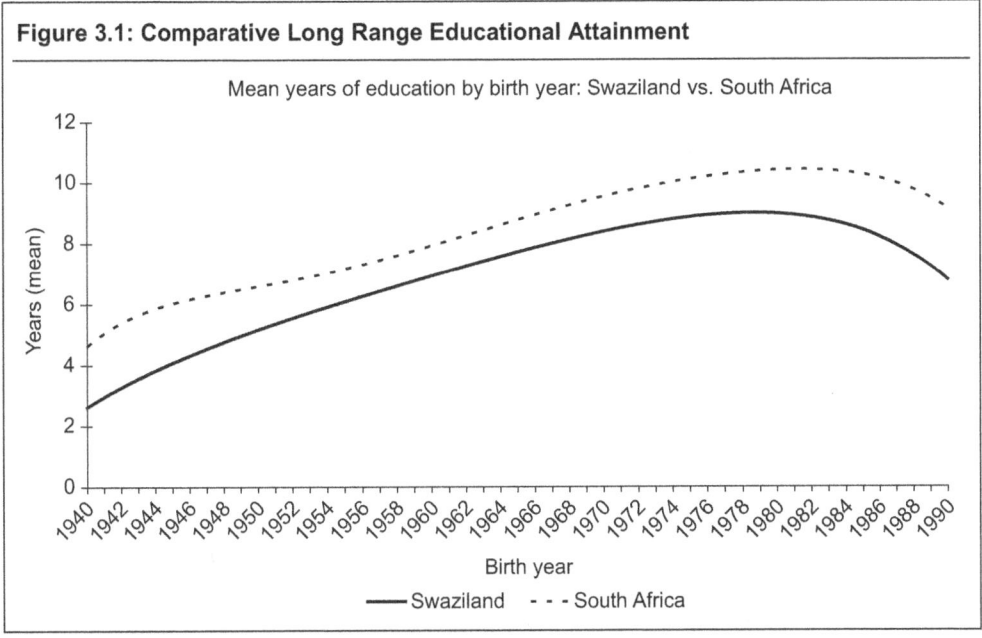

Source: DHS2006/7 and South African Labour Force Survey 2007a.

Between 2004 and 2008, primary school enrollment increased by nearly 8 percentage points (see table 3.1). Junior and senior secondary enrollments increased by 19 and 24 percentage points respectively. This expansion notwithstanding, access is still too low to support Swaziland's growth acceleration and to empower the poor. About 16 percent of children of eligible age are still out of primary school, and a staggering 74 percent and 88 percent are out of junior secondary and senior secondary levels respectively (table 3.1). These levels of access are too low to enable Swaziland to attract high-end FDIs, improve productivity and to be globally competitive.

Table 3.1: Recent Trends in Primary and Secondary Education Enrollment by Gender

Year	Primary education				Jnr. secondary enrollment				Snr. secondary enrollment			
	Total	% F	GER	NER	Total	% F	GER	NER	Total	% F	GER	NER
2004	218,352	...	111	....	48,523	....	54	....	18.286	....	35	....
2005	221,596	48	113	....	51,238	51	58	....	20,106	48	39	....
2006	229,686	48	118	....	54,813	51	63	....	22,167	49	43	....
2007	232,572	48	120	....	60,002	47	69	....	22,834	48	44	....
2008	235,044	....	122	84	57,847	....	67	26	22,731	....	43	12

Source: EMIS. 2004 to 2007. CSO. 2008, DHS 2006/2007.

Second chance opportunities for GET

The Sebenta Institute (SI) offers nonformal universal primary education (NUPE) programs. It runs a level I siSwati language program, level II English language program and level III combined languages programs and primary school subjects. Six

NUPE subjects are required for learners to complete an equivalent of grade 7. Table 3.2 shows enrollment in recent years. Learners who complete NUPE subjects have to re-enter a formal primary school in order to sit for the primary school certificate examination (PSCE). *In practice, this blocks adult learners from taking the examination and from using it to progress through to secondary education and beyond.* This may explain the low enrollments beyond the 'basic level' as adults probably loose the incentive to continue with their studies. The SI and other nonformal institutions also offer basic training opportunities which were elaborated on in Chapter 4.

Table 3.2: Sebenta Enrollment

Programs/levels	2004	2005	2006	2007
Basic	1,305	2,055	2,264	2,408
Post Basic	584	326	315	388
NUPE	35	404	440	480

Source: Sebenta National Institute Strategic Plan, 2008–2011.

An affordable and quality second chance- secondary education opportunity is offered by the Emlalatini Development Centre (EDC) which provides face-to-face and distance learning. The centre follows the same curriculum as that of formal secondary schools with learning materials converted to a distance-learning mode for ease of use by the learners. EDC programs respond to the needs of diverse learners from those requiring a second chance to those who seek to upgrade their examination grades to improve chances for university and/or TVETSD entry. Enrollment has increased steadily since 2004, but is still low relative to very low NERs for junior and senior secondary education (table 3.3).

Table 3.3: Enrollment by Level and Year

Year	J.C	O'Level	Total
2008	320	380	700
2007	310	230	540
2006	211	340	551
2005	252	371	623
2004	240	350	590

Source: Annual Report Emlalatini Development Centre. 2008.

The current coverage of the nonformal programs is also too low relative to that of other small population AMICs such as Namibia and Botswana. Between 1997 and 2007, the Namibia College of Open Learning (NAMCOL) enrolled a total of 24,000 learners in its secondary education programs. While the swelling enrollments are partly due to the poor quality of formal education and the resultant demand for second-chance education, enrollment levels signal Namibia's capacity relative to Swaziland. Moreover, this capacity can be used for other LLL needs as the quality of general education improves. In 2007, the National Literacy Program in Namibia (NLPN) enrolled 23,323 learners across its levels 1, 2 and 3, while the Adult Upper Primary

Education (AUPE) program enrolled 6,810 learners. Between 2002 and 2007, the Botswana College of Distance and Open Learning (BOCODOL) enrolled 29,280 secondary education learners and 4,418 VET trainees.

Beyond the limited coverage, a key weakness of Swaziland's NFE system is its weak articulation with the formal GET. This limits student movement between the two subsectors. For instance, the Namibia level 3 literacy is equivalent to lower primary education—grades 1 to 4—in the formal sector, while the AUPE is equivalent to grade 7. The Botswana system better demonstrates the articulation between the formal and nonformal GET and the facilitation of student movement across the two (see figure 3.2).

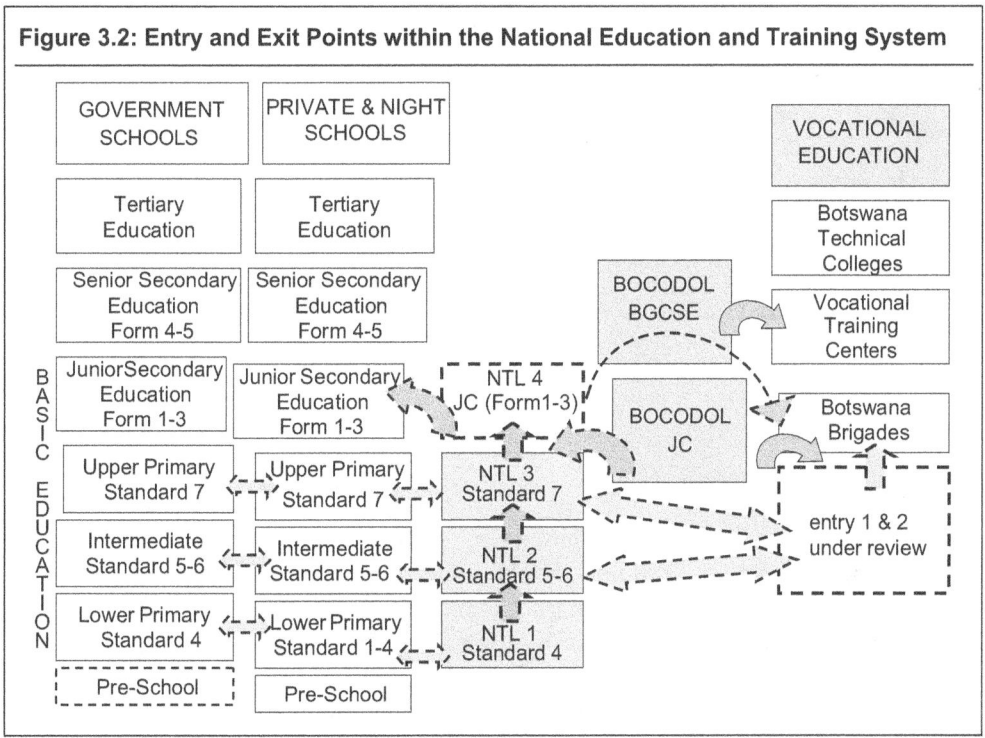

Figure 3.2: Entry and Exit Points within the National Education and Training System

Source: Ministry of Education. 2008. Botswana.

International comparison of access to formal GET

In 2006, the level of the GET access lagged behind that of SADC MICs, especially South Africa with which Swaziland competes for the same labor market. It was also lower than for LMICs with similar levels of resources available for education provision (table 3.4).

Table 3.4: Enrollment Rates in Selected Countries (2006)

Countries	GER Preprimary	GER Primary	GER Secondary	NER Primary	NER Secondary
Botswana	...	108	75	86	61
Mauritius	101	102	86	95	79
Namibia	31	107	57	76	35
S. Africa	38	106	95	88	...
Swaziland	17	106	47	78	32
Brazil	63	140	106	95	78
India	39	115	54	88	...
China	39	111	76	...	...
S. Korea	96	105	96	98	94
Malaysia	122	100	72	99	72
Japan	85	100	102	100	100
Ireland	...	104	112	95	87
Finland	59	100	111	99	95
LMI	34	107	61	85	54
SSA	16	93	31	68	25
HI	78	101	101	95	91

Source: The World Bank. 2008. World development indicators. Washington DC.

Equity of access

For formal GET, gender inequalities in enrollment are quite small until about age 16. Thereafter, more boys remain in the school system longer than girls (figure 3.3). For the age group 17-20, enrollment of boys considerably exceeds that of girls. In contrast women constitute 90 percent of enrollment in NUPE programs. Going back to the earlier-mentioned link between levels of education and women's chances of contracting HIV and, to the age bracket that is most susceptible to contract the virus, this trend presents a serious threat to efforts to redress the spread of the virus and is simply unaffordable.

Age-specific enrollment in the formal GET also differs little between urban and rural areas (figure 3.4). However, as noted, the lack of opportunity for adults to register for SPSCE is a disincentive for them to proceed with their schooling using the nonformal pathway.

Rural dwellers also have limited second chances for secondary education. The EDC has very few rural centers except for one at the Sugar Milling Company at Simunye which helps employees acquire higher qualifications. Other than that, the EDC draws most of its students from Mbabane and Manzini. Therefore, the urban bias of formal GET gets repeated in the nonformal secondary education system.

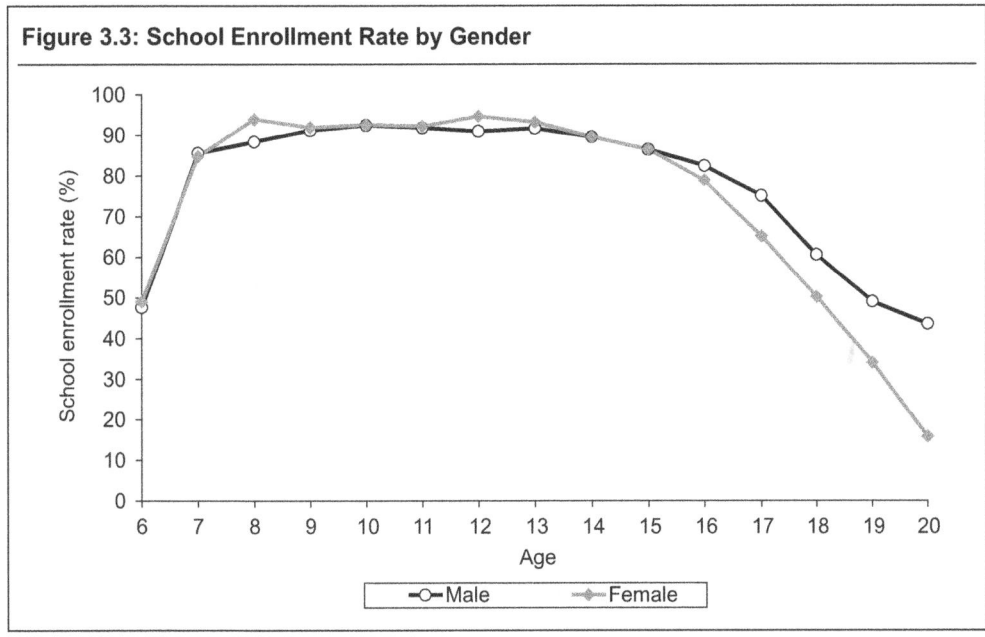

Figure 3.3: School Enrollment Rate by Gender

Source: Calculations from DHS2006/7.

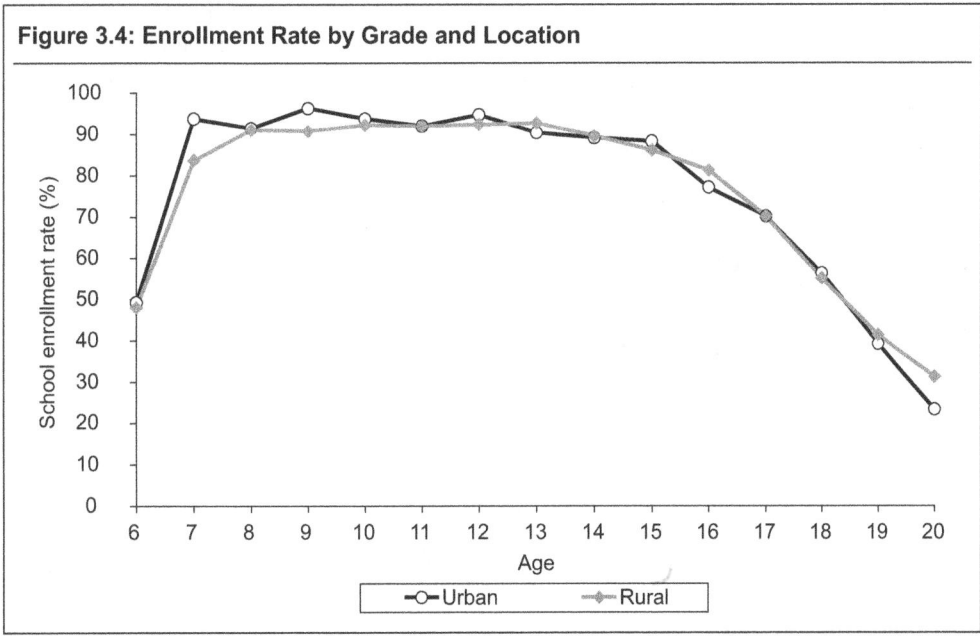

Figure 3.4: Enrollment Rate by Grade and Location

Source: Calculations from DHS2006/7.

Educational attainment of urban dwellers considerably exceeds that of rural dwellers despite the fact that figure 3.4 shows very little differences in enrollment patterns between these two locations (figure 3.5). It is likely that repetition and dropout rates are far lower in urban areas, suggesting better education quality and better social background factors in urban schools.

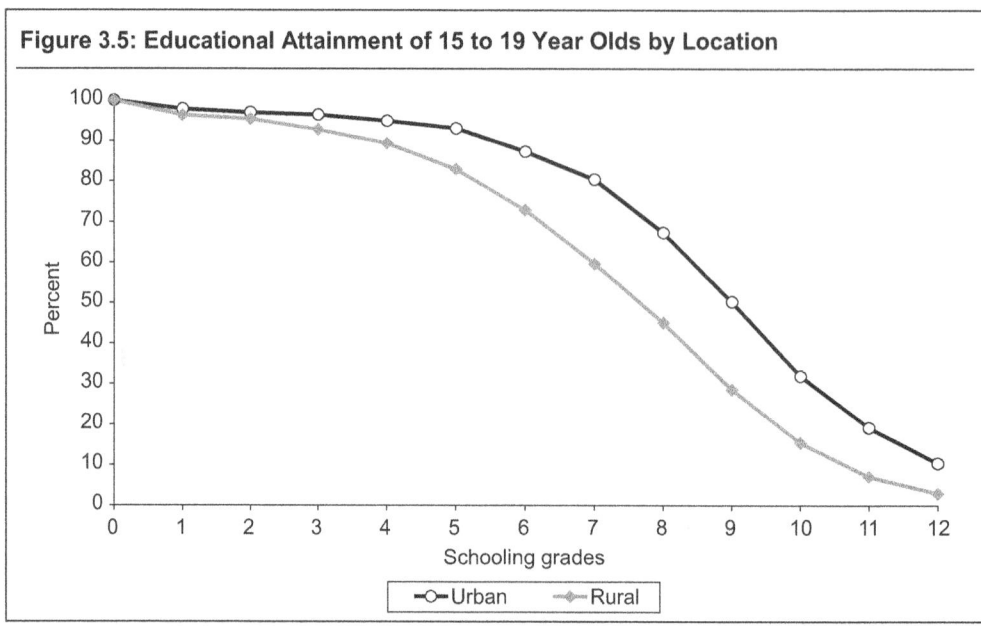

Figure 3.5: Educational Attainment of 15 to 19 Year Olds by Location

Source: Calculations from DHS2006/7.

Regional enrollment patterns vary more across age groups (figure 3.6), but the small size of individual cells in the DHS (each cell referring to individuals of a specific age in a specific region) may partly explain the somewhat erratic patterns here. The only clear conclusion is that unlike the other regions, Shiselweni region never reaches enrollment rates above 90 percent for any age group. Nonenrollment and dropping out of school seems to be a bigger problem in this region.

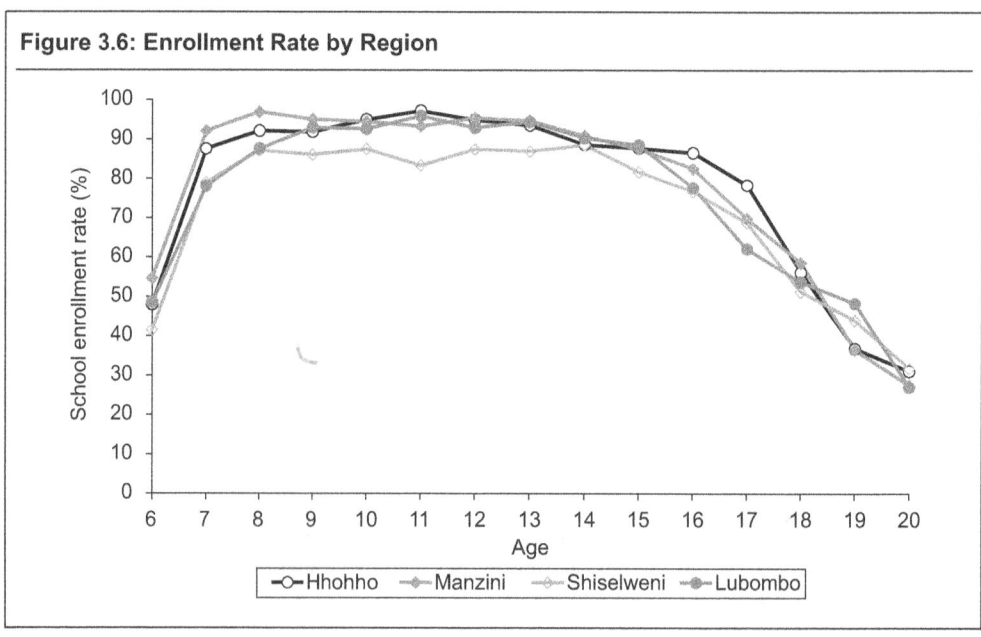

Figure 3.6: Enrollment Rate by Region

Source: Calculations from DHS2006/7.

Socio-economic inequalities in enrollment are large, particularly when comparing age-specific enrollment of children from the poorest quintile (Quintile 1) to those of other quintiles. Figure 3.7 shows that children from the poorest quintile are less likely to enroll at virtually all age groups and that enrollment for this quintile peaks at a fairly high age (13-14 years). Differences between the other four quintiles are not as severe, although Quintile 5 (the richest quintile) has a noticeable advantage compared to others.

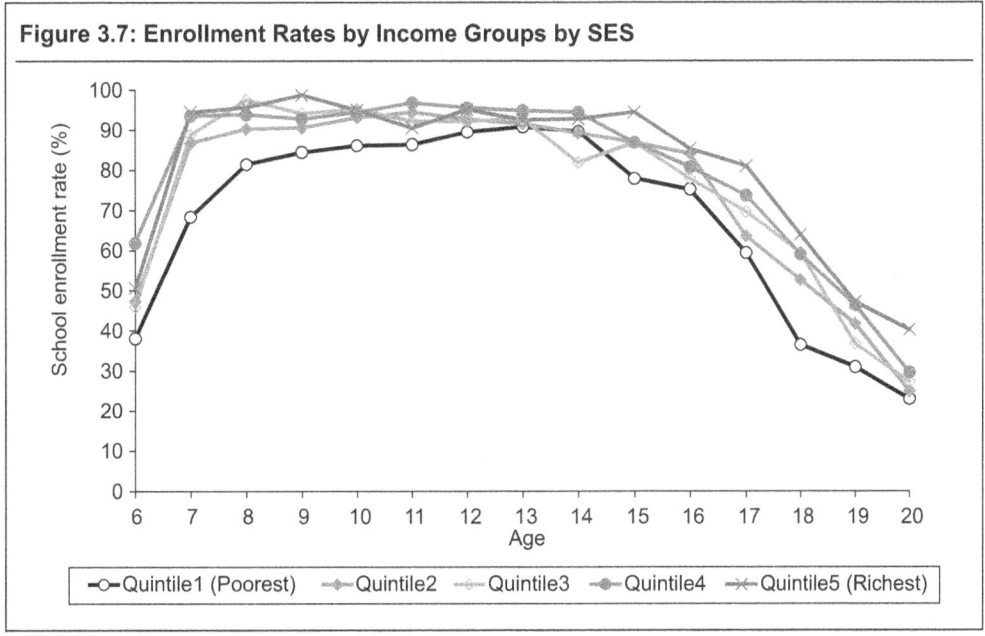

Source: Calculations from DHS2006/7.

Logically, educational attainment of the richest quintile is far better than for the rest, and that of the poorest quintile is far lower than for the rest.[5] Whereas only 37 percent of the poorest quintile amongst this age group had successfully completed primary school, the figure for the richest quintile was 83 percent. For the whole age group, the primary completion rate was 63 percent, as against the 89 percent for a similar age group in South Africa[6] (figure 3.8).

In Table 3.5, a multivariate analysis of determinants of access show substantial and positive association with SES after controlling for age—in linear and quadratic form—gender, location and region—using Lubombo as a reference region. The coefficient for the Bottom40 and Middle40 indicate that higher enrollment is largely associated with pupils in the top quintile—used as a reference group. The probability of being enrolled is 7 percent lower for a child from the middle group than for one from the top quintile, after other factors have been considered, and 14 percent less for a child from the lowest two quintiles. Boys have a slightly better probability of being enrolled. Surprisingly, once other factors have been considered, rural children are more likely to be enrolled than urban ones, indicating an enrollment deficit in urban areas once their SES advantage and other factors have been considered. This may reflect under-enrollment of the urban poor and the need for interventions that focus on them as a specific client group. The only region which appears to be statistically significantly different from the reference region—Lubombo—is Shiselweni, which has significantly lower enrollment for given SES levels and other factors.

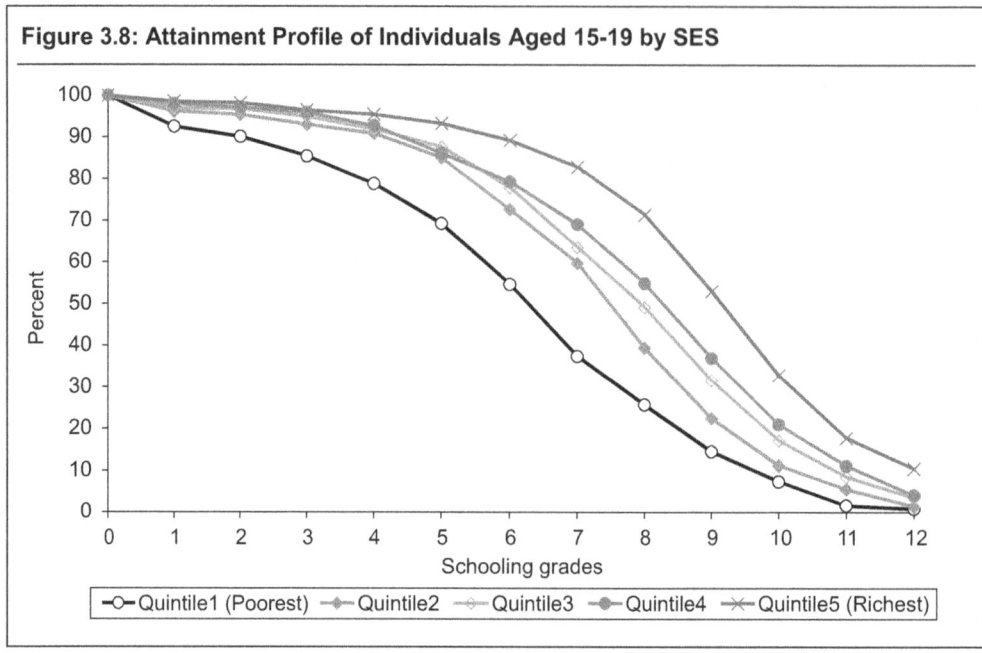

Figure 3.8: Attainment Profile of Individuals Aged 15-19 by SES

Source: Calculations from DHS2006/7.

Table 3.5: OLS Regressions on Enrollment (ages 6-20), Attainment (ages 20-24)

Explanatory variables	DHS Enrolled ages 6-20	DHS Attainment aged 20-24*
Male (1 = male; 0= female)	0.03 (3.65)*	0.02 (0.11)
Bottom40	−0.14 (−9.77)*	−3.52 (−15.64)*
Middle40	−0.07 (−5.69)*	−1.63 (−7.87)*
Urban (1 = urban, 0 = rural)	−0.08 (−5.92)*	0.06 (0.33)
Hhohho	0.01 (0.83)	1.19 (5.63)*
Manzini	0.01 (1.12)	1.48 (7.39)*
Shiselweni	−0.04 (−3.73)*	1.55 (6.97)*
Age	0.24 (38.65)*	.
Age2	−0.01 (−42.77)*	.
Constant	−0.34 (−8.38)*	9.48 (36.75)*
Observations	8 978	2 136
R^2	0.22	0.17

Source: Calculations from DHS 2006/7.

* In the case of educational enrollment and attainment, Urban refers to the area in which the individual lives and not the area in which a school is located (as was the case for performance in Maths and English and enrollment). The same applies to the regional dummies *Hhohho, Manzini,* and *Shiselweni*.

SES is also positively associated with educational attainment. Individuals in the bottom 40 percent of the wealth distribution attain approximately 3.5 less years of education than those in the top quintile, and those in the middle of the wealth distribution attain 1.6 years less. Gender does not play a statistically significant role, once other factors have been accounted for. Interestingly, the type of area in which individuals live does not have a statistically significant effect on their educational attainment. However, in all three other regions, educational attainment is higher than in the reference region, Lubombo. People living in Hhohho, Manzini and Shiselweni attain 1.19, 1.48, and 1.55 more years of education respectively than do people living in Lubombo, once the other explanatory variables have been considered. It therefore appears that the regional patterns observed in the earlier analysis are somewhat reversed once other factors are taken into account. Manzini performs surprisingly poorly, after controlling for its urban status and pupil SES, indicating that the advantage it had seemed to have in univariate analysis resulted from higher SES and level of urbanization. Once this is taken into consideration, Manzini actually underperforms, and Lubombo performs much better than expected given its SES and low urbanization.

A limited number of schools (4) enroll 350 learners with special needs against an estimated 57,000 learners who could benefit from inclusive education. The low access is evident in levels of educational attainment. The National Population Policy Framework for Swaziland (March 2002) estimated that 49.6 percent of people with disabilities had no formal education. Only 32.2 percent had primary education and 9.6 percent had secondary education. Only 24.1 percent were classified as employed because the disabled population has no marketable skills to offer the labor market. The government subvents E84 000 per year to the Examination Council towards assisting learners with special education needs. For examples, the visually impaired pupils have their examination papers transcribed to Braille. In addition, the government has the appropriate policy orientation to integrate learners with disabilities into the mainstream. However, these interventions are yet to translate into effective access.

Education Quality and Equity

Recent evidence highlights education quality and not just attainment as a critical determinant of growth and individual labor market outcomes.[7] However, Swaziland lack both the quantity and quality of GET required to support its growth strategy.

Student quality

For a range of reasons, Swazi children start school without the requisite level of readiness and, they continue schooling without adequate facilitation. As documented in Chapter 2, a limited proportion of children has access to quality and internally-relevant ECCD. Significant proportions are raised in poverty. They are malnourished and, they are exposed to psychosocial stress, emanating mainly but not exclusively from poverty and HIV/AIDS.

Despite the odds against them, Swazi 6th graders performed better on the 2000 sub-regional SACMEQ tests than their better-provided-for counterparts in SADC MICs, with the exception of Seychelles and Mauritius, though less well than counterparts from countries that invest much less in education. There is a strong possibility that this high performance is due to selectivity and less so to the quality of the system. All the same, the system seems to have a better base for building quality GET than its immediate neighbors.

Teacher qualifications

Over recent years Swaziland seems to have substantially reduced the proportion of unqualified teachers especially at the secondary level. On average, about 8 percent of primary school teachers were unqualified in 2007 relative to about 2 percent at the secondary level. This progress is also evident in the qualified teacher to pupil ratios of 37:1 at the primary level and 19:1 at the secondary level. For secondary education in particular, the current stock of qualified teachers could be better used to expand access (tables 3.6 and 3.7). In addition, qualified teachers are almost evenly distributed across regions with Lubombo and Shesilweni having a slightly higher proportion of unqualified primary school teachers.

Table 3.6: Distribution of Primary School Teachers by Qualification and Region (%)

Region/ Year	Graduate	Post-matric plus training	Primary teaching certificate	Primary higher certificate	Primary lower certificate	Primary lower upgrading	Uncertified	Pupil to qualified teacher ratio
2005								
Hhohho	10	37	27	8	0	10	8	39
Lubombo	11	39	22	10	1	7	10	37
Manzini	10	32	31	8	4	9	6	34
Shiswileni	9	31	26	11	5	9	9	33
2006								
Hhohho	14	29	31	11	0	8	6	38
Lubombo	10	39	22	10	2	7	10	40
Manzini	11	32	31	7	4	9	6	37
Shiswileni	9	32	26	10	5	9	9	34
2007								
Hhohho	16	30	30	11	1	7	5	36
Lubombo	11	38	21	11	2	7	10	41
Manzini	13	32	30	7	3	9	6	37
Shiswileni	10	31	26	10	5	9	9	34

Source: Ministry of Education. 2005. 2006. 2007. EMIS.

The negative side is that not all secondary school teachers are qualified for the subjects they teach. There are acute shortages of qualified teachers for mathematics, science, ICTs, and for prevocational subjects such as design, technology, and business studies. The 2005 estimate ratio of student to qualified mathematics and science teachers was 84:1. A Bachelor of Science program at the UNISWA was established in 2006 to address this challenge but this still constitutes a long-term solution for an immediate and urgent challenge. Therefore, Swaziland needs to consider short terms solutions such as the importation of qualified mathematics, science and ICTs teachers.

Table 3.7: Proportion of Secondary School Teachers by Qualification and Region (%)

Year / region	Graduates	Post-matric plus training	Pre-matric plus training	Untrained	Student to qualified teacher ratio
2005					
Hhohho	52	46	1	1	17
Lubombo	58	41	0	1	19
Manzini	49	45	2	4	17
Shiswileni	53	45	0	2	16
2006					
Hhohho	53	45	1	1	26
Lubombo	49	50	0	1	24
Manzini	52	44	1	3	19
Shiswileni	59	40	0	1	27
2007					
Hhohho	53	45	1	1	19
Lubombo	49	50	0	1	22
Manzini	51	44	2	3	18
Shiswileni	58	41	0	1	18

Source: Source: Ministry of Education. 2005. 2006. 2007. EMIS.

Teacher quality/competency

Other than the formal certification, Swaziland does not have a well defined set of skills and competencies that teachers should have in order to teach at a certain level or even to be considered to have current knowledge and skills. This is primarily because school curricula do not clearly stipulate skills and competencies that learners should acquire at each level and consequently knowledge and skills that teachers must have to facilitate such acquisition. There is also no systematic process of checking teaching quality other than inspectors' reports, which provide scant information at best. Given the frequent disconnect between formal qualifications and teacher competencies, formal qualifications may not always be indicative of teacher quality. The lack of a systematic way of checking the level and currency of teacher knowledge and competencies suggests that teacher pre- and in-service training programs may not necessarily address critical weaknesses that impede teaching effectiveness. This is compounded by the fact that Swaziland does not have a systematic teacher continuous development programs (CDPs) as do neighboring countries.

School inspectors' reports for the years 2004 to 2008 point to weak teacher skills, and competencies with respect to: English proficiency, learner-centered pedagogy, facilitation of higher order thinking skills, use of teaching aids, close monitoring of student homework, lesson preparation, regular testing and continuous assessment. The reports also point to weak work habits among some teachers. As presented later in this chapter, the high student repetition rates—while there may be many causes—suggest weak teacher quality and/or poor teaching effectiveness.

Deployment of teachers

The above-reported average qualified teacher to student ratios masks inequities in teacher deployment across schools. Most teachers are unwilling to be deployed to schools in remote rural areas and positions can lay vacant for years. In 2004, it was estimated that 20 percent of teachers in rural areas were unqualified relative to a national average of less than 10 percent.[8] In addition, the administrative process for assigning teachers to schools is often long prolonging vacancies. There are no substitute teachers for regular teachers on prolonged sick leave. These issues have resulted in an unbalanced distribution of teachers.

The curriculum

The 2006 Bank report documented common curricula weaknesses and these still persist. Key among them are subject overload especially at the secondary school level. This results in a lack of qualified teachers, especially for prevocational subjects, inefficient teacher utilization and, the questionable long-term affordability of secondary school prevocational curriculum

Beyond these generic problems, a striking weakness in Swaziland's curricula is the dearth of blueprints that clearly link children's education experiences with the broader country development strategy and sector strategy. or that spell out the rationale, philosophy, objectives, scope, sequence, balance, vertical and horizontal articulation, pedagogy, assessment and the nature of outputs at each phase—lower, middle, higher primary, junior and senior secondary. Because curricula do not clearly characterize the nature of output from each phase in terms of the knowledge, skills, and competencies to be acquired, it is very difficult to judge their effectiveness and relevance to higher levels of the system, labor market demands, as well as national and global development challenges. It is equally difficult to guide pedagogy, assessment, and teacher training. The closest to a definition of outputs is found in the aims of the senior secondary curriculum.[9]

Swaziland now has a broad national development framework in the form of the PRSAP which should orient curricula. Examples of PRSAP actions with direct curricula implications include growth acceleration, productivity growth especially in agriculture, social equity imperatives, efforts to re-attract FDIs and to promote science and technology. Beyond the PRSAP, Swaziland is part of a regional and global labor market whose changing demands should also orient curricula. The Bank's ICAs show that Swaziland's immediate neighbors—South Africa, Botswana, Namibia—have acute skills shortages and in areas where science and mathematics are base subjects— engineering, medical and health professions, mathematics and science teachers. National, regional, and global labor markets are not only becoming skill intensive, but also demand a broad spectrum of skills than can be acquired through Swaziland's subject dominated curricula. Box 3.1 below gives examples of key changes in global labor markets and workplaces which are already evident in Swaziland.

Box 3.1: Labor Market and Workplace Changes already Evident in Swaziland

Labor market changes	Changes in the work place	Impact on individuals' lives
• Diminishing pure blue-collar jobs as they get replaced by automation • More skill intensive industries and jobs • Skill biased employment creation • Creation of unskilled and semi-skilled jobs dependent on the availability of highly skilled labor • Shrinking job opportunities along expanding work opportunities • Occupational identities getting blurred • limited space for narrow specialists • Life-long careers diminishing …	• Flat structures • Small task groupings instead of specialized departments • Working in fluid teams • Demand for a range of skills and not just credentials • Directly facing clients and handling human relations • Directly facing problems and designing solutions rather than routine tasks • Improvising fit-for-purpose and responding to diversity rather than mass production • Designing total solutions • Demand to learn on the job • Appraised 360^0	• Transformation into knowledge worker • Uncertain job security and steady upward mobility • Multiple jobs at any one time • Multiple careers in a life time • Coping with rapid change and uncertainty • Work-study mismatch and constant need for up-skilling and re-tooling • Blurred professional identity • Precarious income • Varying networks instead of single employer • Specific to Swaziland….rapid ascension into high position without the benefit of experience or mentorship and • Coping with psychosocial stress …

Source: Data compiled by author.

Changes summarized in box 3.1 demand a range of skills exemplified in box 3.2, most of which are not considered in current school curricula and, should therefore be considered to guide reforms. In addition, curricula should adopt a competency based approach. Clearly defined learner competencies should be used to guide the reform of teacher education curricula, mechanisms for monitoring and fostering the adequacy and currency of teacher competencies, pedagogy, assessment, and curricula articulation.

Box 3.2: Skills and Competencies for Consideration in Curricula

Basic skills	Generic skills	Behavioral skills	Occupational skills
• Numeracy • Literacy • E-literacy • Life skills …	• Critical thinking • Problem solving • Self-educability • Communication • Harvesting heritages • Surfing networks …	• Adaptability • Team work • Initiative • Multi-tasking • Risk taking • Self-management • Time management • Managing relationships	• Languages • Mathematics • Sciences • Ethics, values, morals • Social sciences • Fine arts • World religions …

Source: Data compiled by author.

Swazi employers reported the importance of these skills and competencies among their employees (table 3.8).

Table 3.8: Employer Ranking Importance of Employee Basic Skills

Basic skills & competencies	Not important				Extremely important
Communication skills:			4.3	21.3	70.2
English language skills	2.1	2.1	17.0	29.8	44.7
Literacy:		3.2	12.8	31.9	46.8
Numeracy:		4.3	14.9	31.9	44.7
Computer skills:	12.8	4.3	17.0	31.9	29.8
Problem solving skills		2.1	14.9	29.8	46.8
Analytical thinking:	6.4	8.5	19.1	23.4	38.3
Ability to work independently		2.1	19.1	36.2	40.4
Customer relations skills:	2.1	4.3	4.3	34.0	53.2
Teamwork skills			6.4	27.7	61.7
Time management skills:	2.1	2.1	12.8	34.0	48.9
Self management skills		2.1	21.3	29.8	46.8
Skills to directly face and work with clients	2.1	6.4	17.0	21.3	48.9
Skills for integrated total solutions to problems	2.1	4.3	23.4	27.7	36.2
Skills to design creative solutions	8.5	6.4	17.0	25.5	36.2
Skills to learn on the job	2.1	6.4	21.3	31.9	38.3
Skills to learn on demand and under pressure		2.1	23.4	27.7	40.4
Multiple skills / broad base skills	4.3	10.6	21.3	23.4	31.9
Deep narrow specialization	17.0	17.0	23.4	12.8	19.1
Adaptability to changing work contexts	2.1	4.3	19.1	31.9	38.3

Source: Data compiled by author.

On the positive side, current primary and secondary curricula have mainstreamed HIV/AIDS and life skills. By 2005, 78 percent of primary school teachers were trained and had acquired knowledge and awareness of HIV/AIDS. Eight-Seven percent had received training in both HIV/AIDS and life skills. The proportions for secondary school teachers were 86 percent and 11 percent respectively. While awareness about the transmission of HIV is relatively high among the general population, this has not yet translated into behavior change. What remains a challenge is the monitoring of effective delivery to students (and their parents) and of impact on behavior. Preparatory work for re-introducing guidance and counseling into curricula is also advanced. However, the integration of these areas into teacher education programs and the inspectorate training programs is yet to take place.

In response to public criticism of the academic bias of secondary education, prevocational subjects have been introduced in 16 schools. In addition the IGCSE curriculum entails a range of practical subjects. The downside of these subjects is their unsustainable cost implications, doubtful relevance, and the implied inefficient use of teachers.

A critical weakness in the efforts to improve curricula relevance is the omission of ICTs. Information Technology (IT) and Computer Studies are part of the IGCSE curriculum. But in 2007, less than 10 secondary schools had registered for IT and Computer Studies.[10] There are no IT teachers on the government payroll. Schools that teach IT have to hire teachers at their own expense. Only 4 students—all males—took the O' Level examinations in Computer Studies in 2006.

Although there is no policy for ICTs in education, the National Information and Communication Infrastructure (NICI) policy lists objectives and targets for the sector. According to the NICI, all teacher training institutions were to offer basic computer studies to the 2008 incoming trainees. An examinable secondary education computer studies curriculum was to be in place by 2008. All primary and secondary schools are to have computer laboratories with Internet access by 2012. In response, the MoE has created ICT lecturer posts in all teacher training institutions. The first cohort of teachers trained in ICTs will graduate in 2010. ICT curricula, syllabi and training manuals were developed for primary and secondary education. However, as of 2008, they had not been approved by the Curriculum Coordinating Committee (CCC). Nonetheless, the Ministry supports computer literacy programs in which some schools have enrolled. A roll-out plan for meeting set targets for schools is yet to be developed. The MoE has established a Senior Inspector for ICT position to work out the roll out plan.

Books and instructional materials

The provision, distribution, and management of books and instructional materials lack policy guidance and management procedures, leaving the system inequitable and vulnerable to mismanagement. Provision and management are guided by occasional circulars, but most head teachers are reportedly not aware of them. Therefore, schools range from organized systems of management and control of book provision to no evidence of any system at all. Head teachers' textbook requisitions are based on annual enrollment projections. The MoE centrally procures books and instructional materials in accordance with government procurement procedures. Textbooks are expected to last four years, during which period schools may make replacement orders for lost and damaged books. The allowable proportion of book replacement is not set and this may lead to wastage.

All the same public provision of primary school books has substantially improved since the government's 2002 initiative to provide free textbook, and the 2004 extension to provide exercise books and stationery. The learner to textbook ratio is assumed to be 1:1 but there are no records to prove this nor does the EMIS collect information on the stock of textbooks.

Although provision has improved, primary school learners have limited independent study time with books. This may adversely affect learning, especially for learners from homes without libraries. Perhaps in a bid to reduce book losses and damages, learners are loaned books to use during school hours. Only grades 5 to 7 are allowed to take books home for study purposes.

Secondary school books are still privately provided by parents through fees. It is assumed that students have all the prescribed books but this is highly unlikely given the cost of providing books and the levels of poverty. The 2006 World Bank report documented that schools often owed bookstores because of difficulties in collecting fees. Beyond the process of prescribing books, provision is mostly unguided. Subject panels approve a prescribed list of books from which senior secondary schools have the discretion to choose. Junior secondary books are centrally prescribed. Book lists for different subjects are prepared by the inspectorate and reviewed annually.

Due to lack of a book policy, the management of secondary school book provision varies widely across schools. Some schools annually rent textbooks to students for a quarter of their cost yet others require students to buy books. For rented books, inspectors' reports show that schools vary widely in their ability to collect books at the end of each year. Failure to collect books artificially shortens the life span of books and increases replacement costs. Some head teachers order books directly from bookshops yet others provide students lists so they may buy books directly. The unevenness in provision and management as well as problems with fee collection suggests that accurate data is required on the state of book provision. Beyond provision, inspectors' reports are very scant on the effective use of books and instructional materials other than just highlighting the lack of teaching aids in some schools. Yet effective use is really what determines the impact of books and instructional materials on student learning.

Currently secondary school books are imported and are therefore very costly. A recent initiative to develop books locally is expected to bring down costs. However, a potential risk with the system is that although curriculum subject panels would actually produce the books, publishers, and not the MoE would hold the copyright. The authors would receive a once-off payment and the MoE would receive royalties. Because publishers would retain the copyright any revisions that may be required to suit curricula changes may come with an unreasonably high price tag for the MoE and ultimately parents.

Physical teaching and learning environment

Unlike its neighboring countries—Namibia and South Africa—the Swaziland EMIS does not routinely capture the state of provision of the physical teaching and learning environment and the extent to which it may affect teaching and learning. Lack of accurate information of such provisions makes it very difficult to plan for provision and to track equity in provision.

School inspectors' reports for the period 2004 to 2008 document poor maintenance and up-keep of school infrastructure. The reports also show acute shortage of school furniture. Available spaces are said to not necessarily fit the purpose. Most schools are said to lack the physical facilities and equipment required to effectively deliver the IGCSE curriculum. Unavailable facilities include special teaching rooms such as required for design and technology, agriculture, home economics, computer studies, libraries, and multi-media centers. Consequently, most secondary schools do not offer IGCSE practical subjects or do so inadequately. This defeats the goal to equip secondary school learners with practical skills. Because most school infrastructure is provided by communities to very uneven standards, available structures do not easily lend themselves to adaptations and/or renovations to suit practical subjects.

Teacher housing

Provision of teacher housing is inadequate, especially in rural areas where teachers—even families—often share available housing. The lack of housing in close proximity to schools could contribute to teacher tardiness and absenteeism as some teachers have to travel as far as 100 kilometers to and from school daily using public transport. This situation also adversely affects participation in after school tutoring, remedial teaching and co-curricular activities.

School management and accountability

Formal management training is not a pre-requisite for promotion to head of department or head teacher posts. Moreover, school heads receive little to no support from Regional Education Officers (REO). In 2006, only 33 of the 199 secondary schools were inspected. Not surprisingly, recent inspectors' reports highlight that most head teachers are ill equipped for their positions. Key weaknesses pertain to school management and administration, financial management, human resources management, time management, instructional leadership, clinical supervision of teachers, and management of student time.

Recently, the MoE introduced the Head Teacher Management Training Program (HMTP) for new appointees. Inspectors' reports note remarkable improvements of graduates of these courses with respect to school, financial and teacher management. Improvements are also noted with instructional leadership and professional support for teachers. However, the bulk of old head teachers who do not benefit from this course are observed to be weak in key aspects of their responsibility. It would appear that they too could benefit from such a course.

As with teachers, there is no systematic approach to monitoring head teachers' accountability for student learning. Head teachers do not have any performance targets to work towards and to be evaluated against. A combination of these factors makes head teachers' appraisals a bit of an inconsistent exercise and one with no structured follow up. As with teachers, Swaziland should carefully consider articulating competencies for school heads, setting them performance targets and placing them on performance contracts.

Learning outcomes

Performance on the Swaziland Primary Certificate (SPCE) Examination

Overall pass rate on the 2006 SPCE is an impressively high 88 percent and has kept at the same level since 2003 (table 3.9). Most students attain a second or third class. However, a third class is not adequate for admission into secondary school, so nearly 70 percent of candidates acquire passes that make them eligible for secondary school places.

Table 3.9: Primary Certification Examination Pass Rates by Level (%)

Year	Pass levels				Total passes	Total failures	Total entries
	Merits	First	Second	Third			
2004	2.56	10.95	55.59	18.98	88.0	11.93	21,040
2005	3.41	12.53	54.97	17.02	87.93	12.07	22,264
2006	2.49	10.48	56.23	18.90	88.10	11.90	22,281

Source: Swaziland Examinations Council.

Performance on Junior Certificate Examination (JCE)

In line with a broad curriculum, a wide range of subjects (19) is offered for the JCE. The number of candidates increased by 36 percentage points between 1996 and 2006, showing a steady expansion in access. Overall passes increased by 10 percentage points. This is quite an achievement because often, an expansion of access is accompanied by a decline in learning outcomes. Total passes are high, having averaged 83 percent since 2003 (table 3.10). Second class passes dropped by almost 2 percentage points and third class passes increased by almost 3 percentage points.

Table 3.10: Junior Secondary Examination Pass Rates by Level (%)

Year	Pass level				Total		
	Merits	First	Second	Third	Passes	Failures	Entries
2004	3.87	9.84	58.81	10.70	83.21	16.79	10,113
2005	3.80	9.42	59.83	10.89	83.94	16.06	11,093
2006	3.32	8.67	57.92	13.37	83.28	16.72	12,172

Source: Swaziland Examinations Council.

Learning outcomes are inequitably distributed across regions (table 3.11). Students from Manzini and Hhohho perform better than those from Lubombo and Shisleweni. Hhohho has the highest percentage of merit passes followed by the Manzini region, while Shiselweni and Lubombo have the highest failure rates.

Table 3.11: Distribution of Learning Outcomes by Region

District	Merit	First	Second	Third	Fail	Total
Hhohho	149	346	1,862	456	461 (14.1%)	3,274
Lubombo	51	148	1,277	321	464 (20.5%)	2,261
Manzini	141	351	2,140	502	542 (14.7%)	3,676
Shishelweni	63	215	1,815	410	456 (15.4%)	2,959

Source: Swaziland Examinations Council.

Ordinary Level Examination (O Level)

Again an alarmingly high number of subjects (30) were registered for; some by very few candidates. Overall pass rate was over 70 percent. For 2006, pass rates were particularly low for mathematics (45%), siSwati (9%), Biology (67%), and English Literature (48%).

Student performance on international assessments

Swaziland outperformed other SACU countries on Mathematics and Reading SACMEQII tests (table 3.12).[11]

Table 3.12: Average Pupil Performance on SACMEQII Reading and Mathematics Tests

	Reading	Maths
Botswana	522	513
Kenya	548	563
Lesotho	450	446
Mozambique	517	530
Malawi	428	430
Namibia	448	429
Swaziland	530	516
Tanzania	546	522
Uganda	483	506
South Africa	492	486
Zambia	439	432

Source: IIEP 2004.

Figures 3.9 and 3.10 compare Swaziland's distribution of reading and mathematics scores with those of South Africa and Lesotho. The vertical line represents the SACMEQ average score of 500. The scores were calibrated to give a standard deviation of 100. Only a small proportion of Swazi pupils could not achieve a score of 400, i.e. one standards deviation below the average, whereas a large proportion of South African students and a fair proportion of Lesotho pupils performed below this level. Looking at the higher ranges, a fair proportion of Swazi children performed above a score of 600 in reading, but fewer did in mathematics.

Figure 3.9: Kernel Density Curve for Swaziland, Lesotho and South Africa, SACMEQII Reading Scores

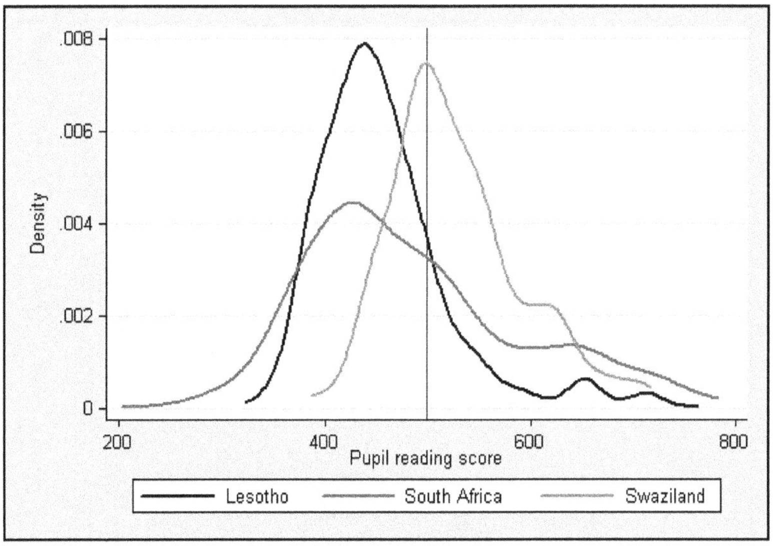

Source: Calculated from IIEP 2004.

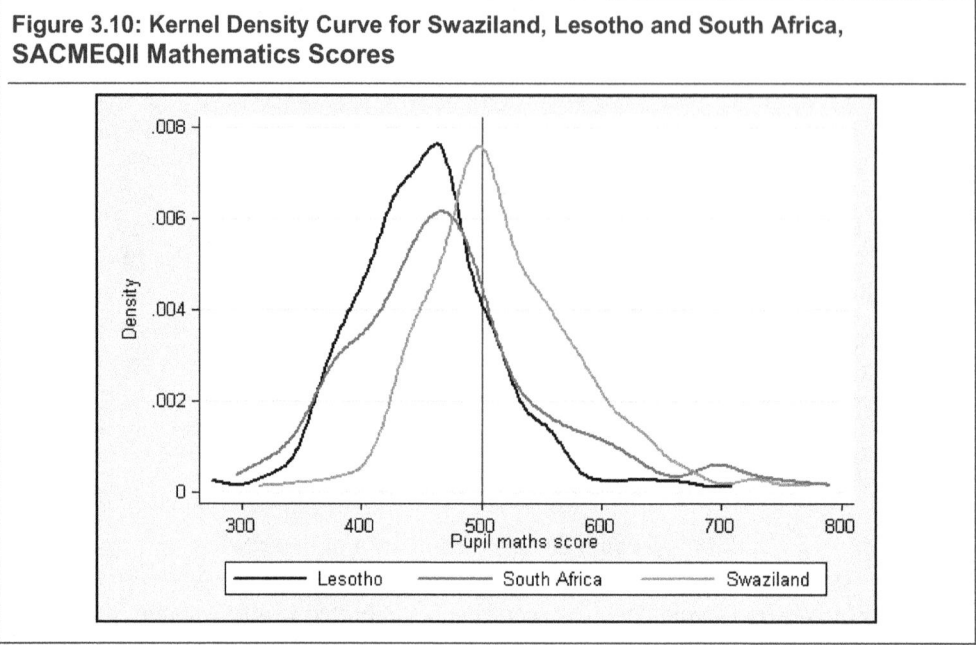

Figure 3.10: Kernel Density Curve for Swaziland, Lesotho and South Africa, SACMEQII Mathematics Scores

Source: Calculated from IIEP 2004.

SACMEQ reading and mathematics scores are higher for urban than for rural children (figures 3.11 and 3.12). This is not surprising, given that the earlier analysis has shown few differences in enrollment patterns between these two area types, but major differences in attainment patterns.

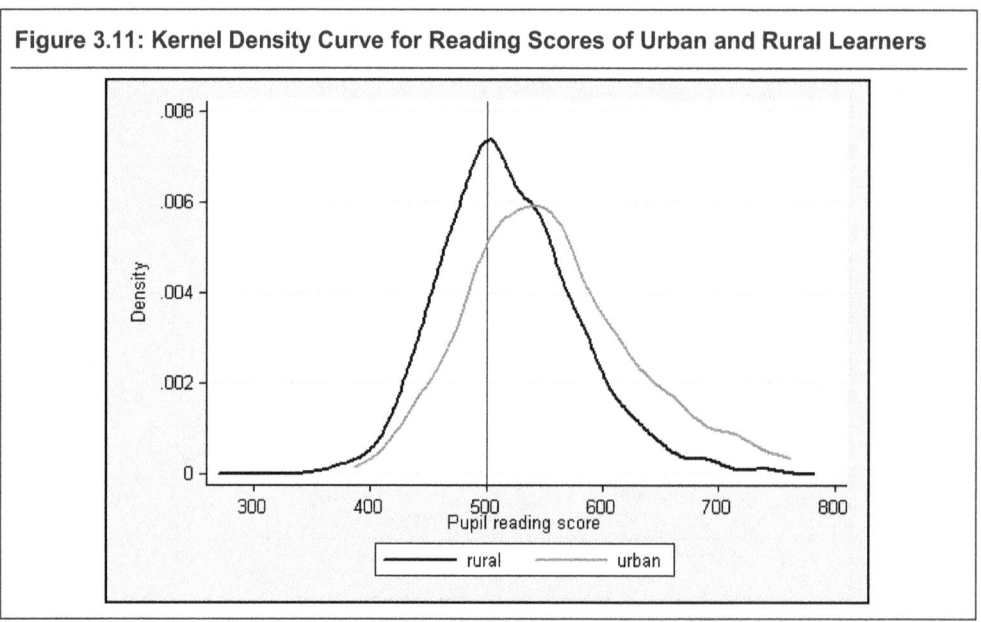

Figure 3.11: Kernel Density Curve for Reading Scores of Urban and Rural Learners

Source: Calculated from IIEP 2004.

Figure 3.12: Kernel Density Curve for Mathematics Scores of Urban and Rural Learners

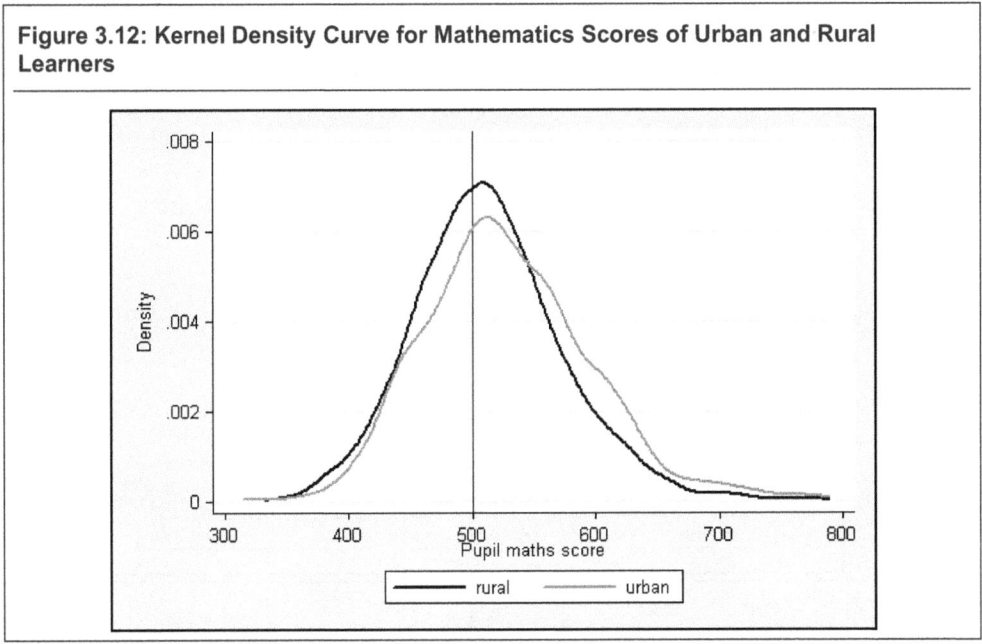

Source: Calculated from IIEP 2004.

Regional performance on the SACMEQ tests differed less, as can be seen from figures 3.13 and 3.14. Shiselweni students did slightly worse than others in reading, but surprisingly students from Lubombo appeared to do the best of the four regions. A similar pattern applies in mathematics, but here the differentials are even smaller.

Figure 3.13: Kernel Density Curve for Reading Scores by Region

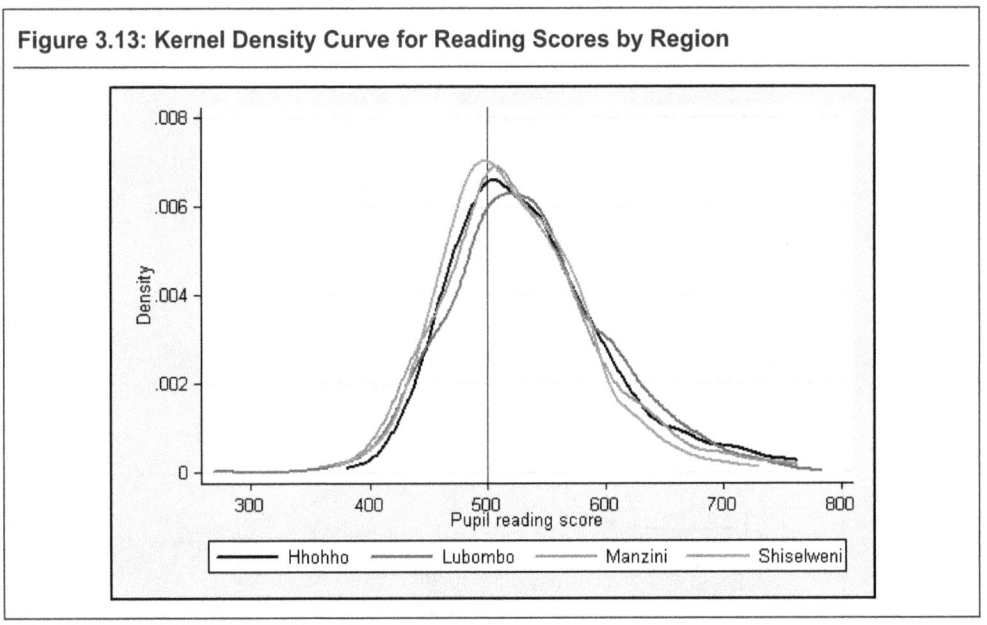

Source: Calculated from IIEP 2004.

Figure 3.14: Kernel Density Curve for Mathematics Scores by Region

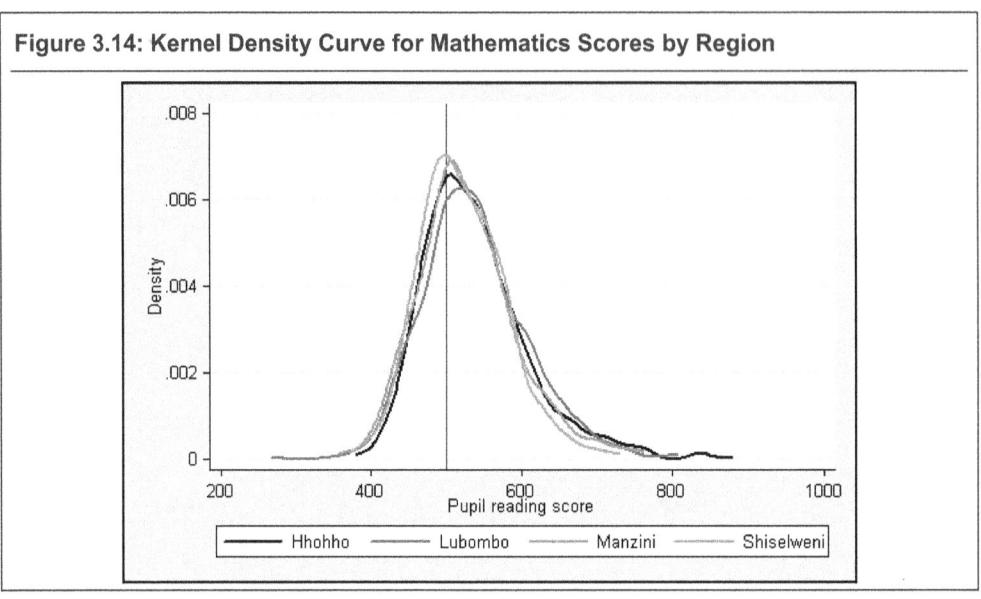

Source: Calculated from IIEP 2004.

SES is significantly associated with higher SACMEQ Scores: Figures 3.15 and 3.16 show the patterns of test scores for three socio-economic groups, the poorest—bottom two quintiles of pupils—the middle group—quintiles 3 and 4—and the richest quintile. Substantial differences in performance are apparent. This indicates that socio-economic status (SES) influences not only enrollment patterns, but also the quality of education. The poorest group struggle much harder to perform well in tests, though Swaziland has been relatively successful in containing inequality in educational *quality*, compared to some of its neighboring countries.

Figure 3.15: Kernel Density Curve for Reading Scores by SES Group

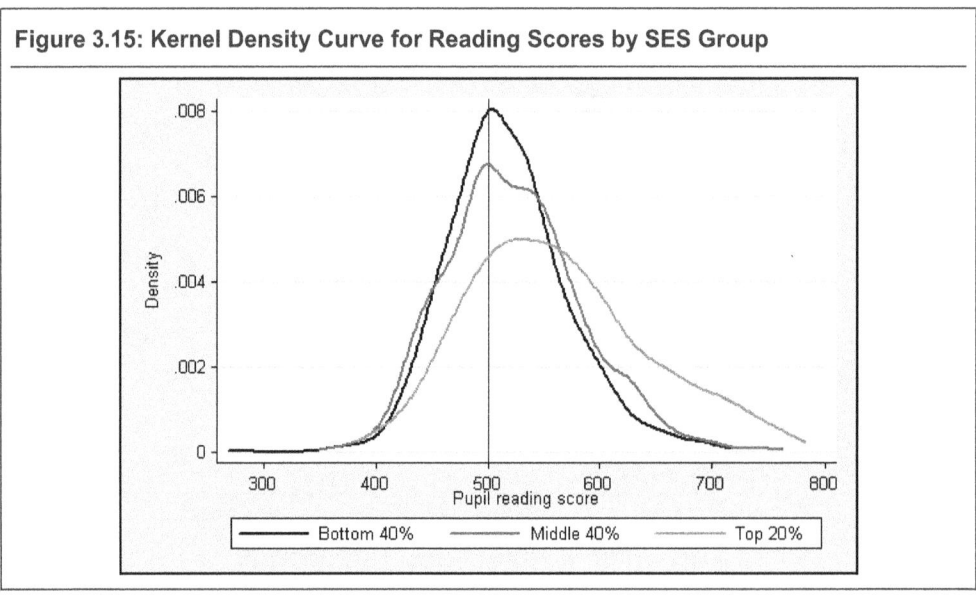

Source: Calculated from IIEP 2004.

Figure 3.16: Kernel Density Curve for Mathematics Scores by SES Group

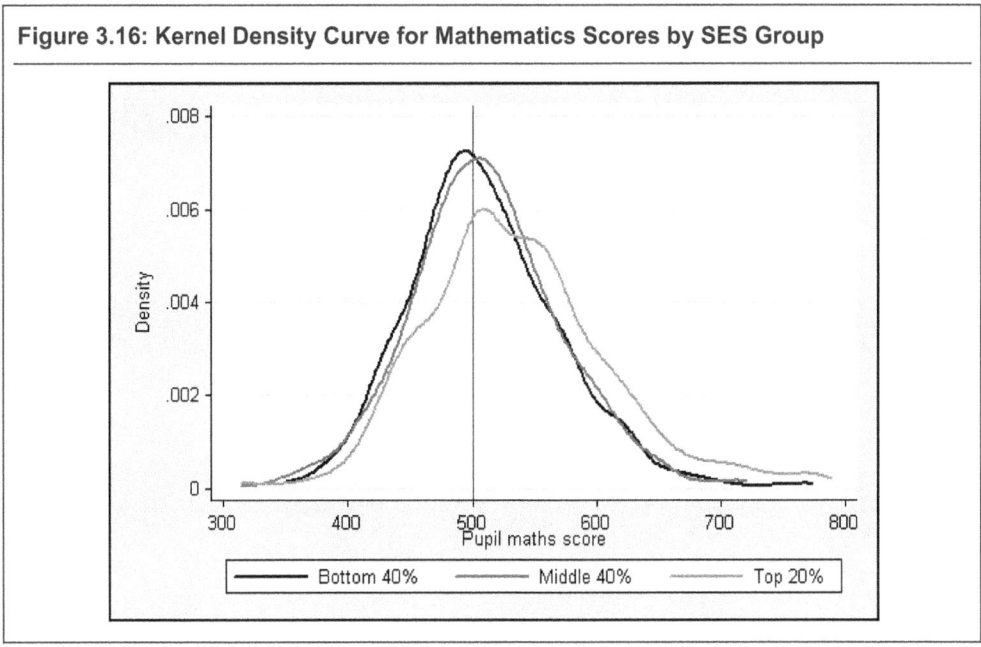

Source: Calculated from IIEP 2004.

Multivariate analyses of test scores

Table 3.13 indicates that after controlling for other factors, boys do not perform significantly better in mathematics than girls. On the other hand, pupils from the bottom and middle 40 percent—Bottom 40 and Middle 40—of the income distribution perform significantly lower than their wealthier counterparts, scoring roughly 30 points lower. Interestingly, however, the similarity in these coefficients indicates that the performance of pupils in the bottom and middle 40 percent of the income distribution is almost the same. Pupils in urban schools performed better in mathematics tests than did those who attended rural schools, with urban schools learners scoring on average, 7 points—or 0.0722 standard deviations of all the SACMEQ pupils—higher. Pupils attending schools in areas other than Lubombo achieved lower mathematics scores, though for Hhohho not significantly lower. The margin by which Manzini and Shiselweni fell below Lubombo was about 20 and 17 points respectively.

With respect to reading scores, girls outperform boys by almost 10 points, once other factors—location, region and SES group—have been considered. SES again plays a substantial role, with students in the bottom 40 percent of the income distribution scoring 47 points below those from the richest 20 percent and, students in the middle 40 percent of the income distribution scoring 40 points below the richest. The top quintile therefore has an enormous performance advantage. Pupils attending schools located in rural areas score 24 points higher than their counterparts in urban schools, while the same two regions (Manzini and Shiselweni) fall well below Lubombo once other factors are considered.

Table 3.13: OLS Regression on SACMEQ Reading and Mathematics Scores

Explanatory variables	Mathematics	Reading
Male (1 = male; 0= female)	3.77 (1.61)	−9.87 (−4.31)*
Bottom40	−30.30 (−8.96)*	−46.79 (−14.17)*
Middle40	−30.52 (−9.14)*	−39.82 (−12.22)*
Urban (1 = urban, 0 = rural)	7.22 (2.04)*	24.45 (7.09)*
Hhohho	−0.77 (−0.22)	−1.18 (−0.34)
Manzini	−19.89 (−5.57)*	−19.72 (−5.66)*
Shiselweni	−17.20 (−4.79)*	−13.19 (−3.94)*
Age	.	.
Age^2	.	.
Constant	547.52 (142.13)*	573.92 (152.60)*
Observations	3 138	3 139
R^2	0.06	0.12

Source: Own calculations from DHS2006/7 and IIEP 2004.
Note: Statistics in parentheses; *significant at 1%; The reference group is females in the top 20% of the wealth distribution living in rural areas in the Lubombo region.

Internal Efficiency

Repetition rates

The repetition policy allows for no more than 10 percent of the learners to repeat any grade. However, levels of repetition presented in table 3.14 suggest that the policy is not implemented. They also suggest that teaching and learning are fairly ineffective across the system. Repetition rates are particularly high at the first grade suggesting that a substantial proportion of learners enter grade 1 without the requisite primary school readiness. This is not surprising given low access to ECCD and the generally doubtful quality of ECCD programs.

Across the two years, the average repetition rate for primary schools is about 17 percent and about 10 percent for secondary education. Reducing these rates is critical to realizing efficiency gains that could be applied to expand access and improve quality.

Table 3.14: Repetition Rates 2006 and 2007 (%)

Grade	2006	2007
1	20	22
2	16	19
3	20	21
4	18	18
5	17	19
6	17	18
7	7	7
8	12	10
9	13	12
10	4	4
11	13	11
12	...	...

Regional comparison of repetition rate

The following cross-country comparison of repetition suggests that Swaziland's average grade repetition is among the highest in the sub-region (table 3.15).

Table 3.15 Percentage of Pupils who are Repeaters in the Region

	UIS primary	UIS secondary	SACMEQ primary
Botswana	5	1	6
Kenya	6		15
Lesotho	19	13	15
Malawi	21	9	14
Mozambique	5	15	21
Namibia	16	9	12
South Africa	8	14	10
Swaziland	**17**	**12**	**15**
Tanzania	4	3	6
Uganda	13	2	13
Zambia	7	5	12
Average	13	8	13

Source: UNESCO: UIS (2008); IIEP: SACMEQ (2004).

Dropout rates

Recent dropout rates illustrate that the schooling system is relatively good at retaining pupils up to around age 14. In 3 of the regions, the age-specific enrollment ratio (ASER) for children aged 8 to 14 is close to 95 percent. However, the fourth region, Shiselweni, does considerably worse. In this region the ASER never exceeds 90 percent. Dropping out begins to occur on a large scale after age 14, and in particular after age 15. For instance, between age 16 and 17, the drop-out rate is well above 10 percent for all regions except Hhohho.

Summary of enrollment and attainment in GET

Completion rates are low and years-input per graduate are too high: Figure 3.17, which combines the ASER and attainment ratios, indicates that historically around 25 percent of the population have not completed primary school (Grade 7). Moreover, of the estimated 75 percent who do complete this grade, most do so much later than they should. With no repetition, by age 13 all pupils should have completed Grade 7, yet currently this is only true for around 10 percent of the age cohort. Even by age 17 there are still students who have yet to complete Grade 7. This pattern implies that there are many over-aged pupils in schools. Historically, only around 50 percent of the population completes Grades 10 (lower secondary schooling), and fewer than 40 percent complete Grade 12 (upper secondary schooling).

For greater internal efficiency to be realized, the picture in Figure 3.18 needs to change. The arrows reflect necessary changes. Enrollment of children aged 6 to 15 should be 100 percent. Moreover, it is reasonable to expect that by age 16, all children should have completed Grade 7. This would allow for some repetition, but much less than what currently pertains. Completion of Grade 10 should be substantially increased. And there should be no, or extremely few, pupils aged 20 and above within the schooling system.

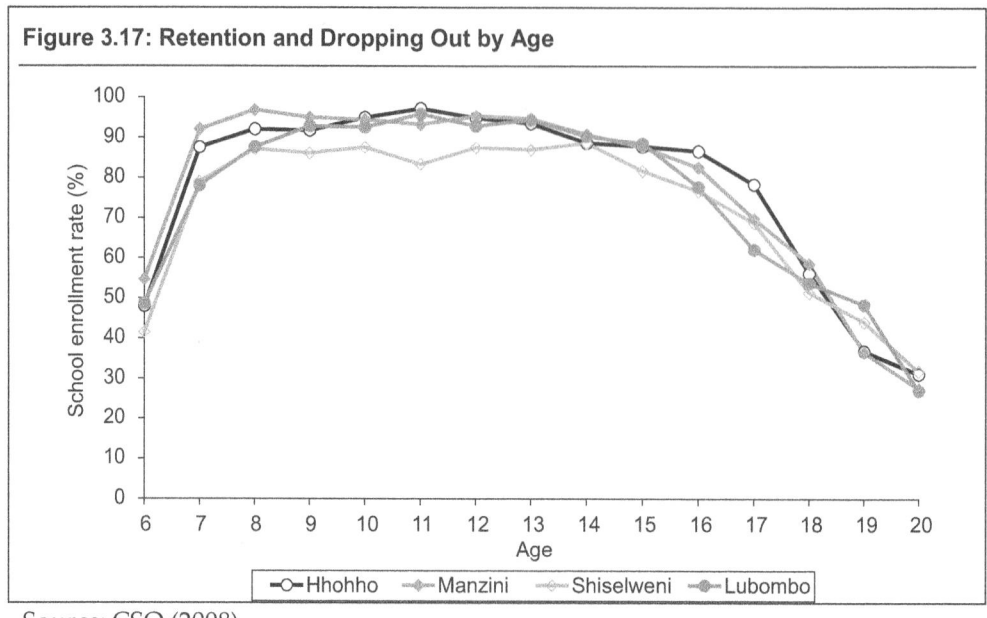

Figure 3.17: Retention and Dropping Out by Age

Source: CSO (2008)

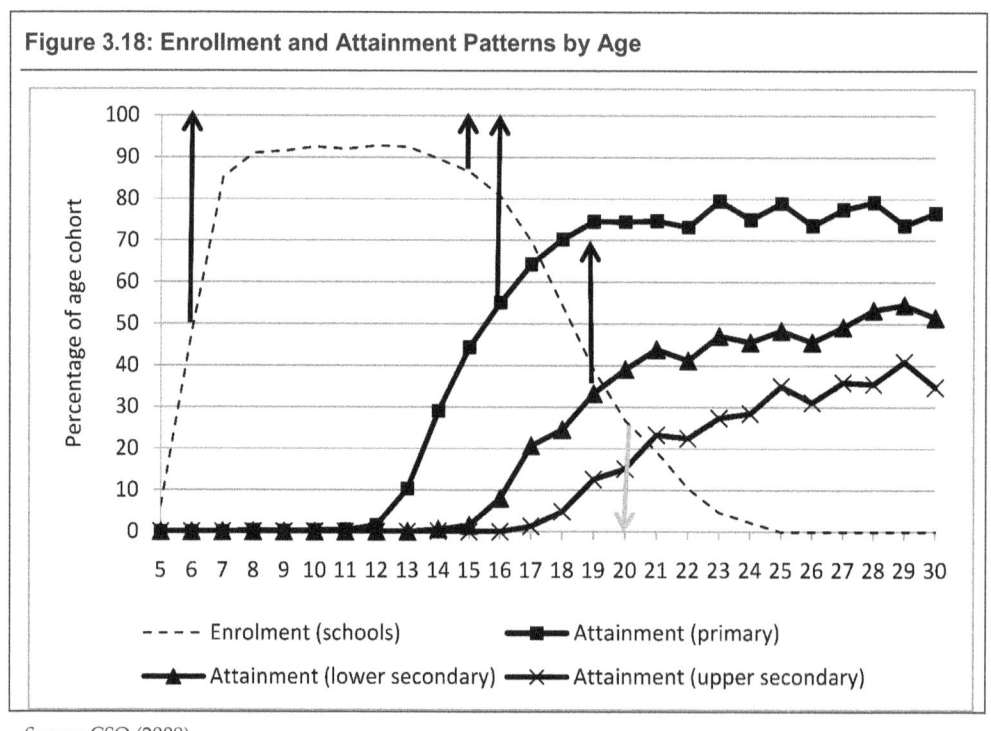

Figure 3.18: Enrollment and Attainment Patterns by Age

Source: CSO (2008).

Years-input per graduate values, as defined by UNESCO, also show a rather striking indication of the cost of internal efficiencies. The years-input per Grade 10 graduate, which should be 10 years, is instead 23 years. This means that if one takes into account grade repetition, and the fact that many pupils drop out before Grade 10, then for each successful graduate, 23 years of education have been spent. The years-input value for a Grade 12 graduate is a staggering 40 years. By any reasoning, these are staggering levels of system inefficiency.

Conclusion

Over the years Swaziland has invested substantially in increasing access to education and training. Success is evident in the increase in education attainment with each subsequent generation. However, current levels of access to GET are too low to supply Swaziland with the skills required to complement technology—within a conducive investment climate—to stimulate, innovation, productivity and accelerate growth. Access and attainment are pro-rich, especially at the senior secondary level. The private and public cost of GET is a key impediment to access. Limited and pro-rich access limits the redistributive effect of the ETSDS. Relative to SACU countries, Swaziland has maintained a reasonable level of quality education. However, learning outcomes favor the rich and this is evident in the thinning out of children from low income households at the top of the ETSDS ladder. Due to selectivity of the system, public subsidies to secondary level are pro-rich. GET is resource inefficient and this is most evident in low PTRs, high repetition rates and staggering years-input per graduate. High repetition rates also cast doubt on the quality of the system. Impressive progress has been made toward being socially responsive. HIV/AIDS and life skills are mainstreamed in the curriculum. Curricula have also integrated practical subjects in terms of prevocational subjects and practical subjects that are part of the IGCSE curriculum. However the sustainability of these subjects is seriously in doubt.

Notes

[1] Verspoor A. M. with SEIA Team. 2008. At crossroads. Choices for secondary education in sub-Saharan Africa. The World Bank, Washington D.C. (p. 89).
[2] Ibid.
[3] Marope. M.T. 2005. Namibia human capital and knowledge development for growth with equity. The World Bank. Washington DC. NB: The higher returns in Namibia could reflect the scarcity premium.
[4] World Bank. 2002. Education and HIV/AIDS: A window of hope. Washington, D.C. The World Bank.
[5] Note, though, that because many of these individuals had not yet completed their schooling, attainment levels at higher grades were still low.
[6] This is based on an analysis of the South African Labor Force Survey of 2007a.
[7] Ibid. Fasih T. 2008. Linking education policy to labor market outcomes. Washington DC. The World Bank. Hanushek E. and Wößmann. 2007. Education quality and economic growth. Washington DC. The World Bank. De Ferranti et. al. 2003. Closing the gap in education and technology. Washington D.C. The World Bank.
[8] World Bank. 2006. Swaziland: Achieving education for all challenges and policy directions. Washington DC. The World Bank.

[9] These are to enable pupils to: (a) acquire knowledge, develop confidence and ability to assess their personal strengths and weaknesses and be realistic in choosing appropriate career/employment opportunities and/or further education and training; (b) develop skills to assist in understanding economic, social, political and spiritual issues relating to day-to-day life and exercise democratic values; (c) develop desirable attitudes and behavioral patterns in interacting with the environment and their fellow men in a respective and tolerant manner; (d) acquire attitudes and values, develop skills and understanding to allow for the execution of rights and responsibilities as good citizens of Swaziland and the world at large; (e) acquire knowledge, skills and practices to encourage good family and healthy practices including awareness and management of epidemics like HIV/AIDS, that prepare them for productive life; (f) develop life-skills such as problem-solving, critical thinking, communication, enquiry, team work and being adaptive in a changing world.

[10] This is based on the examinations council's registry of examinable subjects across schools.

[11] Zanzibar was tested separately from mainland Tanzania and is here considered like a separate country, as school education in Tanzania is decentralized to the two separate federal units.

CHAPTER 4

Technical and Vocational Education, Training, and Skills Development

Introduction

Good quality, broad based and market responsive technical and vocational education, training, and skills development (TVETSD) programs supply the skills and competencies that immediately respond to labor market demands and that drive growth in post-industrial economies. Skilled labor is critical for its capacity to apply knowledge and technology to realize higher value added productivity which is the base for sustainable growth. Skills are determinants of employability including self-employability and therefore income distribution, poverty reduction and shared growth. Therefore by enhancing the skills base, the TVETD subsector can contribute to several of the PRSAP pillars: empowering the poor to generate income, macroeconomic stability, growth acceleration, human capital development, improving the quality of life and fair distribution of the benefits of growth.

Policy Orientation

Swaziland lacks a national policy statement to guide the development of its TVETSD system and to link it to the national development reform agenda and to labor market demands. A number of documents, most of which date from the 1980s, contain some policy elements. These are the Vocational and Industrial Training Act (1982), the National Educational Commission Review (1984), the NDS (1997), the National Policy Statement on Education (1999), the Human Resource Development and Planning Bill 2003, and the PRSAP (2006). Key policy themes that emerge from these documents, include the need to:

- improve management and resource efficiency through enhanced system coordination and better utilization of existing institutions;
- widen access to TVETSD by removing financial barriers such as excessive fees and "academic" barriers like the requirement for a high pass in English for entry to some TVETSD programs;
- improve the relevance of TVETSD through greater collaboration between industry, government and providers of TVETSD programs;
- enhance articulation between education, training and the world of work;

- establish links between industries and training institutions;
- foster entrepreneurial development to provide people with the skills to find meaningful self-employment and review courses in public institutions to gear them towards self employment skills;
- integrate vocational training into the general education curricula by including vocational skills in the primary curriculum and vocational training options at the secondary level;
- promote education and career pathways as well as work opportunities for young people;
- enhance the status of TVETSD.

These elements are yet to be brought together in a coherent TVETSD policy. A draft policy has been prepared and will be finalized based on this analysis. Hitherto, the absence of a policy has led to ad hoc developments with the result that the TVETSD subsector lacks strategic direction and is not effectively integrated with the overall ETSDS, the national development strategy and national and regional labor markets.

Legal Framework

As with policy, the legal framework for TVETSD comprises isolated and fragmented pieces of legal instruments, the collective of which is not adequate to provide a comprehensive legal framework for the subsector. One of these pieces is the Vocational and Industrial Training Act of 1982. The Act established the Industrial and Vocational Training Board (IVTB) and provides a legal framework for apprenticeships and trade testing. It also includes provisions for a levy system to support skills development—which was rejected—and guidelines for the commencement of training schemes

Another key legal instrument is the Human Resource Development and Planning Bill of 2003. The Bill aimed, inter alia, to produce a more coherent enabling and regulatory environment for TVETSD. It provided for the creation of a National Training and Qualifications Authority (NTQA) with responsibility for: establishing a National Qualifications Framework (NQF), setting standards, registering standards-generating bodies, registering providers, quality assurance and overseeing a training fund financed through a levy on employers. If enacted, this Bill could have catalyzed a series of significant and progressive reforms.

The lack of a national TVETSD legal framework has led to very weak regulation and quality control of public and private training provision. At present, public provision of TVETSD is regulated through circulars mainly from the MoE and the MoEE. Private provision is largely unregulated. As with "illegal" GET schools, private training providers do not have to register, except as businesses with the MoEE. They do not have to seek accreditation for their programs with any authority. This leaves the nature and quality of training to their discretion and trainees vulnerable to abuse.

Organizational and Management Framework

Figure 4.1 summarizes the organizational structure of TVETSD.

Figure 4.1: Structure of Swaziland's TVETSD Sector

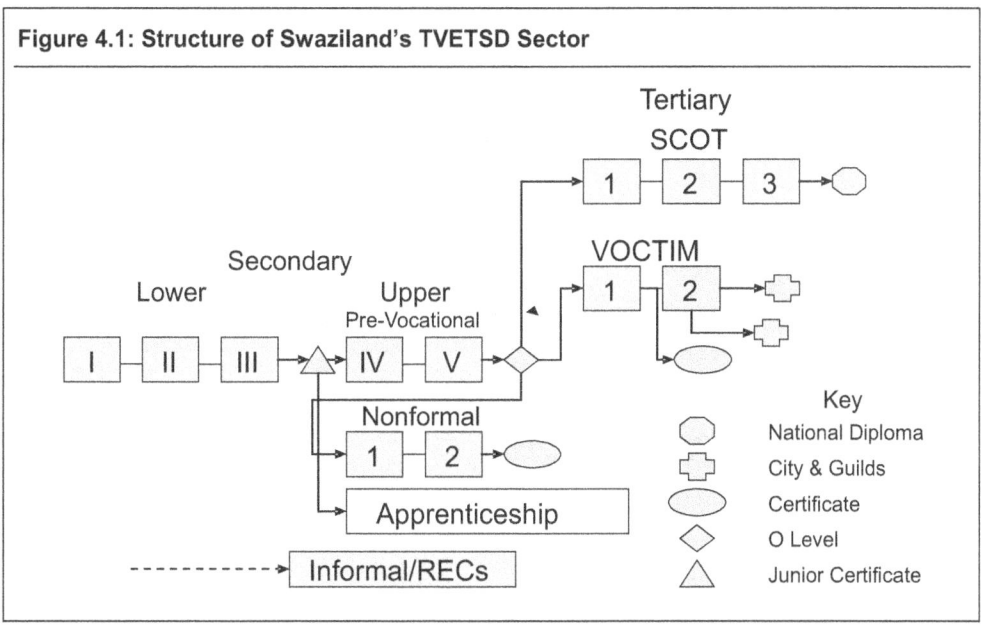

Source: MOE.

The management of TVETSD is characterized by heterogeneity and fragmentation. At least eight public organizations have some role in the management of TVETSD and none has the overall mandate for systemic coordination. Proposals to restructure the management of TVETSD have been in draft for some time but details of the responsibilities are yet to be gazetted. Two public institutions, the MoE and the MoEE, could be said to have the bulk of the responsibility for TVETSD. Table 4.1 provides examples of the types of programs offered by line Ministries and the number of trainees enrolled.

The current fragmentation in the management of TVETSD leads to a range of unaffordable risks, including:

- duplication and wastage in terms of curriculum development and training provision;
- restrictions on government and industry attempts to ensure that providers meet minimum quality standards in terms of staff qualifications, program design and assessment;
- undermining of attempts to ensure national consistency in training provision
- limiting the development of articulation and credit transfer arrangements both within the TVETSD and with the schools and higher education sectors;
- segmentation of training supply;
- training provision that is isolated from market forces; and
- diminished industry confidence in the outputs of the TVETSD.

Table 4.1: Examples of Programs Offered by Line Ministries

Line Ministry	Type of training	Duration in months	Total Trainees	% Female	Instructors	Trainees per Instructor	Annual Output
Agriculture	Cooperatives Development Center (CODEC) - fulltime certificate course in cooperative management	10	39	6	6	6.5	39
	Farmer Training Centers	24	61	39	5	12.2	61
Home Affairs	Vocational Rehabilitation Centers for people with physical disabilities.	12	94	34.04	8	11.8	94
Regional Development and Youth Affairs	Women in Development Training Center offers craft, business and basic trade skill programs for women	9	100	88	15	6.7	100
Public Works	Training programs for roads technicians	n.a.	n.a.	n.a.	n.a.	n.a.	n.a.
Public Service and Information	Short- and long-term training programs for civil servants	n.a.	n.a.	n.a.	n.a.	n.a.	n.a.

Source: Relevant Line Ministries.
n.a. Not applicable.

Access and Equity

Demand for TVETSD is met through 57 publicly-supported and 27 private institutions. These 84 institutions are complemented by enterprise-based training, trade tests, and apprenticeships/traineeships. For Swaziland's population size (1.1 million), this seems to be a more than adequate supply; however, collectively these institutions are not able to meet current demand. Each year, about 7,500 students terminate their studies after Grade 7, Form 3 and Form 5. In addition, 6,500 students drop out of secondary education. These 14,000 individuals and thousands of adults in need of basic skills, re-tooling and/or up-skilling frame the potentially unmet demand for TVETSD. The 14,000 school leavers must compete for less than 1,000 places in TVETSD institutions. Only about 7 percent of school-leavers may therefore gain access.

Range and Levels of Provision

Publicly funded provision

The 57 publicly-funded providers enroll about 2,858 trainees. They comprise 1 public technician level training institution, 1 public artisan / trade level training institution, prevocational programs in 16 senior secondary schools, 19 government training institutions, and 20 nonformal nongovernment training institutions, 18 of which are publicly aided. Table 4.2 provides an overview of providers.

Table 4.2: Overview of Publicly Funded TVETSD Provision (2006 or most recent year)

Type of provider	No. of Providers	No. of Trainees	% Female	No. of Trainers	Trainees/ Trainer Ratio	Annual Trainee Output
Public technician level training institution – SCOT	1	314	32.7	43	7.3	114
Public artisan / trade level training institution – VOCTIM	1	157	20.3	33	4.8	224
Secondary schools offering prevocational programs	16	720	na	67	10.7	na
Government-owned training centers	19	664	45.0	75	8.8	664
Nonformal government training centers – government assisted	18	813	56.0	56	14.5	378
Nonformal government training centers – not government assisted	2	190	43.0	23	8.3	190
Total	57	2,858	40.0	297	9.6	1,570

Source: Enrollment records of respective institutions.

In addition to limited spaces, the extended duration of most programs is a disincentive for prospective adult trainees. Most programs demand two to three years of fulltime study. This limits the extent to which the system can provide just-in-time training for initiates and/or working adults. Yet Swaziland's responsiveness to fast changing and unexpected demands for skills presented by FDIs and/or prospects for small businesses depends on such courses. Table 4.3 provides a summary of courses by duration.

Table 4.3: Summary of Public Provision by Duration

Type of provider	Providers	Duration of programs
Public technician training institution	SCOT	3 years.
Public formal vocational training institution	VOCTIM	1–2 years.
Secondary schools offering prevocational programs	High Schools	2 years
Government-owned training centers	Rural Education Centers	1 year.
	National Handicrafts Training Center	9 months.
	CODEC	10 months
	Farmer Training Centers	2 years
	Vocational Rehabilitation Centers	1 year
	Women in Development Training Center	9 months
	SPTC Training Centre	12–18 months
Nonformal government training centers – government assisted	Swaziland Skills Training Centers—MITC, NASTIC & SITC	2 years.
	MVTC	2 years.
	NPYTC	1–3 years.
	SEBENTA	12 months
Nonformal government training centers – not government assisted	Bosco Skills Center	2 years
	Likusasa	12 months

Source: MOE.

Formal technical and vocational education and training

Prevocational programs

The prevocational program seems to not be meeting its aim to extend vocational training opportunities to senior secondary students. Very few learners take this option. Since 2004, when the pilot ended, enrollment has averaged 4 percent (table 4.4). Plans to take the pilot to scale were changed because of the need to first evaluate the program.

Table 4.4: Examined Trainees as Indicative Enrollment in Prevocational Programs

Subject	2004	2005	2006	2007
Agriculture	90	65	109	92
Business Studies	70	31	41	43
Entrepreneurship	302	235	302	298
Home Econ.	60	51	58	57
IT	294	229	281	279
Tech. Drawing	64	60	64	63
Total	880	671	855	832
% of total senior secondary enrollment	5	3	4	4

Source: Examinations Council.

Due to lack of vertical articulation, the prevocational program has not been successful in helping its graduates to access higher levels of TVETSD. As further challenge confronting this program is financial viability. Its low student uptake translates into unsustainably low STRs and unaffordable unit cost of senior secondary education.

Artisan or trade level training

Access to artisan or trade level training programs is limited and has been on the decline since 2003 with signs of recovery beginning in 2006 (see figure 4.2). Unaffordable fees are cited as a cause of the declining enrollment. As discussed under the section on system efficiency, this represents a substantial underutilization of training capacity against unmet demand for places.

Vocational and Commercial Training Institute Matsapa (VOCTIM) enrollment is high in programs for which there is little labor market demand. The bulk of trainees take commercial subjects. Enrollment figures for automotive training and electrical training have remained more or less the same over time, while there has been a steady decline for woodwork and mechanical engineering. The rest of the courses follow the overall trend of a peak in the early 2000s followed by a sharp decline and then a slight recovery starting in 2006, but never reaching the initial high (figure 4.3).

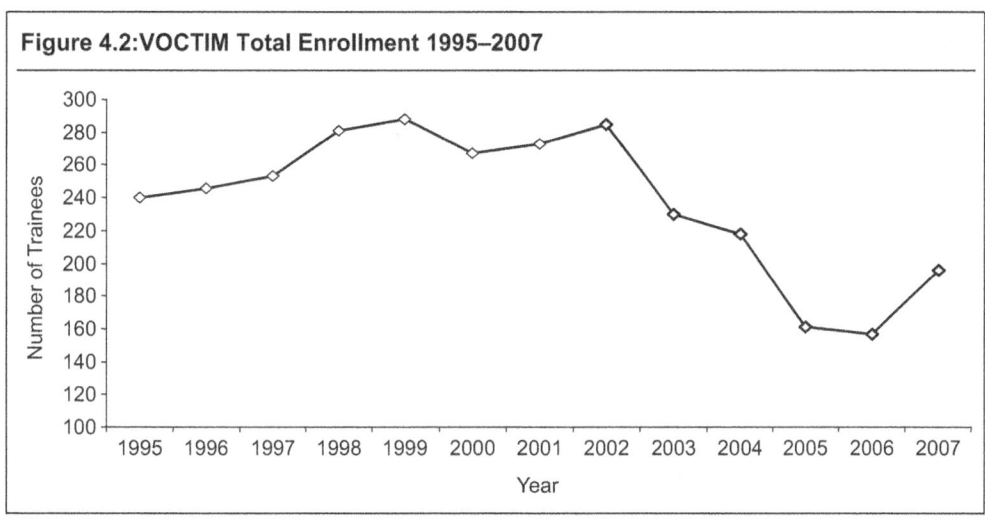

Figure 4.2: VOCTIM Total Enrollment 1995–2007

Source: VOCTIM administration.

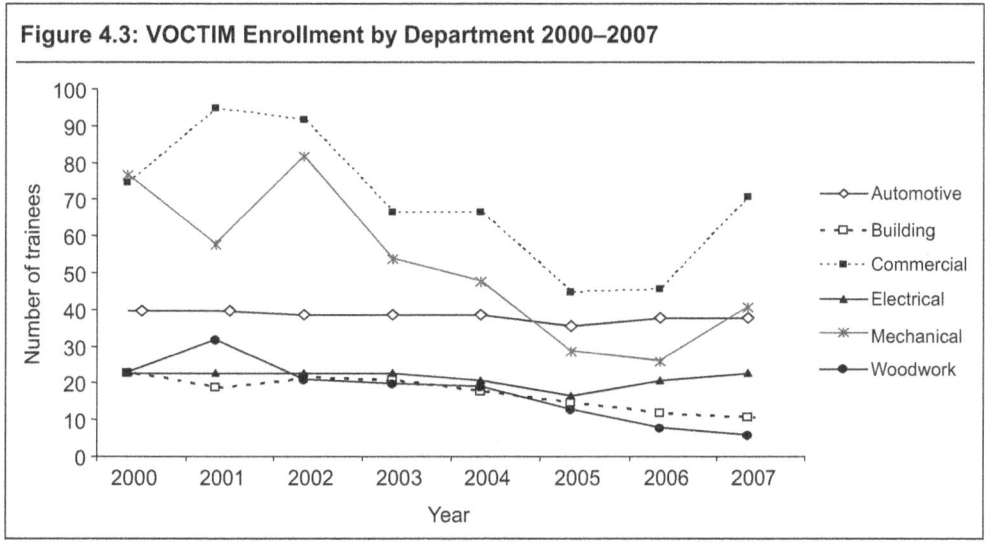

Figure 4.3: VOCTIM Enrollment by Department 2000–2007

Source: VOCTIM administration.

Technician level training

SCOT is the only institution that offers technician training. With capacity for 1,500 students—including newly-renovated residential accommodation for 1,200 students—it enrolls 314 trainees or operates at 21 percent of its capacity (figure 4.4).

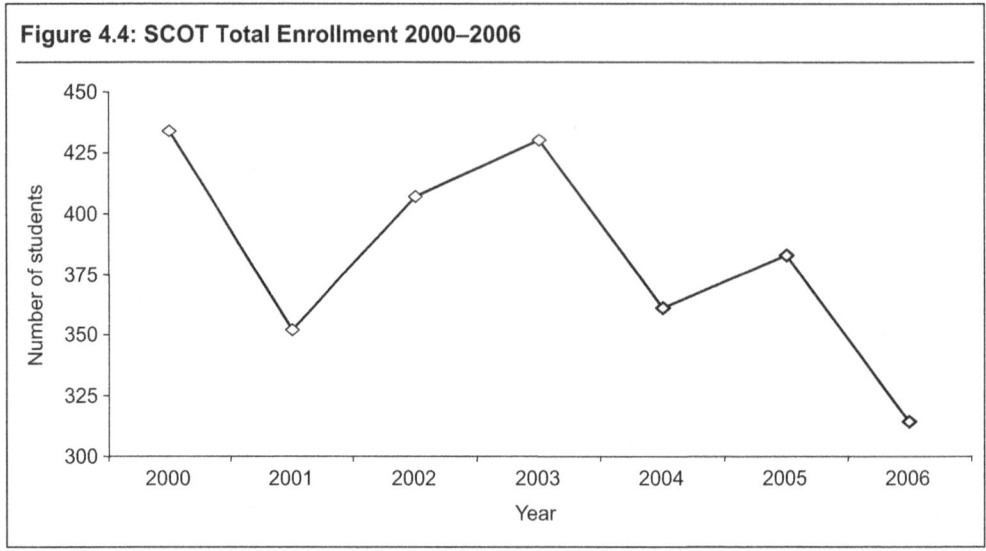

Figure 4.4: SCOT Total Enrollment 2000–2006

Source: SCOT.

Table 4.5: SCOT Enrollment by Year of Study, 2000–2006

	2000	2001	2002	2003	2004	2005	2006
Year 1	233	166	156	184	51	170	103
Year 2	88	159	135	143	163	93	150
Year 3	113	27	116	103	147	120	61
Total	434	352	407	430	361	383	314

Source: SCOT.

Nonformal vocational training

Government provided no- formal vocational training

Rural education centers (RECs), are the main providers of adult basic training and skills development. Their enrollment has also been on the decline since 2001 (figure 4.5). Because of their good geographical coverage—two per region—RECs present an opportunity to expand access to VET for rural dwellers and to collaborate with senior secondary schools in the provision of prevocational programs.

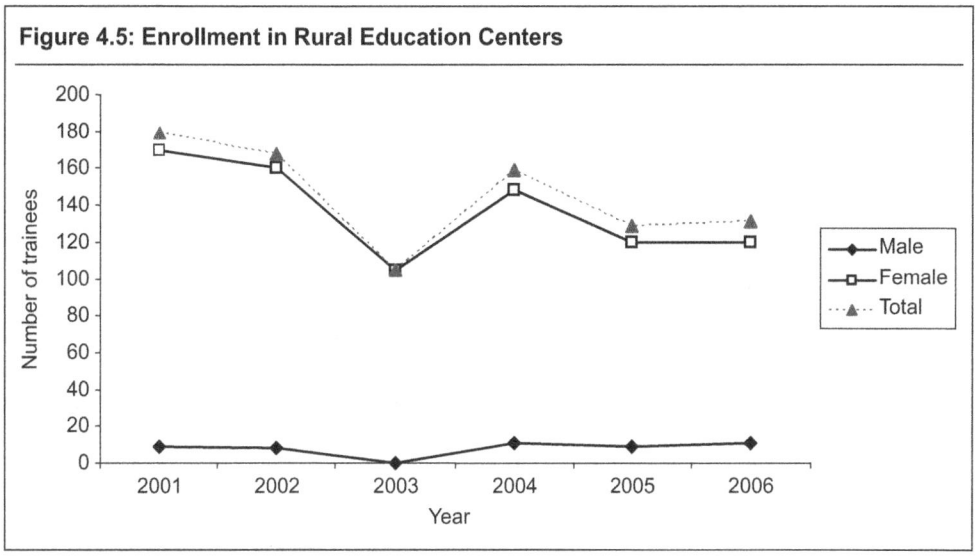

Figure 4.5: Enrollment in Rural Education Centers

Source: Ministry of Education.

Government assisted no-formal vocational training

Eighteen nonformal providers receive government assistance in the form of instructor salaries. These centers also charge trainees nominal fees. They include three Swaziland Skills Centers—Manzini Industrial Training center (MITC), Nhlangano Agricultural Skills Training Center (NASTIC), Sitegi Industrial Training Center (SITC)—and SEBENTA adult education institute. Collectively, they enroll about 800 trainees a year. These centers tend to offer shorter entry-level skills training programs, and therefore, an opportunity to elaborate them into just-in-time programs that could enable Swaziland to respond to unanticipated shifts in labor market demands. This would considerably enhance the provision of entry level skills training for adults, upgrading and re-tooling opportunities, and second-chance training opportunities for youth.

Private nonformal vocational training

Two nongovernmental privately-financed institutions—including The Bosco Skills Center—enroll about 190 trainees. The Bosco Skills Center offers strongly market-focused vocational training with emphasis on entrepreneur development. This program provides free office/workshop space to entrepreneurs across seven types of businesses in return for the training of apprentices. Each workshop trains from 4 to 12 apprentices over 2 years. The apprentices pay a nominal fee (about E700) but receive this back in weekly allowances. Employers receive not only free work space but also free labor for the duration of the training. Employers are monitored to ensure that reasonable training takes place. The expansion of programs of this type would do much to enhance the market relevance of entry level skills training in Swaziland.

Enterprise-based training

The 2007 investment climate assessment (ICA) shows that firms in Swaziland tend to train their workers more than those in Botswana or Namibia but less than those in

Mauritius, South Africa and other countries (table 4.6). About 50 percent of the firms provide training compared to 72 percent of firms in China, 76 percent in Thailand, and 64 percent in South Africa. Training programs include: (i) apprenticeships conducted through SCOT and the directorate of industrial and vocational training (DIVT), (ii) agricultural extension programs, notably in the sugar industry, (iii) HIV/AIDS awareness and counseling, (iv) supervision and management training offered by regional training providers that lead to formal recognition by qualification authorities, such as the South African Qualifications Authority (SAQA), (v) adult basic education programs, and (vi) generic customer service and product knowledge training particularly in the hotels sector. While there is a significant level of enterprise based training most is conducted in-house and does not lead to a formal recognition. The lack of formal recognition of training can jeopardize the trainees' future chances of securing other jobs.

Table 4.6: Prevalence of Firm-based Training as a Percentage of Trained Workers

Country	% Firms offering training	% Skilled workers who are trained	% Unskilled trained
Botswana	37	57	41
Malaysia	42	81	76
Namibia	44	68	41
Swaziland	**49**	**64**	**27**
Mauritius	62	34	18
South Africa	64	45	47
China	72	48	25
Chile	72	34	25
Thailand	76	---	---

Source: Swaziland ICA Survey, Volume 1, 26 and Volume 2, 58.

Swaziland is also in the top tier of the distribution of all countries in terms of the proportion of the skilled workforce that gets trained. A recent labor survey shows that 78 percent of employees received training since they were employed. Firms with more than 10 workers are 40 percent more likely to provide training than smaller firms. This could be because small firms cannot afford the substantial fixed costs associated with training. Exporting firms are about 40 percent more likely to provide training than nonexporting firms. Firms that invest in HIV-prevention interventions are about 64 percent more likely to provide training. Employees with more formal schooling are more likely to receive firm-based training.[1]

Apprenticeships and traineeships

The number of apprentices is low and enrollments and completions have been static over the past decade (figure 4.6). There are about 200 apprentices each year, 50 of which are new recruits and 50 are completers. Like many African countries—Namibia, Benin, Ghana, Kenya, South Africa, and Tanzania—Swaziland has enacted formal apprenticeship laws which regulate the following: official registration of contracts, access to apprenticeships, training duration, skills assessment, and certification procedures. However, these arrangements are only applied in a small number of enterprises. Part of the reason for low participation is the elimination of tax incentives that employers used to receive for taking apprentices. There are 28 apprentice trades, of which 20 are active. Apprentices who complete the program are awarded Grade II trade certification. According to DIVT other reasons behind low apprenticeship/traineeship numbers are: (i) a lack of guidelines on the level of training expected; (ii) difficulty in identifying employers who are willing to engage apprentices/trainees; (iii) concerns by employers about apprentice / trainee contractual obligations; and (iv) economic conditions limiting employer capacity to engage apprentices/trainees.

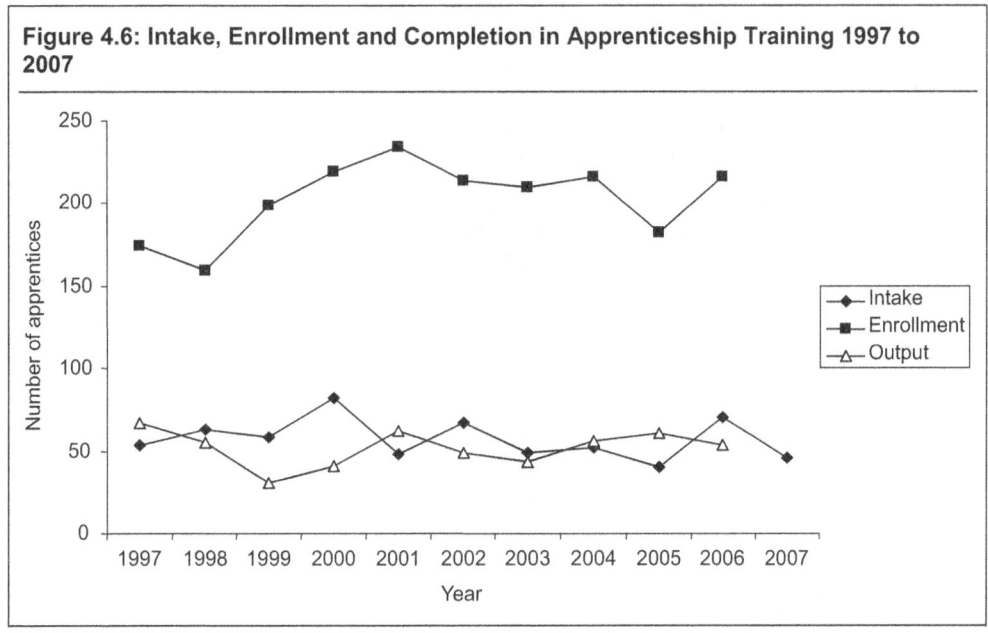

Figure 4.6: Intake, Enrollment and Completion in Apprenticeship Training 1997 to 2007

Source: Ministry of Education.

Trade testing

Trade testing tends to focus on the certification of lower level skills and there are no supporting skill development programs for individuals who wish to gain higher level skills. Between 600 and 800 people undertake trade tests each year and these cover 21 occupations. DIVT administers the trade tests at government training institutions throughout the country on a fee for service basis. About two thirds of tests are conducted at the lowest level—Grade III.[2] There are incentives in the labor market for artisans to gain higher levels of trade test grades. However there are no courses to assist artisans to move from Grade III to Grade I. According to DIVT, the main constraints on trade testing are: (i) a lack of serviceable equipment, particularly at SCOT; (ii) cost;[3] (iii) inadequate budget; and (iv) a lack of capacity to develop and maintain occupational and training standards.

Private commercial provision

Private commercial organizations are increasingly becoming major providers of TVETSD. A 2008 survey identified 26 training institutions with estimated enrollments of 2501 trainees. Most of the 175 courses offered by these providers were in business (45.1 percent) and IT related fields (23.4 percent). Seven of these providers had total enrollments exceeding 200 trainees, which means that these institutions have more trainees than do public institutions such as VOCTIM. The largest provider in this category had a total enrollment of 324 learners which is comparable to the public TVETSD institution, SCOT. The distribution of these providers has an urban bias with 17 of them based in either Mbabane (11) or Manzini (6).

In 2008, enrollment in private commercial providers was almost the same as the number of trainees in the public TVETSD system (2,501 trainees). Private training is unregulated much along similar lines of the so-called "illegal" schools. This raises important questions about management and teaching quality, the relationship between training programs and industry skill demands, and the employability of graduates. It is worth noting that other countries in the region, such as Uganda, and internationally, such as Australia, where there has been rapid growth in private TVETSD provision have experienced problems with the quality of some programs. In both cases, attempts have been made to improve the quality of training through the development of professional associations. In Uganda, where private training providers train more than 80 percent of trainees, the Uganda Association of Private Vocational Institutions has made significant efforts to improve the capacity of its members to deliver good quality services and to improve their relevance to the labor market. Similarly in Australia, the Australian Council for Private Education and Training plays an important role in promoting quality training and professional development for its members, and in advocating on behalf of private training providers.

Access and equity

Urban dwellers, who also tend to be more affluent, have better access to formal TVETSD. Nearly all the private providers and the two major public training providers—SCOT and VOCTIM—are in Mbabane and Manzini. This is offset to some degree by the presence of non formal TVETSD institutions in rural areas. However these organizations tend to focus on basic skills training. Therefore, rural dwellers tend to have access to lower level training than their urban and more affluent counterparts. Given the association between training, employability, and income, this hardly works towards reducing social inequalities as intended in the PRSAP.

Overall, females comprise about 40 percent of total TVETSD enrollment in publicly-supported TVETSD institutions. This compares favorably with Mozambique and Namibia, where females comprise respectively, 29 percent and 19 percent of trainees.[4] However, females' participation is concentrated in lower-level training offered by SI and RECs, and in the so-called female-orientated programs—sewing for instance. They account for only 33 percent of enrollment at SCOT, and 20.3 percent of enrollment at VOCTIM, both of which provide more traditional, longer-term TVETSD programs. This does not support the gender parity goal of the PRSAP.

The user charges of private and some publicly supported providers, such as VOCTIM, are a potential barrier to access for lower-income families. Trainees at

VOCTIM, the only public institution offering formal craft training, are self-sponsored. VOCTIM fees range from SZL4,500 to 10,500 per year, in addition to other charges. This represents a significant financial barrier to participation in TVETSD, and has contributed to low enrollment at VOCTIM.

As with female trainees, people from low income households have better access to lower level training offered by the SI and RECs. These institutions also offer programs for disadvantaged youth who are not able to continue with an academic career.[5] Most NGO training institutions charge low fees, thereby encouraging participation from lower-income groups. For example, at SI, trainees pay a registration fee of E50.00 plus SZL100.00 per month. For a 12-month program, this would be a total cost of E1,250. Therefore, the upgrading of RECs and STCs into VTCs therefore has a compelling equity imperative when one considers their clientele base—women, rural dwellers, disadvantaged youth, and the poor.

Adults have limited access to skills development due to inflexible provision in terms of course duration, time of delivery and content. Courses for income generation and livelihood improvement are limited. The main public TVETSD providers, SCOT and VOCTIM, are essentially pre-service providers for young people completing secondary education.

Quality of TVETSD

Curricula and programs

Swaziland does not have a national TVETSD curriculum, national occupational standards, or a national qualifications framework (NQF). This means that there is no national specification for the skills required in particular occupations. This limits student mobility and makes it difficult to compare the quality of training provision across providers. Certification is fragmented, usually given by the provider itself. Programs offered for the same occupation by different providers vary in terms of duration, content, assessment and certification. Lack of a clear qualifications framework and occupational standards also places Swaziland at a competitive disadvantage in the region. It also perpetuates the lack of recognition of technician training, which is not identified as a distinct level of occupation in Swaziland.

A standards-based NQF, like those in South Africa, Botswana, and Namibia, would clearly specify the competencies required for particular occupations, and set levels for artisans, technicians, and professional or degree equivalent. It would also provide a national set of benchmarks for TVETSD programs, provider assessment arrangements, and trade testing. If Swaziland decides to implement such a framework, it must be careful to avoid complexity, particularly in the generation of unit standards, credits, and qualifications packaging.

In the absence of certification based on national standards, employers and TVETSD providers use externally accredited examinations and certificates offered by international awarding bodies, such as City and Guilds, and Pitman. These examinations give an indication of the relative quality of a limited number of training programs.

Instructor qualifications

The adequacy of instructor qualifications is uneven across the TVETSD subsector. There is shortage of qualified prevocational instructors but for those who are there, 50 percent hold degrees and another 50 percent hold diplomas. This is an exception because for upper levels, most instructors lack appropriate qualifications. At VOCTIM, 13 of the 38 teaching staff (34.2 percent) have only an advanced certificate or less. Almost half of the instructors (45.2 percent) at SCOT have only advanced diploma or lower (table 4.7). Other than the low qualifications, most SCOT trainers do not have pedagogical training. The potential adverse effects on trainee quality are unaffordable if Swaziland should take the route of exporting skilled labor as proposed in this report.

Table 4.7: Instructor Qualifications for Selected Institutions

Qualification	SCOT	VOCTIM	Prevocational Program
Masters	6	2	
Bachelors	23	7	31
HND/Advanced	8	5	
Diploma	7	11	35
Full technological certificate	6	5	
Certificate	3	8	1
Total number of instructors	53	38	66

Sources: SCOT, VOCTIM, and MoE, 2008.

A major upgrading of staff qualifications, especially at SCOT, is required in order to ensure that: (i) staff have the technical competence to deliver higher level technician programs; (ii) programs offered by SCOT are of comparable regional and international standards; and (iii) graduates of SCOT are competitive in the region and internationally.

Instructor competencies

TVETSD instructors either lack or have very limited, irrelevant or outdated industry experience. This means that many instructors are either out of touch or unaware of contemporary work practices or are unclear about the standards that apply in the workplace. This severely limits their capacity to train and assess learners to workplace standards. Again, this does not help Swaziland to build exportable skilled labor.

In mature TVETSD systems, in the region and internationally, instructors are expected to possess training and assessment competencies, technical competencies in the relevant occupational area and appropriate industrial experience. In Namibia for instance, the proposed new qualification system for TVETSD instructors has been designed on the assumption that people seeking to become TVETSD instructors have (i) a qualification aligned with a NQF Level 4 in the relevant occupation or technical area and (ii) a minimum of 3 years work experience in the relevant occupational area.

In Australia, a mandatory quality assurance framework has been established, which is called the Australian Quality Training Framework (AQTF). All training providers seeking to offer national qualifications must meet requirements and are subject to ongoing audit and monitoring against the standards that comprise this framework. A key provision of the AQTF requires training providers to demonstrate that training and assessment are "conducted by trainers and assessors who: (i) have the necessary training and assessment competencies; (ii) have the relevant vocational competencies at least to the level being delivered or assessed; and (iii) continue developing their vocational and training and assessment competencies to support continuous improvements in delivery of the RTO's services;" These provisions in the AQTF are designed to ensure that assessors have appropriate skills and access to ongoing professional development. This is designed to ensure that TVETSD instructors have up-to-date knowledge of both their technical area and developments in training and assessment.

There are no national occupational standards for TVETSD instructors. Countries in the region such as South Africa and Namibia and internationally, such as Scotland, Australia and New Zealand have developed national occupational standards and related qualifications for instructors that form part of a NQF (see box 4.1 for a Scotland example). The development of national occupational standards for TVETSD instructors in Swaziland would provide a basis for: (i) identifying the skills required by a vocational trainer workforce; (ii) identifying skills gap; (iii) designing professional learning pathways; (iv) providing career progression for vocational trainers, and (v) ensuring that instructors have the skills to design programs, deliver training and assess learners in line with industry standards.

Box 4.1: Scotland—Occupational Standards for TVETSD Instructor

In Scotland the Employers National Training Organisation (ENTO) is currently responsible, on behalf of Lifelong Learning United Kingdom (LLUK), for the development and maintenance of the Learning and Development National Occupational Standards and the associated Scottish Vocational Qualifications (SVQs). The SVQ in learning and development are made up of groups of unit standards that describe the key functions of vocational trainers working in a range of institutional and work place settings. There are six interrelated SVQs in learning and development that are designed for particular groups of vocational trainers. For example the *Level three in direct training and support* is directed at people delivering training in a workplace or training centre, whereas the *Level 5 in learning and development* is designed for those with responsibility for management of an organization's learning and development programs.

Each SVQ in learning and development comprises a mix of core and elective units. This enables the qualifications to be structured to suit the differing needs and job roles of the relevant group of vocational trainers. For example the *Level three in learning and development* comprises nine core units which are: Evaluate and develop own practice, Identify individual learning aims and programmes, Agree learning programmes with learners, Develop training sessions, Monitor and review progress with learners, and Create a climate that promotes learning. In addition, three elective units must be selected. These must be drawn from the following set of electives: Enable learning through presentations, Enable learning through demonstrations and instruction, Enable individual learning through coaching, Enable group learning, Support learners by mentoring in the workplace, Support and advise individual learners, Assess candidates using a range of methods, Support competence achieved in the workplace, and Review health and safety procedures in the workplace.

Source: Data compiled by author.

Physical training environment

Physical inputs in government owned and/or government supported institutions are generally inadequate, particularly at SCOT. Over-reliance on government financing and declines in government support at SCOT have led to the de-capitalization of the institution. The extreme lack of furniture, equipment, and even weather-proof facilities has sparked several student protests. The new library at VOCTIM has not been used for 5 years because of lack of furniture and books.

Management of publicly supported TVETSD institutions

Central control has stifled innovation, isolated TVETSD institutions from labor markets and delayed the resolution of operational problems. The over-centralized control of SCOT and VOCTIM has led to a low sense of "ownership" of the institutions on the part of managers. It is also a disincentive for fund raising which translates into an unsustainable dependency on the government. Devolution of authority to these training institutions, within clear expectations for performance, would enable them to set tuition policies, establish pay scales, generate and retain income and find their own markets. In short, there is a need to empower these institutions and provide incentives for them to innovate and solve problems. Many examples exist in the region of post-secondary technical institutions that have autonomy and operate under independent boards of governors, including the Polytechnic of Namibia, technical colleges in Botswana, technikons in South Africa and institutes of technology in Tanzania.

Central government places few if any performance conditions on the transfer of resources to institutions like SCOT and VOCTIM. Subsidies are transferred based on previous budgets regardless of the number and quality of trainees enrolled and graduated. There is very little evidence of financial transfers being conditional on meeting agreed performance criteria. This is a critical system weakness. The funding of TVETSD should be performance based in order to ensure accountability and to enhance performance by training providers. Consideration should be given to the adoption of a performance based funding model, such as the purchaser-provider financing model that is used in Australia (see box 4.2 for an example).

Box 4.2: Purchaser Provider Financing Model for TVETSD

The purchaser/provider model of service delivery is becoming more common in financing TVETSD systems. Broadly defined, it involves two separate agents. The first is the purchaser who decides what will be produced. The second is the ultimate provider who delivers the agreed outputs.

In this system, government decides what services it wants, and then seeks a provider for those services. In the case of TVETSD, the service being sought might be the delivery of training in a particular industry or occupational area, the development of occupational standards for an industry or research in a particular field. The provider may be a public or private training provider, depending on who can offer the service in a timely manner, at a competitive price, and at an acceptable standard of quality.

Under this arrangement, the Ministry of Education would purchase training from a pool of accredited training providers who would be selected through a competitive tendering process.

A purchaser – provider financing model for TVETSD would ensure that (i) training providers are responsive to demand, (ii) realistic and transparent pricing is established for training programs, (iii) performance standards are met by the providers of the training programs or other service, and (iv) the MoE has a mechanism for improving the quality of program provision.

Source: Data compiled by author.

Instructional processes

Swaziland stands out among countries in the region in its extensive use of "training through production" (see box 4.3 for elaboration on the approach). Nongovernmental training institutions, particularly Swaziland Skills Centers and Don Bosco, train almost exclusively through production. The practice appears balanced, does not succumb to the risk of income generation overwhelming the teaching process and generally should be considered a key strength of the system. It also has the advantage of equipping learners with skills to establish and grow their own businesses, improve their incomes, survive as entrepreneurs and create employment for others.

Box 4.3: Training Through Production

This approach to vocational training involves using production activities to develop technical and generic skills. In this approach, instruction is fully integrated with the production of items for sale in local markets using indigenous materials and appropriate technology. Trainees are involved in all stages of production, including: design, product development, production, promotion, sales and record keeping. As products are designed, produced, and marketed, the necessary technical skills for each step are identified and built into the instruction. This allows the trainer to adjust the instruction on an ongoing basis. In 'training through production,' trainees gain technical skills as well as the experience and skills necessary to start and manage their own small businesses.

Key benefits of 'training through production' include:

- trainees learn to use available technology and local materials in the creation of products. Thus the trainee learns skills that enable him or her to succeed in the context of the informal sector.
- training is more affordable because trainees can offset the cost of their training by earning money while they learn.
- training providers can earn income which helps meet the cost of training provision.

Providers using training through production approaches should be careful not to compete with local businesses.

'Training through production' techniques are also used in more mature TVETSD systems. For example, in Australia, the Hot Glass Studio, which was established in 1975, employs 'training through production' techniques in the training of hot glass workers. Trainees and staff work together on the production of various types of glass products. These include corporate awards and gifts, custom one-off commissions, architectural work and small production runs.

Source: Data compiled by author.

Assessment and assessment quality assurance

The subsector lacks a systemic approach to assessment and assessment quality assurance. Assessment is therefore conducted against different criteria, under varying conditions, using different assessment instruments and is administered by staff that may or may not have assessor competencies. In some cases, assessment quality assurance is managed through external examinations set by international awarding bodies, such as the City and Guilds and international professional bodies, such as the Association of Certified Chartered Accountants. In other cases, such as nonformal training institutions and apprenticeship training, assessment is quality assured by the trade tests administered by the DIVT. These tests are recognized by industry and some employers require diploma graduates from SCOT to take the appropriate trade test to demonstrate their competencies. However it is generally acknowledged that DIVT has inadequate resources and capacity to adequately maintain these tests. Overall assessment quality assurance in the TVETSD system is weak.

Learning outcomes and outputs

Performance trends on national examinations

As with general education, performance on examinations and tests appears to be high. However the lack of national standards, the use of trainers with limited industry experience and inadequate qualifications, and poor assessment quality assurance raises questions about the quality of the outputs of the training system. At SCOT, 95 percent of third year candidates successfully complete their courses. Percentage passes are high across board (table 4.8). The certified accounting technician program recently achieved a distinction, reaching fourth highest in the world on the ACCA (UK Chartered Accountants) examination.

Table 4.8: SCOT Percentage Pass Rates by Year and Faculty

Faculty	2003/04	2004/05	2005/06	2006/07
Building & Civil	97	97	100	93
Business Administration	93	89	69	86
Education	100	95	97	95
Engineering Science	97	100	94	97
Total	96	95	93	95

Source: SCOT Administration.

At VOCTIM, the pass rates on the City and Guilds examinations have fluctuated from year to year but increased from 64 percent in 2003 to 81 percent in 2006 (table 4.9).

Table 4.9: VOCTIM Percentage Pass by Year

Year	Total	Pass	Fail	% Pass
2003	1,091	699	392	64
2004	396	340	56	86
2005	646	450	196	70
2006	224	182	42	81

Source: VOCTIM Report, 2007.
Note: The large fluctuation in the number of candidates cannot be explained, probably in part because of inaccuracies in data sets.

During the period, 2004–2006 the overall pass rates on trade tests rose from 64 percent to 73 percent. The largest number of these tests is conducted in the following occupations: electrical wireman, motor mechanic, blocklayer/plasterer, welder, carpenter and plumber (figure 4.7).

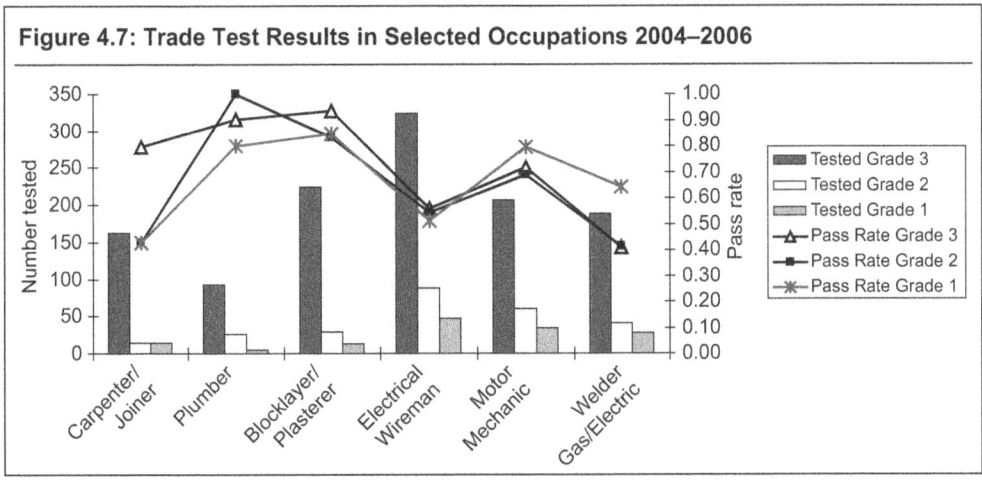

Figure 4.7: Trade Test Results in Selected Occupations 2004–2006

Source: DIVT.

Pass rates were highest in plumbing and blocklaying, averaging between 80 and 100 percent and lowest in welding and in electrical wireman—approximately 50 percent. The low pass rate in the latter occupation reportedly reflects the more stringent standards owing to public safety requirements (table 4.10).

Table 4.10: Participation and Pass Rates in Trade Tests 2004–2006

	2004		2005		2006	
Trade test grade	Total	% Pass	Total	% Pass	Total	% Pass
Grade III	430	67	467	73	677	74
Grade II	112	54	128	65	118	69
Grade I	81	64	72	65	61	70
Total	623	64	667	70	856	73

Source: DIVT.

The prevocational programs offered in the 16 senior secondary schools also exhibit relatively high levels of student performance. While pass rates vary across the areas of study over 90 percent of students achieved a pass in the examinations in each year from 2004 to 2007 (table 4.11).

Table 4.11: Examination Pass Rates in Prevocational Programs 2004–2007 (%)

Subject	2004	2005	2006	2007
Agriculture	84.4	96.9	96.3	95.6
Business Studies	82.9	93.6	100.0	100.0
Entrepreneurship	97.4	91.5	93.1	90.9
Home Economics	90.0	98.0	89.7	89.5
IT	94.9	90.4	97.9	95.3
Technical Drawing	95.3	95.0	92.2	95.2
Total	93.4	92.6	95.1	93.6

Source: Examinations Council of Swaziland.

Employer and employee views of TVETSD quality

Despite the high pass rates, the TVETSD seems to not be meeting employers and employees' expectations. A survey of 75 employers and 168 employees views on TVETSD provision, which was conducted as part of this sector review, revealed that:

- Swazi companies are experiencing difficulty in hiring technicians, particularly mechanical, electrical, and electronic and computer technicians. Twenty-eight percent of employers stated that this was due to a lack of training provision, and 29.3 percent said it is because of the low quality of the outputs of the training system. These results tend to call into question the validity of the relatively high levels of student achievement that are reported in national examinations and trade testing programs.
- A significant proportion of employers (54.2%) rated the performance of SCOT, which is the nation's major public provider of technician and paraprofessional training, as average or below average. No equivalent data was collected for VOCTIM. However 22.1 percent of employers described VOCTIM as having "... little knowledge, low competency, low level, no aptitude, inadequate teaching aid, declining standards, no vocational education, and low computer literacy."
- Over half of employers (57.3%) rated the quality of public secondary schooling, which may be viewed as a proxy indicator of generic skills such as communication, as average or below average. This is particularly important when it is considered that employers rated generic skills in areas such as communication (70.2%), teamwork (61.7%), customer service (53.2%]) and problem solving (46.8%) as being extremely important for employees.
- Practical skills training appears to be a relative but not overwhelming strength of both.
- Graduates from both SCOT and VOCTIM appear to have inadequate information technology (IT) skills. 22.1 percent of employees and 12.6 percent of employers cited concerns about the level of skills of graduates of VOCTIM and SCOT, respectively.
- The TVETSD curriculum offerings, particularly at SCOT, are outdated, lack a sound theoretical base and do not include adequate workplace experience.

The survey also revealed that many TVETSD graduates receive retraining or skills upgrading once they are employed, and that the cost of this is carried by employers. Seventy-eight percent of employees who responded to the survey indicated that they had received training since being hired by their current employer. This took the form of on-the-job training (43.9%) or formal training within the company (19.5%). In most cases (73.1%), this additional training was paid for by the employer. This is an additional cost to industry and is further evidence that the TVETSD system is not producing workers with the type, level or quality of skill required by companies. This is consistent with the findings of the investment climate assessment undertaken in 2007 which showed that companies in Swaziland (64%) are more likely to provide training for skilled workers than firms in either Mauritius (34%) or South Africa (45%).

Relevance

Internal relevance and implications for pathways

TVETSD lacks internal relevance in the sense that lower levels seem to not prepare trainees for higher levels. The internal irrelevance emanates from poor to no vertical curricula/program articulation. At present, trainees finishing SSTC and trade level III programs do not have ready access to VOCTIM. Similarly, VOCTIM graduates cannot carry over credits to SCOT. Learners from prevocational courses in secondary schools get no special consideration for entrance to SCOT despite their exposure. In fact, taking prevocational subjects may hinder the ability of learners to go onto tertiary education, as entrance requirements focus on academic qualifications.

Poor internal relevance and/or poor vertical articulation of programs limit the pathway arrangements required to facilitate trainee movement across levels of TVETSD, and between TVETSD and higher education. This does not mean that all or most learners should progress to the next higher level of training, what it does mean is that there should not be unnecessary barriers to progression.

A key objective for introducing NQFs in the region and internationally[6] has been to enhance learner mobility within and across the different formal and nonformal ETSD subsectors. For instance, recent sector reforms in Namibia have seen the introduction of a ten-level qualification framework. Under this standards-based framework, TVETSD trainees have open access to level 1 programs and can progressively attain the full range of TVETSD and higher education qualifications using a combination of 'training and assessment' and 'assessment only' pathways.

Market relevance

TVETSD is supply driven. All too often program offerings are based on the availability of workshops and instructors rather than on demand. Courses offered by both formal and nonformal providers focus on traditional entry-level skills in areas, such as mechanics, automotive, electrical, building, commerce and sewing. They do not adequately cater to emerging areas such as: services, tourism, child care, health care and higher level technician skills.

Part of the constraint to market relevance is that demand is low and unclear. About 14,000 new school leavers enter the labor market each year. However, between 1999 and 2005, there was only a net gain of 580 new wage jobs each year. Because the wage economy is not generating sufficient new jobs, the majority of new entrants to the labor market will need to find work in the informal sector or outside the country. For TVETSD to play its role of empowering the poor to generate income, Swaziland needs an aggressive employment creation strategy. Strengthening supply, as intended in this report, without strengthening demand, is an unsustainable approach, which may exacerbate the emerging phenomenon of the "educated/trained unemployed."

Even in a context of low employment creation, Swaziland companies are reportedly experiencing shortages of artisans, technicians and some professionals. This shortage is reportedly met by employing expatriates. A third of the companies in the employer/employee survey had recruited expatriate workers in the preceding 12 months.

For the few new available jobs, employment creation is becoming progressively skill-biased. Among the new wage jobs created in Swaziland between 1999 and 2005,

2,000 were for professionals and technicians, and 4,200 were for semi-skilled workers. Wage employment for unskilled workers actually fell by 2,720 jobs. Broad-based skills development is therefore another avenue that Swaziland should exploit in its quest to redistribute wealth.

While demand may be low in Swaziland, neighboring countries have unmet demand for skilled labor, some of which could be met through TVETSD. Preliminary data from the South African Department of Labor indicates substantial and increasing shortages of technicians and trades personnel (128,050 in 2008), community and personal service workers, sales workers, clerical and administrative workers, and machine operators and drivers. In 2008, South Africa had a total of 528,205 vacancies for skilled workers. South Africa also has a shortage of skills in the agriculture sector where Swaziland ought to have a comparative advantage. Demand is high for farm managers and foremen, agriculture educators, extension workers, marketing and economists among others.[7] All these are fields that SCOT and the Luyengo campus of UNISWA could address.

Rapid economic growth and the emergence of new technologies are contributing to skill shortages in technical fields in neighboring Mozambique. A recent Organization for Economic Co-operation and Development (OECD) report on Mozambique concluded that mega-project development in the country has ":...increased the demand for medium to high skills, especially in the areas of the metal, gas and telecommunication industries, where about 10,000 to 20,000 jobs have been created.".[8] A further report released in May 2008 by the Association for Development of Education in Africa (ADEA), titled, The Challenge of TVETSD Reform in Mozambique: Goals, Options and Constraints, noted that the country is experiencing a severe shortage of appropriately skilled and qualified workers as a result of rapid economic development. This report highlighted demand for: (i) skilled artisans including welders, hydraulics, piping, electricians, plasticians; carpenters and bricklayers (ii) technicians such as instrumentation technicians, PLC implementers; (iii) biofuels, sugar and food processing engineers, technicians, and professionals; (iv) mining engineers, technicians, and professionals, and (v) hydro-electric engineers, technicians and other professionals.

The increased information and communications needs in the sub-region are creating demand for ICT professionals. A recent study on ICT skill needs in Botswana highlighted critical skills shortages amongst network engineers, IT support and maintenance staff, software engineers, and telecom engineers. The report also noted that there was unmet demand for programmers, analysts, technicians, and web designers.[9] Similar demands for technical staff are emerging in Namibia, where Telecom Namibia, the country's major telecommunications provider, noted in its 2005-06 annual report that the company had "...experienced problems of not being able to recruit and place suitably qualified persons as the Namibian labor market has an acute shortage of suitably trained and qualified persons in the fields of telecommunication, electronic engineering, information technology and internet protocol."[10] The shortage of technical skills in Namibia was highlighted in the 2007 OECD country report on Namibia, which confirmed earlier findings by the World Bank (2005) and ICAS (2007). The OECD report noted that "...the Namibian labor market is characterized by a severe lack of skilled labor and wide-spread unemployment among semi-skilled or unskilled workers. A recent study has projected a continuing substantial deficit in the supply of a large range of professionally qualified workers: IT technicians, professional nurses, financial practitioners, technicians, semi-professionals, engineers, physicians and dentists."[11]

Skills shortages are emerging in the health field in a range of Southern African nations. The International Organization for Migration reported that in 2003, there were 32,000 vacancies for nurses in South Africa, and that the government had sought to address shortages in the public health sector by recruiting health workers from Iran and Cuba to work in provinces.[12] A more recent study by Gerein, Green and Pearson in 2006, on the demand for health professionals in the region noted that "... estimates of how many additional doctors, nurses and midwives are needed in sub-Saharan Africa to provide essential health interventions related to the Millennium Development Goals range from 1 to 1.4 million. Projecting future needs, WHO estimated that substantial shortages of professionals with midwifery skills need filling in sub-Saharan Africa to scale up to universal coverage for maternal, newborn and child health."[13]

The existence of skill shortages in artisan, technician, and para-professional occupations in neighboring countries provides an important opportunity for Swaziland to develop as a supplier of high-level technical skill. Swaziland could seek to position itself as a provider of artisan, technician and para-professional skills to neighboring countries experiencing critical skill shortages. In the short term this would provide an important source of employment for Swazi workers and foreign exchange earnings for the country, whereas in the longer term, it would raise the overall skill base of the Swazi workforce and potentially increase the country's attractiveness as a destination for FDIs. As noted, investing in skills has proved to be an important development strategy for a number of countries. While all countries have unique circumstances and face different constraints, it may be useful for Swaziland to consider how investment in skills contributed to the growth of Singapore and Ireland. In 1961, skills development was moved from Singapore Polytechnic. Over the next 20 years, the government made concerted efforts to link economic and workforce development by focusing on training and development, forging partnership between TVETSD providers and employers and adopting a strong export orientation. By 1990, this system was clearly paying off, and a country with no natural resources except the talent of its own people became a world leader in productivity in a range of manufacturing and service areas.

The overall impression is that Swaziland's TVETSD subsector has not responded to national or regional demand for skilled workers. TVETSD programs are focused on inappropriate skills, are too long, do not reflect industry standards, and are delivered by people who lack contemporary industry experience. There is significant demand for high level artisan, technician and para-professional skills both within the country and the region and an opportunity exists for the TVETSD system, at least in part, to focus on the production of high skill – high value outputs. If Swazi workers are to compete effectively for these high skill – high value jobs, they require technician level skills that meet industry standards. This means that the TVETSD system must deliver high quality technician-level programs that are: (i) focused on domestic and regional industry needs; (ii) future-orientated; (iii) flexibly structured; and (iv) delivered in a timely and cost-efficient manner.

This is not to say that there should not also be a focus on lower- and middle-level skill development. Like other countries in the region, Swaziland needs to adopt a multi-pronged approach to skill development. For example, in Namibia the government has established the National Foundation for Community Skills Development Centers (COSDECs), which administers a national network of community-based training centers. They focus on providing short, hands-on, competency-based training programs that equip trainees with skills, entrepreneurial acumen, and productive competencies needed for employment in the formal and informal sectors of the economy. Similarly, the Nigerian Government, through the National Open Apprenticeship Scheme (NOAS), provides vocational training to unemployed youth and school leavers in over 100 trades. Between 1987 and 2000, over 600,000 unemployed youths had participated in these programs with over 400,000 starting their own enterprises.

Swaziland needs to categorically address factors that reduce the national and sub-regional responsiveness of its TVETSD programs. Key among these factors are: (i) little to no private sector involvement in the development and management of TVETSD; (ii) lack of timely, accurate and informative national labor surveys and graduate tracer studies; (iii) inexperience in developing customized training solutions to meet industry/enterprise specific requirements; and (iv) the limited capacity to offer higher level technician training. TVETSD provision also needs to be restructured so that it is both responsive and has the capacity, in terms of staff, programs, and physical facilities, to meet industry skill needs at domestic and regional level.

As already noted, the other key gap in the TVETSD system is the lack of training opportunities for adults. Training provision is overwhelmingly focused on pre-employment training for youth. There is very limited provision for adults to acquire or upgrade their skills. All too often, the available training is provided at inappropriate times, is too long, and is geared towards induction or foundations skills. Adult learners require short, modular, competency-based training programs that address specific skill requirements and steadily accrue credits toward formal qualifications.

The move to introduce modularized training programs by countries in the region such as South Africa, Botswana and Namibia and internationally such as New Zealand, Scotland, Singapore and Australia, has greatly expanded training opportunities for adults. In these modularized systems, adult learners are able to undertake short programs rather than the lengthy two-year programs, which are a feature of the Swazi TVETSD system. In addition, the move to more flexible forms of training delivery has meant that adult learners are able to undertake these short programs at a time and place that is suitable for them. For example, in New Zealand adult learners may enroll at a private or public provider to undertake a single or small group of unit standards in an occupational area, such as, Build a straight brick wall or Prepare rooms for guest at a hospitality establishment. Trainees may undertake these programs at a training provider or through distance delivery using a combination of training manuals, computer aided instruction and mentor support.

Social relevance

There is little evidence that TVETSD providers have mainstreamed HIV/AIDS in their programs. Programs also do not include pastoral care and counseling for trainees and instructors. This is in stark contrast to other countries in the region. In South Africa, Botswana and Namibia, credit-rated, unit standards on HIV/AIDS awareness and the management of HIV/AIDS in the workplace are incorporated in national qualifications for semi-skilled workers, artisans, technicians and vocational trainers. The relative absence of education and counseling on HIV/AIDS in TVETSD programs is a deficit that calls for urgent attention.

Currency and responsiveness of training programs

Beyond responsiveness, TVETSD programs need to be current. However, in Swaziland, maintaining the currency and responsiveness of training programs represents a major challenge for TVETSD providers. Currently, providers are responsible for the maintenance of their own training programs. In those cases where the programs are purchased from external awarding bodies, such as City and Guilds, maintenance is undertaken by the owner of the program. Program maintenance is a major cost for providers, and it is clear that the programs and the associated assessment materials used by many providers are out of date. For example, DIVT has indicated that a major constraint on the trade testing system is a lack of funding to maintain the standards and assessment items in key occupational areas. Lack of program maintenance serves to undermine the relevance and responsiveness of training programs and devalues the qualifications awarded to learners. In mature TVETSD systems the quality of national occupational standards is underpinned by a systematic maintenance process. For example, in Australia, all standards are reviewed 3 years after endorsement. Through the continuous improvement policy, changes may be made during the life of standards in response to feedback from users or changes in industry practices.

System Efficiency

Trainee progression

As with pass rates, completion rates in TVETSD appear to be relatively high. At SCOT and VOCTIM, most learners who start a program finish it successfully. At SCOT, dropout reportedly is minimal between entry and year three of studies, and 95 percent of year three learners pass their final examinations. In part, this high throughput is a reflection of extreme selectivity at entry. Only about 20 percent of applicants are admitted. At VOCTIM, the overall completion rate of entrants is estimated to be about 80 percent.

Instructor to trainee ratio

Public TVETSD in Swaziland is characterized by low numbers of trainees per instructor and the consequent inefficient use of plant and equipment. Overall, government support to TVETSD has declined from 2.7 percent of recurrent expenditures in 2000 to 1.7 percent in 2005, a reduction in relative terms of 37 percentage points. This has led to limits on trainee intake while staffing has remained constant. This means that the number of students per teacher has decreased. For example, at SCOT the trainee-instructor ratio is 7.7:1. For VOCTIM, the ratio is 4.8:1. This is low compared to an international average of about 15:1 and the OECD average of 13.2:1. It suggests that there is underutilization of existing training resources and raises questions about the financial viability of some programs

As noted, inefficiencies are evident in the use of physical space. SCOT's actual enrollment is only 21 percent of its capacity (314/1500). Moreover, SCOT facilities are used only between 08:00 and 16:00, with only limited evening classes between 17:30 and 19:30, and only during weekdays. VOCTIM operates at only two-thirds of its capacity. The reason for underutilization of facilities at SCOT is the dependence on public financing which is tightly constrained, whereas under-subscription at VOCTIM reflects the high cost of tuition.

Such inefficiencies are not as apparent amongst the private commercial providers. For example, of the 26 private commercial providers surveyed in 2008, the ratio of trainees to instructors ranged from 5:1 to 48:1. While this is broadly comparable with the international average (15:1), it does mask some inefficiencies and also highlights a possible quality issue associated with conducting TVETSD programs with trainee/instructor ratios exceeding 40:1.

Sustainability

Even though TVETSD provision is generally expensive, the two main TVETSD institutions, VOCTIM and SCOT, have unsustainably high unit cost: E38,105 and E37,515 respectively. Enrollments are unsustainably low: 314 and 157 respectively in 2006. These institutions are, therefore, unable to realize the required economies of scale that make investments in the hiring of specialist trainers, the maintenance of facilities, the purchase of IT equipment systems and the acquisition of specialist equipment worthwhile.[14]

Problems of sustainability also confront the national trade testing service. In 2006 for instance, trade testing generated an estimated gross income of E140,400 (table 4.12). Reportedly, this is far below the cost to government of providing the trade testing service. This has contributed to a situation where DIVT lacks the funds to adequately develop and maintain the tests and relevant occupational standards. This in turns undermines the relevance and usefulness of the trade testing service to industry.

Table 4.12: Trade Testing—Participation and Estimated Fee Income, 2006

Trade test grade	Total	Fee per test (E)	Estimated gross income (E)
Grade III	677	150	101,550
Grade II	118	200	23,600
Grade I	61	250	15,250
Total	856		140,400

Source: DIVT.

Under the circumstance it seems reasonable for Swaziland to reconsider the training levy as provided for by both the Vocational and Industrial Training Act (1982) and the Human Resource Development and Planning Bill (2003). The levy may improve funding for TVETSD providers, finance critical infrastructure and underwrite part or all of the cost of other services such as trade testing.

Conclusion

Despite the rate of employment creation, Swaziland has a shortage of artisans, technicians, some professionals, and enterprise managers. The country is also surrounded by natural resource-rich neighbors with acute skills shortages. The TVETSD system is currently not geared to meet this national and sub-regional demand for skills. Key weaknesses pertain to lack of a policy framework that could chart the strategic direction for TVETSD. National fiscal constraints have led to declines in access at all levels, access that was already limited in the first place. Fiscal constraints are exacerbated by resource inefficiencies of the subsector. Key factors of inefficiency include underutilization of physical facilities and equipment, low trainee-to-instructor ratios, and excessively high unit costs. With limited resources, the system lags behind that of its neighboring countries, which Swaziland should be outplaying to get a share of their labor market.

Access is particularly low for adult learners, rural dwellers, and women.

There are no standards and/or qualification framework that could formalize them and that could articulate TVETSD with other levels of the sector. Lack of standards and an NQF has led to system rigidities and limited pathways within TVETSD, and between it and other tertiary levels. The system provides little to no flexibility, particularly required by adult learners to re-tool and/or up-skill. Most programs cater to pre-employment trainees and are too long in duration.

The system is not responsive on many fronts. It fails to prepare trainees for subsequent levels within it, and for entry into other forms of tertiary education and training. Unlike general education, it has not yet cued to the need to respond to the HIV scourge. For a range of reasons the system is also disconnected from the needs of the national and sub-regional labor markets.

On the positive side, TVETSD is internally efficient on several points. Repetition and dropout rates are low. Pass rates and completion rates are impressively high. Safe for the lack of standards, the system is also of high quality. This is borne by trainee performance on international tests such as Pitman and City and Guilds. Current levels of quality provide a base for expanding access and strengthening relevance.

Notes

[1] Swaziland ICA report, 25-26.
[2] There are three levels of certification, with level one being the highest.
[3] Trade tests are prepared by panel members selected from private sector, parastatal institutions, government ministries and training institutions. DIVT administers the tests at government-controlled training institutions throughout the country using industry experts and trainers. DIVT indicates that the actual cost of providing a test at each level is far above what each candidate pays towards the test. The current fees paid by candidates are: Grade 1-250.00 E, Grade 2-200.00 E, Grade 3-150.00 E. Grade testing fees are reviewed on an annual basis by IVTB.
[4] Sources - World Bank, *Namibia Human Capital and Knowledge Development for Economic Growth with Equity* and ADEA – 2008 Biennale on Education in Africa - *The Challenge of TVETSD Reform in Mozambique: Goals, Options and Constraints.*
[5] Secondary schools require fees which are beyond the means of most low-income parents.
[6] For instance in South Africa, Namibia, Scotland, New Zealand and Australia.

[7] Nicci Earle & Andrew NM Paterson The shape of demand for high-level agricultural skills in the South African labor market in *Development Southern Africa* Vol. 24, No. 4, October 2007.
[8] OECD, African Economic Outlook 2008 – Mozambique Country Report
[9] Mutula, S. and Van Brakel, P., ICT skills readiness for the emerging global digital economy among small businesses in developing countries Case study of Botswana, February 2007.
[10] Telecom Namibia, Annual Report 2005/2006.
[11] OECD, *African Economic Outlook 2008 – Namibia Country Report*
[12] International Organization for Migration, *World Migration Report*, 2008, p.411
[13] Gerein, N., Green, B, and Pearson, S., The Implications of Shortages of Health Professionals for Maternal Health in Sub-Saharan Africa in *Reproductive Health Matters* 2006;14(27):40–50
[14] Gustafsson, M. and van der Berg, S. *Economic and financial aspects of education in Swaziland: Input into World Bank review of education and Training in Swaziland.*

CHAPTER 5

Higher Education

Introduction

Higher education provides high level knowledge workers and research-based knowledge essential to support knowledge driven growth. Experience from fast-developing Asian countries has shown how considerable social and economic development can accrue from investment in knowledge, especially in science and technology. Examples include Korea and Singapore which both emphasized research-based training of scientists and engineers at high levels of academic quality, but also included real life applications of the knowledge, especially in industry. Unfortunately, these countries and their strategies are yet to take root in SSA. Some small European countries, for example Finland and Ireland have also used knowledge to catalyze fast economic development. Ireland in particular, with financial support from the EU, has benefited substantially from this strategy. More recently, some larger countries, notably China and India, have followed a similar path with notable success. The latter two have been hard to overlook, since they dominate the global economic development.

Most African countries, Swaziland inclusive, are yet to build the size and quality of higher education systems that can produce knowledge workers required to lead knowledge-driven growth and spur competitiveness. As such, they lag behind other parts of the world with respect to knowledge-based development. The number of researchers per million people in Africa is about 10 percent of that in China and 1 percent of that in leading industrialized countries. The outcomes of both basic and applied research in Africa are very modest. For example, in 2004/2005 the number of patents obtained by residents in Africa was 16, compared with 67,000 in East Asia. Also Africa's share of international research publications is extremely low.[1] The region produces far fewer science, mathematics, and technology-based professionals than other developing regions. Only 9 percent of university graduates are engineers, while almost 50 percent are trained in Humanities and Social Sciences and 22 percent in Education. In Swaziland, an even smaller fraction (1-2 percent) studies Engineering. If Science is added, the fraction increases to 6 percent, compared with, for example, 50 percent in China.[2]

Other than its contribution to development in general, higher education provides essential professional and technical leaders required for the development of other levels of the ETSDS. Therefore it will be difficult for Swaziland to improve its ETSDS without the support of its higher education institutions.

Historical Overview

Swaziland has a young higher education system whose roots go back to the 1960s with the establishment of the joint University of Basotholand, Bechuanaland and Swaziland (UBBS). UBBS was established in 1963, growing from Pius Catholic University College at Roma; which was a college of the then more liberal University of South Africa (UNISA). The first physical presence of UBBS in Swaziland came in 1972 with the establishment of Faculty of Agriculture in Luyengo. In 1975, and after independence of the three countries, UBBS was reconfigured into a full University of Botswana, Lesotho and Swaziland (UBLS), a union that broke up a year later leading to the formation of the University of Botswana and Swaziland (UBS) in 1976. Through mutual agreement, UBS separated into the two national universities in 1982. This marked the formal establishment of UNISWA.

Since 1982, UNISWA remains the only higher education institution and a dominant provider of tertiary education and training. It accounts for 70 percent of enrollment at this level. This carries a substantial responsibility in terms of technical leadership for knowledge-driven development. It currently has 3 campuses: Kwaluseni, the main campus for most faculties, Luyengo Campus for the Faculty of Agriculture, and Mbabane Campus for the Faculty of Nursing. Across the 3 campuses are 7 faculties: Agriculture, Commerce, Education, Health Sciences, Humanities, Science and Social Science, 2 institutes: Institute of Distance Education (IDE) and the Institute of Post Graduate Studies (IPGS), and the UNISWA Foundation. The Foundation was established in 2004 for resource mobilization with a focus on improving the university infrastructure.

Over its 26 years—1982 to 2008—UNISWA has grown by 440 percent from about 1,000 to virtually 5,440 students.

UNISWA's core mandate is to produce knowledge and skills for the national economy, and this seems to have constituted the rationale for the original selection of programs of study. It remains the formal justification for a major part of UNISWA programs. However, in reality this purpose seems to have progressively received less attention as the focus seems to have shifted to providing young Swazis university qualifications regardless of their relevance to the economy and to overall national development.

Policy Orientation

As with the rest of the sector, the 1999 Education Policy guides current development of the higher education subsector. Identifiable elements that apply to this subsector include the need to:

- provide trained personnel in accordance with the identified social and economic needs of the country;
- institute cost sharing mechanisms between the MoE and beneficiaries of tertiary education;
- structure programs to suit the 'world of work' and self-employment;
- take cost implications and relevance into account when determining the duration of programs;

- impart research skills and inculcate the culture of research for personal, professional and social development."

Other national "policy-related" documents that should guide higher education are Vision 2022, the NDS and the PRSAP. In addition, UNISWA produces periodic strategic plans to guide subsector development—albeit discontinuously and almost consistently late. The previous plan ended in 2005. Its sequel, dated 2008 to 2012, is still in draft. The link between the national development orientation and the subsector strategic plans is at best obscure. This constitutes a key source of disconnect between the national development agenda and university study, research and community development programs. This gap needs to be closed.

Institutional and Management Framework

His Majesty the King Mswati III of Swaziland is the Chancellor of UNISWA and its ultimate ceremonious head. The institution is governed by the University Council (UC) which also oversees its administration. Its chairperson is directly appointed by the King. The current UC is dominated by the public service and has very limited representation of organizations and industries that constitute future employers of its graduates. Such stakeholders' influence on academic, research and community development programs is at best negligible. This is another major source of the disconnect between UNISWA programs and the world that its graduates are to function in. In contrast to the UC, the board of the UNISWA Foundation has a rich representation of business leaders and this constitutes a good practice that can be extended to the UC.

The appointment of UC members is not necessarily merit based. As such, it lacks balance between expertise and experience of the members and the most important sectors of the economy. Moreover, members are appointed for long periods. This limits potential for constant renewal of the institution. The UC is also dominated by men. This does not reflect the gender parity sought after in the PRSAP.

Overall there seems to be little to no political interference with the autonomy and academic freedom of the institution as assured in the University Act of 1983. The Senate, supported by its committees oversees academic affairs. Daily management and administration is overseen by the Vice Chancellor and his management team comprising the Pro-Vice Chancellor, Registrar, Bursar, Deans of respective Faculties and Directors of different Centers, Institutes, and Foundations.

As shown above, the management of critical fields and activities is strengthened through the creation of centers which are lead by Directors. Most Directors oversee these centers part-time, in addition to their regular university responsibilities. The Institutes and the Centers are not reflected in the University Act of 1983 and this provides grounds for its revision. The time commitment that Directors can give to these centers may be too little to promote the field or activity as intended. Figure 5.1 summarizes the overall management structure.

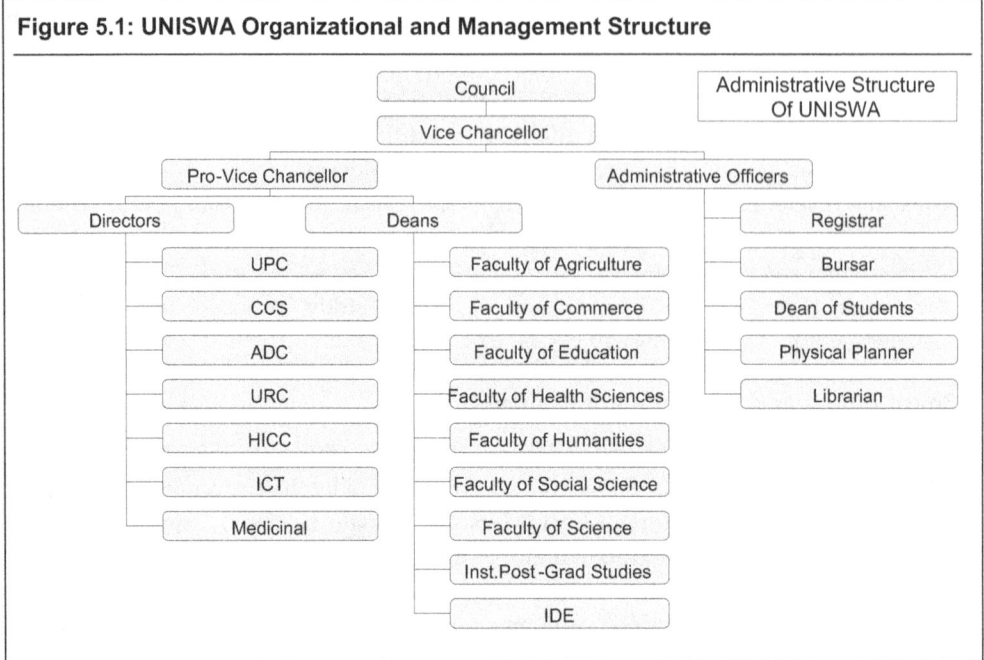

Figure 5.1: UNISWA Organizational and Management Structure

Source: UNISWA.
Notes: UPS: University Planning Center, CCS: Center for Community Services, ADC: Academic Development Center, URC: UNISWA Research Center, HICC: Health Information and Counseling Center, ICT: Information and Communication Technology, Medicinal: Swaziland Institute for Research in Traditional Medicine, Medicinal and Indigenous Food Plants.

The autonomy enjoyed by the overall university is not accorded its lower levels of management. Internal management is highly centralized and grants limited autonomy to the units that produce the university outputs (graduates and research results). This limits efficiency and effectiveness. Virtually all decisions are made at the top, including staff recruitment, budgets, and financing. Many routine decisions are taken at the level of Vice Chancellor, and this is likely to slow down the administrative processes. Even the many vacancies may to some extent be a result of the centralized recruitment process. There is an urgent need to decentralize the organizational management and administrative processes.

The administrative structure of the University has not kept pace with the expansion of enrollments. A simple and transparent management may require much fewer administrative staff members, but there may also be occasional needs for expansion. For example, appointment of a second Pro-Vice Chancellor for administrative affairs would leave the current Pro-Vice Chancellor time to concentrate on academics and research, at a time when the need for new thinking is obvious.

The efficiency of management is also hampered by lack of an accurate and current information management system. This also limits an informed articulation of strategies for future subsector development, effective monitoring and evaluation of such developments and of the institution's performance, and effective impact evaluation of the institution.

Accountability

UNISWA's autonomy and academic freedom could be complemented by a comparable level of accountability for national development, as broadly conceived as possible. As noted, it would seem that the university has trailed from its core mandate to produce technical leaders for the economy. The lines that connect UNISWA to community real-life challenges, national and sub-regional labor markets, industry, national, sub-regional, regional and global development agendas, need strengthening and institutionalization. As noted, the first source of the disconnect lies with the constitution of the UC. Another constraint is the apparent lack of mechanisms for anchoring university programs in the overall national and global development dialogue. The university often cites the lack of a national human resources development strategy that could have guided its programs. However, even without such a strategy, UNISWA can still use national development instruments outlined in Chapter 1, and global knowledge, to orient its programs. More importantly, UNISWA could carve its space in the national dialogue and take a lead in it.

Equity and Access

Access has considerably increased over the last few decades but is still far lower than effective demand, than in other SADC MICs, and, than for countries that effectively use their universities to supply the technical leadership required to propel growth (table 5.1). Between 1982 and 2008, the average annual growth rate in enrollment was 8 percent, which is higher than growth in the population of eligible age. Actual enrollments rose from 1,000 in 1982 to 5440 in 2007/2008. However, access is low, even when considering study abroad, which is quite substantial. Around 2,110 Swazi students were studying abroad in 2004, most of them (1,880) in South Africa.[3] Study abroad could easily raise the GER to around 6 percent, which is still low.

Table 5.1: Tertiary Education Enrollment SADC MICs and in Selected Regions for Selected Years

Country	Net enrollment ratio			
	1991	1996	1999	2004
Botswana	3.1	4.3	2.7	5.1
Mauritius	3.4	5.9	6.2	15.0
Namibia	2.5	6.0	4.5	4.8
South Africa	10.6	13.5	11.6	12.4
Swaziland	3.2	5.2	3.7	4.1
Region				
Southern Africa	9.6	12.4	10.5	11.3
SSA	2.2	2.6	3.1	4.0

Source: UNESCO Institute for Statistics.
Note: Large differences in the numbers may be influenced by national definitions of what constitutes tertiary education.

While over the long term, the increase in enrollment has been substantial, the proportion annual intake of qualified candidates declined from 68 percent in 2000 to 42 percent in 2007 (figure 5.2), due mainly to a lack of GoS scholarships. Relative to eligible candidates, access is declining instead of growing.

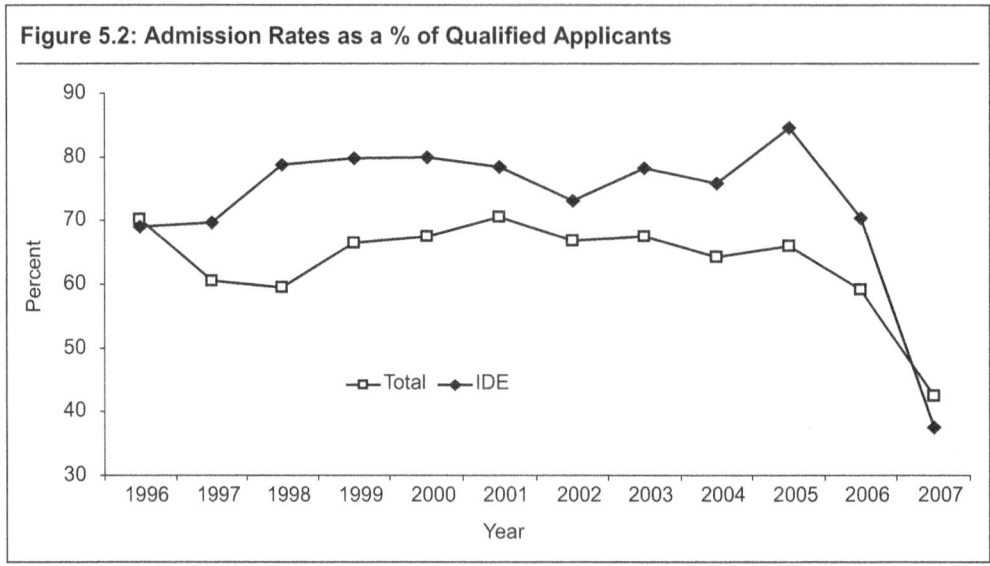

Figure 5.2: Admission Rates as a % of Qualified Applicants

Source: UNISWA.

Enrollments vary significantly across faculties, but it is clear that IDE drives much of the recent increases, followed by the Faculty of Agriculture (table 5.2). The fact that IDE dominates enrollments is a positive development, given its lower unit cost (see Chapter 7), but its intake is also on the decline. IDE was able to accept close to 80 percent of qualified applicants until 2005; since then the share has dropped, reaching below 40 percent by 2007 (see figure 5.2 above).

Table 5.2: Enrollment by Faculty, 2000–2007

	2000/01	2001/02	2002/03	2003/04	2004/05	2005/06	2006/07	2007/08
Agriculture	418	483	556	643	711	761	828	853
Commerce	513	511	564	631	614	597	581	564
Education	341	394	306	313	320	336	358	356
Health Sci.	220	268	287	343	308	317	312	324
Humanities	563	571	554	594	579	574	526	449
Science	294	303	317	329	349	380	349	342
Soc. Sci.	565	575	582	610	648	662	647	643
P.G.S.	32	38	45	55	46	50	47	48
IDE	780	1,055	1,246	1,447	1,595	1,943	2,046	1,860
Total no. of students	3,726	4,198	4,457	4,965	5,170	5,620	5,694	5,439
FTE* in IDE	234	317	374	434	479	583	614	558
FTE Total	3,180	3,460	3,585	3,952	4,054	4,260	4,262	4,137

Source: Vice Chancellor's Annual Reports.
* Full time equivalent (FTE) number of students calculated by multiplying IDE enrollment by 0.3, since IDE programs correspond to 30 percent of the normal load.

A graphic representation of enrollment by faculty and year is shown in figure 5.3.

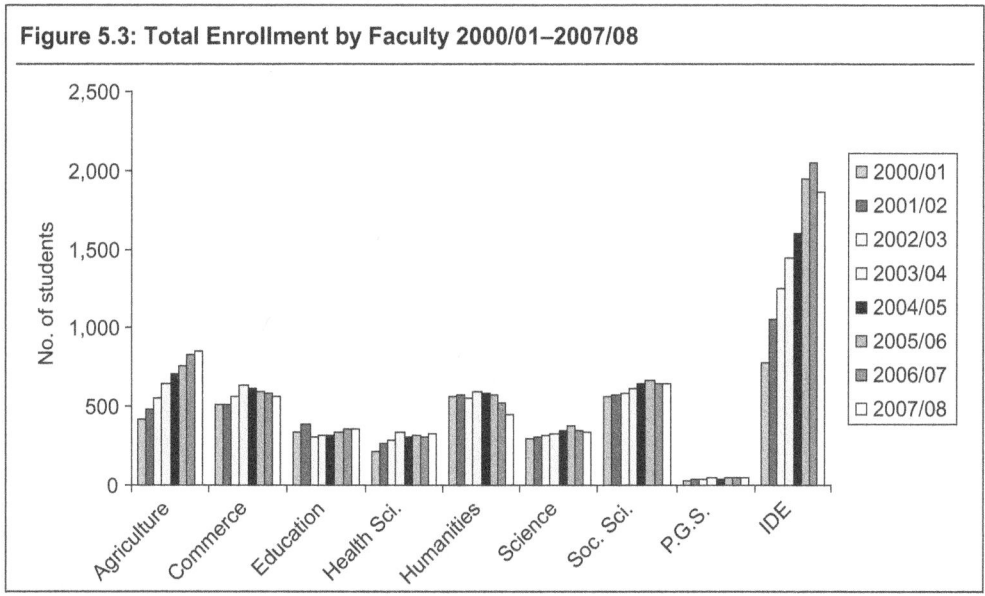

Figure 5.3: Total Enrollment by Faculty 2000/01–2007/08

Source: Vice Chancellor's annual report.

Access is still limited to the undergraduate level of studies with less than 1 percent of students in graduate programs in 2007, except for those in the Post-Graduate Certificate in Education. Therefore, UNISWA does not produce the level of knowledge workers who could spearhead research and who could foster research and development (R&D) partnerships with industry. With limited graduate programs, UNISWA is a predominantly teaching university. This does not do much for improving the research output of the professoriate or for the production of graduates with high-level research and analytical skills. It also calls into question the efficiency of the utilization of professor-level academic staff that should be able to mount graduate programs, produce research outputs and, produce a succession chain of future researchers.

Gender parity has been attained in overall access. The low female participation that persisted through the first decade closed in the late 1990s, resurfaced in the early 2000 but, seems to have closed again in 2007 (figure 5.4). However, women are substantially under-represented in the faculties of science, agriculture, commerce, and in post graduate studies (figure 5.5).

Women are over-represented in humanities and education. Their dominance in fields with low employment opportunities—humanities particularly—risks perpetuating the gender-related inequities in earnings that were outlined in Chapter 1. It also risks the gender equity goal of the PRSAP, while denying households the widely-documented benefits of women's economic power. On the positive side, women dominate the so-called 'female domain' of health, where regional and global demand is currently high, and this may compensate for their sparsity in other scarce skills fields. However, these are still areas of lower earnings than the other science-based specializations.

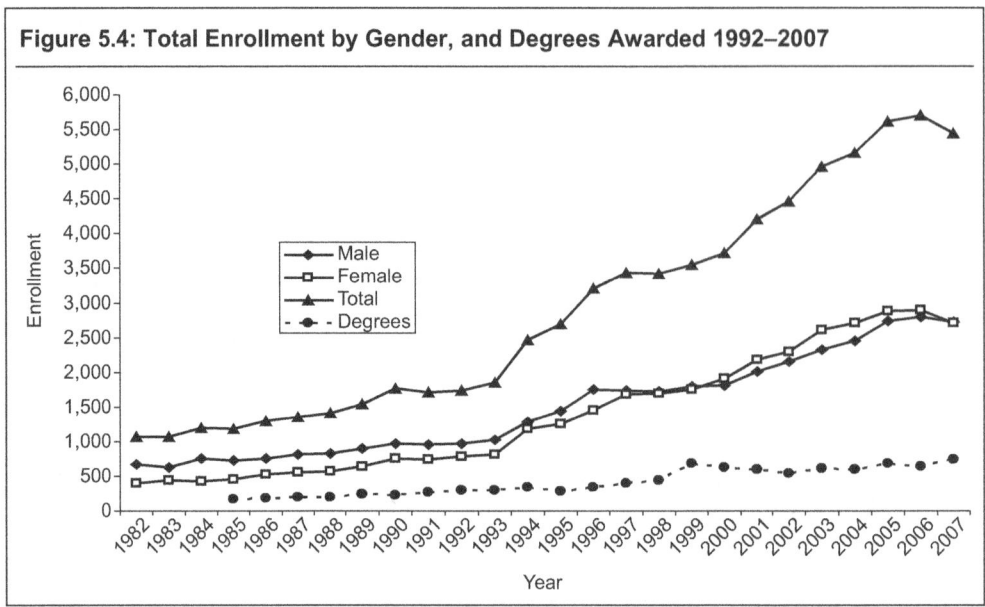

Figure 5.4: Total Enrollment by Gender, and Degrees Awarded 1992–2007

Source: UNISWA.

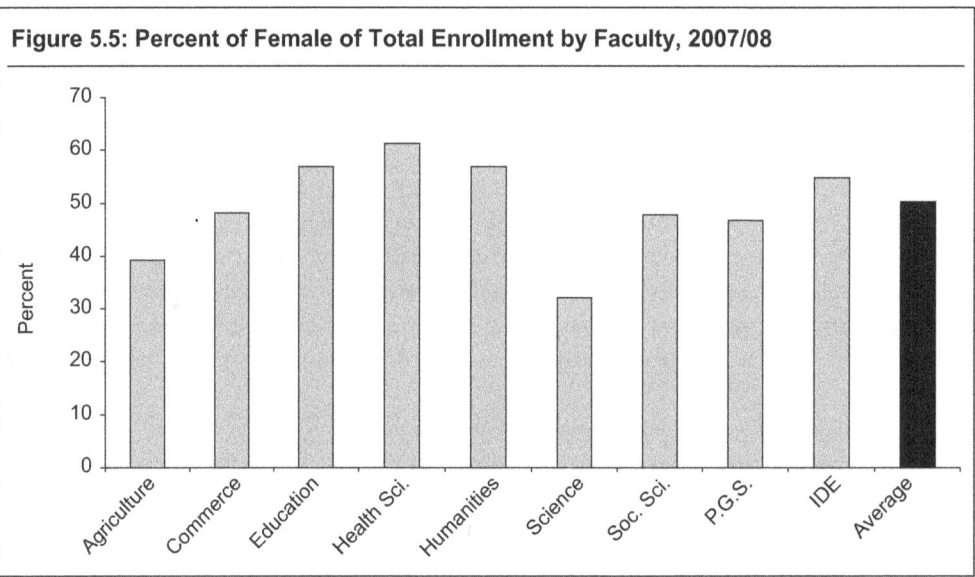

Figure 5.5: Percent of Female of Total Enrollment by Faculty, 2007/08

Source: Vice Chancellor's Report 2007/08.

Access is inequitable by SES to the advantage of children from high-income households. In 2007, nearly 70 percent of UNISWA students were from the highest income quintile, relative to 4 percent from the lowest two income quintiles (figure 5.6).

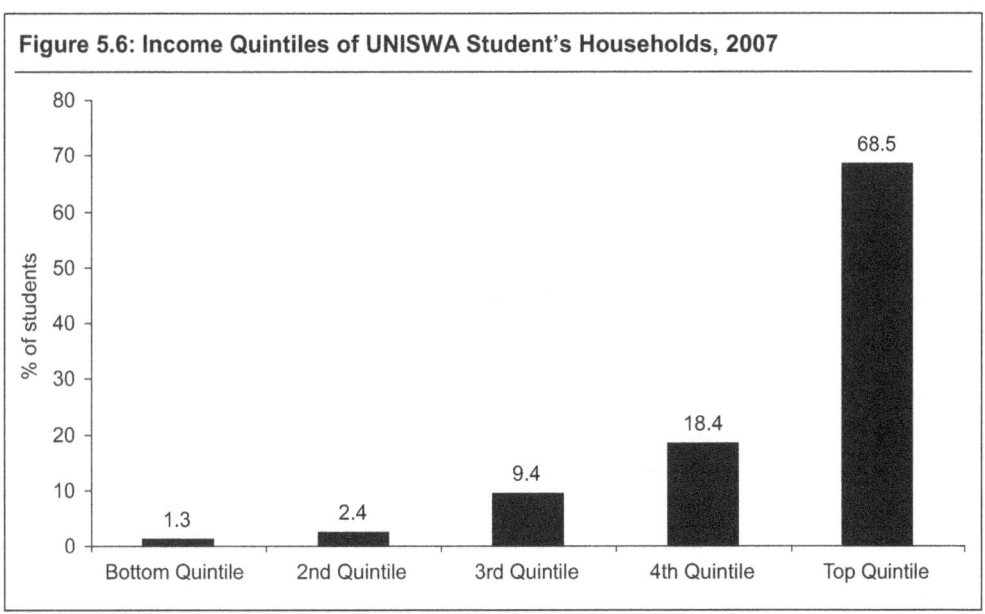

Source: DHS 2006/7.

The low participation of children from low-income households at this level attests their sifting out and exclusion as they struggle to progress through the ETSDS. Given the substantial earnings associated with higher education, this situation demonstrates how the ETSDS could be reproducing social inequalities and cementing the current social class structure. This runs contrary to the spirit and letter of Vision 2022 and of the PRSAP on many dimensions. The fact that gifted children from poor families have little to no access to higher education is not just a personal loss to them and their families, it is an unaffordable wastage of the country's potential human capital base and its associated development impact.

The vast majority of university students comes from rich urban areas, and relatively very few from more remote rural areas. Since secondary schools in remote, rural areas tend to be considerably weaker than schools in urban areas, it is difficult, even for talented children, to qualify for university enrollment. Contrary to the intention of the PRSAP, this pattern of access will make it difficult to close the rural/urban income gap, an impact that could, among others, have accrued from remittances of these excluded children.

While poor access and poor quality of GET cause the sparsity of rural and low SES students at the top, UNISWA could be part of the solution and actually get involved in redressing this trend. Examples of its involvement could include support for rural secondary schools and those in poor areas to produce eligible candidates for university entry. Specific examples of such support include establishing holiday academic camps for particularly talented children from these areas, adopting schools in these areas and instituting admission quotas for near-qualified children from these areas and providing them with academic counseling and support to catch up. Pre-entry programs for learners who nearly qualify for university entrance, particularly in mathematics, science and technology, are yet another untapped option.

Private provision of higher education

The GoS almost solely bears the burden to expand access to higher education with little to no private sector support. Moreover, two most important tertiary institutions, Nazarene Teacher Training College and the College of Nursing, are only partly private, since staff salaries are paid by the Government. The combined enrollment in the private institutions is about 9 percent of the national total tertiary enrollment; this is very low compared to other countries in the region, see table 5.3.

Table 5.3: Share of Private Tertiary Education 2004

Countries	Share of private enrollments (%)	Student numbers
Botswana	100	13,221
Angola	32	4,154
Mozambique	32	7,121
Mauritius	18	3,201
Kenya	13	15,783
Zimbabwe	10	6,022
Uganda	10	8,836
Swaziland	9	590
Madagascar	8	3,371
Tanzania	5	2,147

Source: Global Education Digest 2006, UIS.
Note: Swaziland numbers are for 2005; they were calculated from MOE 2005 Statistics and include the Nazarene Colleges of Nursing and Teacher Training.

Quality and Equity

Curricula/programs/modes of delivery

UNISWA's faculties and institutes offer 35 programs. Each program has a range of courses at the certificate, diploma, degree, post-graduate, and graduate levels. The bulk of the programs are offered at a degree level and extremely few at the certificate and graduate levels. A key issue with the programs is the lack of articulation and the resultant lack of portability of credits within and across levels. Poor articulation also leaves ample room for course overlaps and the associated resource inefficiencies. As with TVETSD, higher education needs to be integrated into an NQF that will integrate it into a seamless LLL system with real pathways and flexibility.

Study programs are quite traditional, dominated by lectures and hardly using the potential offered by ICTs in facilitating teaching and learning. However, a positive aspect is that in the last year of the degree program students undertake a small research project. In addition, many programs include a 10-week internship in local businesses. In the science-based fields, lectures are supplemented by laboratory sessions. Laboratories are generally well-designed and spacious, although some need modernization. However, current provision of equipment is clearly insufficient for a satisfactory preparation of students for modern workplaces. Insufficient and inadequate laboratory equipment is often cited as a limiting factor on student intake in Science and Engineering.

A heavy reliance on lectures and traditional laboratory courses (instead of open-ended work in the laboratories) does not encourage student independent thinking. The requirement of a large number of "passive" class hours reduces their sense of responsibility for their own learning. Independent and group work could motivate students while facilitating higher-level learning and deeper understanding of concepts.

IDE could be used as a platform to diversify delivery modes and to exploit the potential of ICTs. Students have 30 percent of face-to-face contact hours, scheduled mostly on weekends. These are complemented by self-instructional modules. The institute itself does not seem to be using ICTs much in its delivery of programs and this constitutes a lost opportunity.

Student quality at entry

Due to the combined selectivity of the system and the linking of intake to the limited number of GoS, UNISWA has more qualified candidates than it can admit. Exceptions are fields that require high passes in mathematics and science. Student readiness at entry is therefore a challenge that is limited to these fields. With the exception of fields that require mathematics and science, UNISWA intake comes ready to handle university studies.

Staff qualifications

Staff qualifications have improved in recent years. UNISWA academic staff hold reasonably high qualifications and more so for the expatriate staff (figure 5.7). Nearly half (47%) of Swazi staff hold a Masters degrees. Another 47 percent hold Doctoral degrees leaving only 6 percent without the minimum required qualification. For expatriates, over 70 percent have Doctoral degrees and the rest hold Masters' degrees. In 2007/08 UNISWA had 17 staff members on training abroad. Staff also has the option to upgrade their qualifications through the Academic Development Center, but the uptake is generally low.

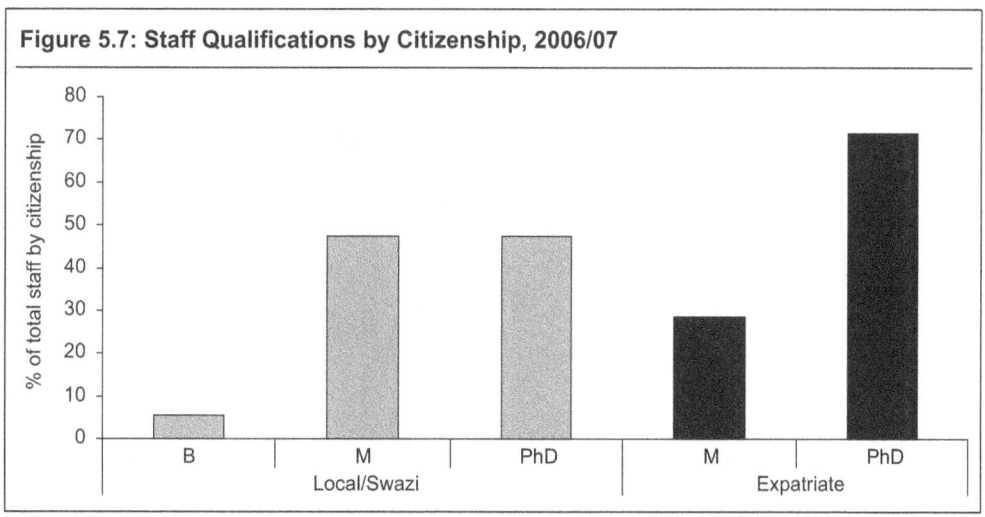

Figure 5.7: Staff Qualifications by Citizenship, 2006/07

Source: UNISWA Planning Center (UPC). B = Bachelor degree; M = Master's degree.

Men dominate the academic staff (65%). In addition, women are concentrated in the lowest positions and this provides a negative role modeling for students, while denying women the income required to realize the PRSAP gender parity goal. Only 13 percent of the top academic positions (professors and associate professors), and less than 33 percent of the senior lecturer positions, are occupied by women. In contrast, women comprise 44 percent of the lowest rank of lecturers (figure 5.8).

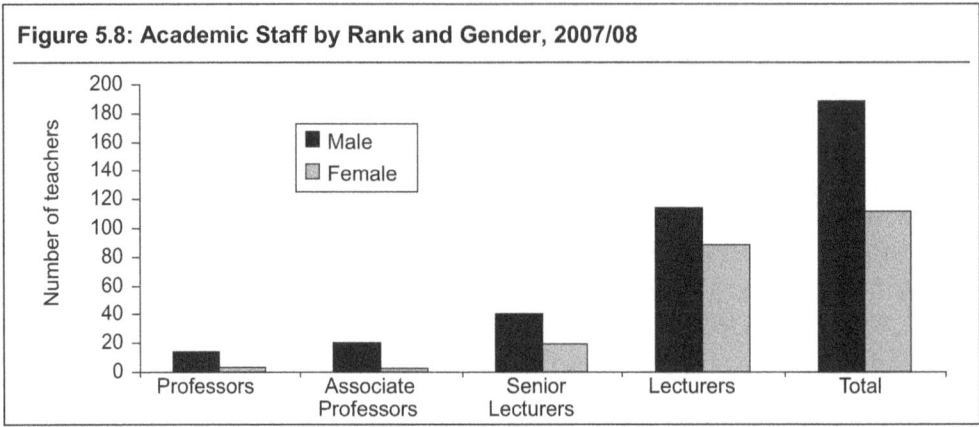

Figure 5.8: Academic Staff by Rank and Gender, 2007/08

Source: Vice Chancellor Report 2007/08. L= Lecturer; SL = Senior Lecturer; AP = Associate Professor; P = Professor

The share of female academics varies greatly across faculties. They constitute 80 percent of the staff in the Health Sciences and less than 20 percent for Science and Engineering. For the gender parity goals of the PRSAP, this is not sufficient. Moreover, it does not present female students the appropriate role modeling they need in order to break the dominance of men at this level. The situation in other faculties is somewhat better, with 30-45 percent female academic staff members (figure 5.9). The overall picture demands a staff recruitment policy that deliberately seeks out qualified and/or trainable women.

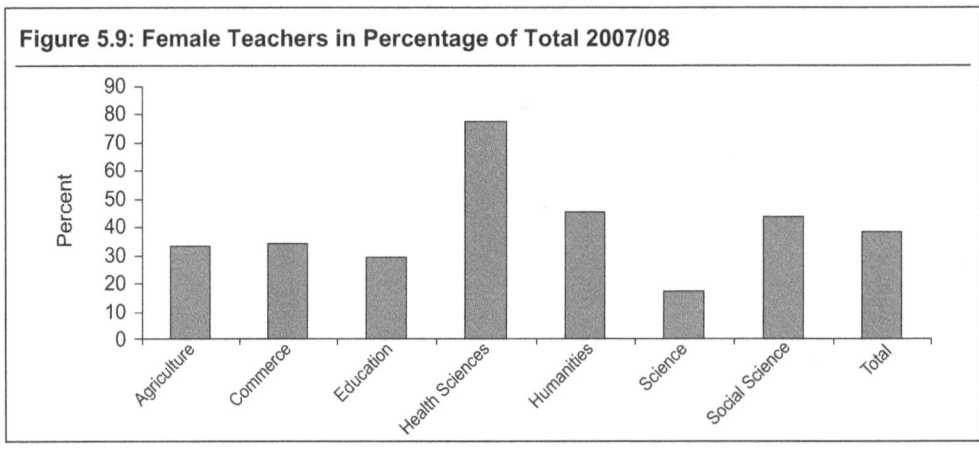

Figure 5.9: Female Teachers in Percentage of Total 2007/08

Source: Vice Chancellor's Report 2007/08.

Consistent with levels of qualifications, the share of Swazis in high academic positions is far lower than foreigners. This situation is only improving slowly. This also warrants concerted redress (figure 5.10).

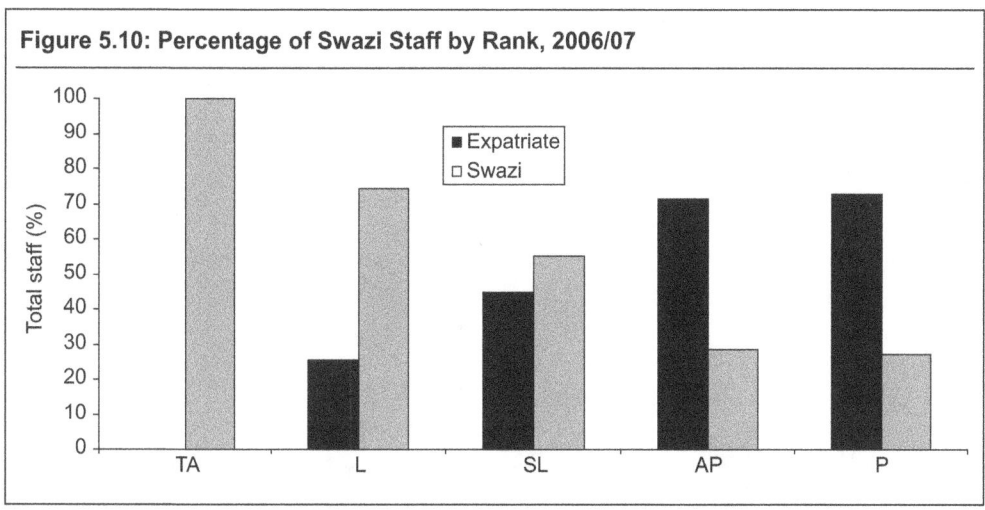

Figure 5.10: Percentage of Swazi Staff by Rank, 2006/07

Source: UNISWA Planning Center (UPC).

Physical facilities

Given increases in enrollment and limited capital budgets, there have been concerns about overcrowding of the physical facilities and its potential impact on teaching and learning effectiveness. Between 1999 and 2005, the average number of square meters per student at the three campuses decreased from 1.3 to 1.1 at Kwaluseni, from 2.0 to 1.3 at Luyengo, and from 3.9 to 1.7 at Mbabane (figure 5.11).

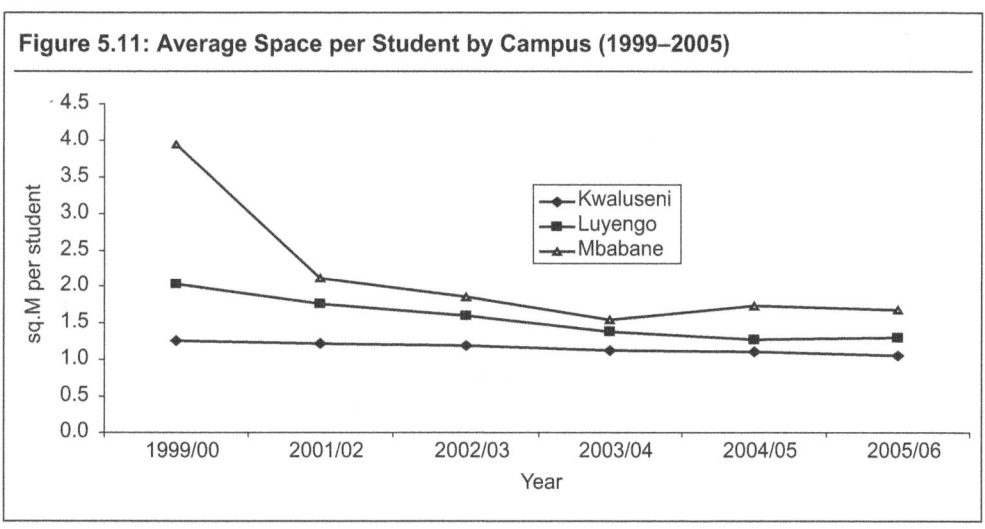

Figure 5.11: Average Space per Student by Campus (1999–2005)

Source: Physical Planning Office.

The available space per student at both the Luyengo and Kwaluseni campuses is below the UNESCO recommended norm of 1.5 m² per student. Overcrowding seems particularly acute in the Faculties of Humanities and of Social Science at Kwaluseni. A report in 2006 by the University Physical Planner stated that, "the area allocated to the Faculties of Humanities and Social Sciences is inadequate even for one Faculty." These two faculties had an average of only 0.5 m² per student in 2005. However, a recent utilization survey showed a different picture, as shown in figure 5.12.

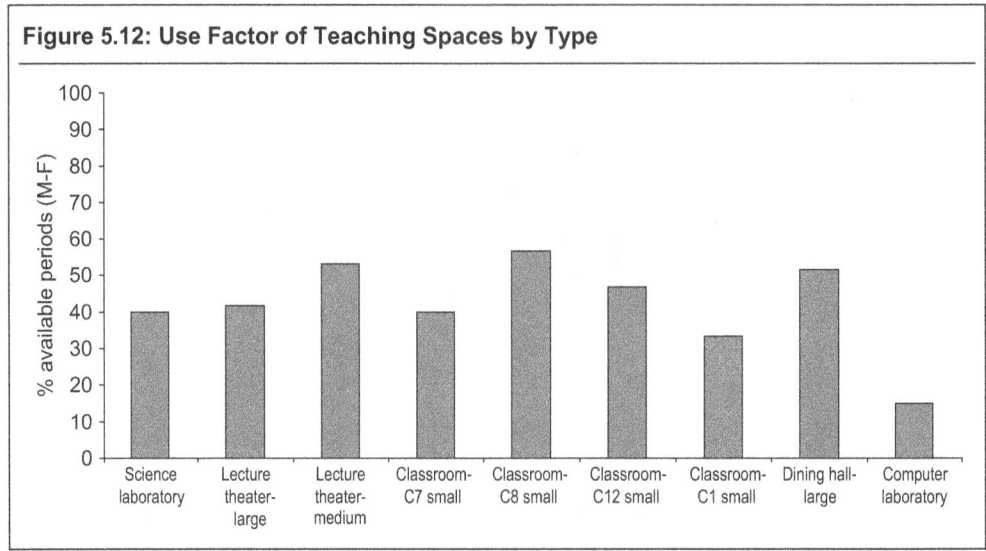

Source: UNISWA survey, excluding Luyengo Campus.
Note: Use factor is defined as the proportion of available class periods per week (Monday-Friday) in which the teaching space was actually used for an official class. The data refer to the first semester August- December, 2007. The maximum use possible is assumed to be 60 periods per week.

The numbers in figure 5.13 do not support a generalized concern with overcrowding. The use of nonteaching spaces—dining hall and common rooms—is notable but all the same, the overall situation does not point to a crisis in teaching spaces. For instance, science laboratories are used only 24 hours per week, primarily because it is a tradition to have laboratory classes only in the afternoons. With better planning it may be possible to expand the use of the expensive laboratories and thus allow for an increase in student intake. However, it must be noted that, in addition to the teaching time, 4th year students use science laboratories for individual project work. This may slightly increase the use factor, but not to a level where it could be said to be efficient.

The under-utilization of computer laboratories for teaching purposes averaging only 9 hours per week, or 15 percent of the available time, is striking, as the mastery of ICTs beyond the level of literacy ought to be compulsory for all university students.

Quality assurance

UNISWA still heavily relies on the old and limited system of external examiners drawn mainly from Anglophone Africa, for its quality assurance. By its nature, this system is inadequate to provide a comprehensive review of the quality and development relevance of programs. Consideration should be given to current quality-assurance systems that offer a comprehensive review of programs, inputs, processes, outputs and outcomes, using a panel of distinguished higher education experts who bring to bear the best international practices. Such reviews should also be periodic—every 3 years—and regularized.

The university is working toward improving its assessment of staff performance. Some envisaged strengths of the system include: clear articulation of staff job descriptions against which they would be assessed, and allowing for student inputs in the assessment of staff. This initiative provides a base for further strengthening of quality assurance.

Outputs and learning outcomes

UNISWA outputs are low and have not grown since 1999. The number of degrees awarded increased considerably in the late 1990s, from 343 in 1996 to 682 in 1999, but have leveled off since then, reaching 638 in 2006. (see figure 5.4).

Ironically, current data sets show reasonably high completion rates for most faculties expect for the science/engineering. Completion rates range from 70 to 90 percent overall and only 60[4] percent for science and engineering as well as for the IDE (figure 5.13).

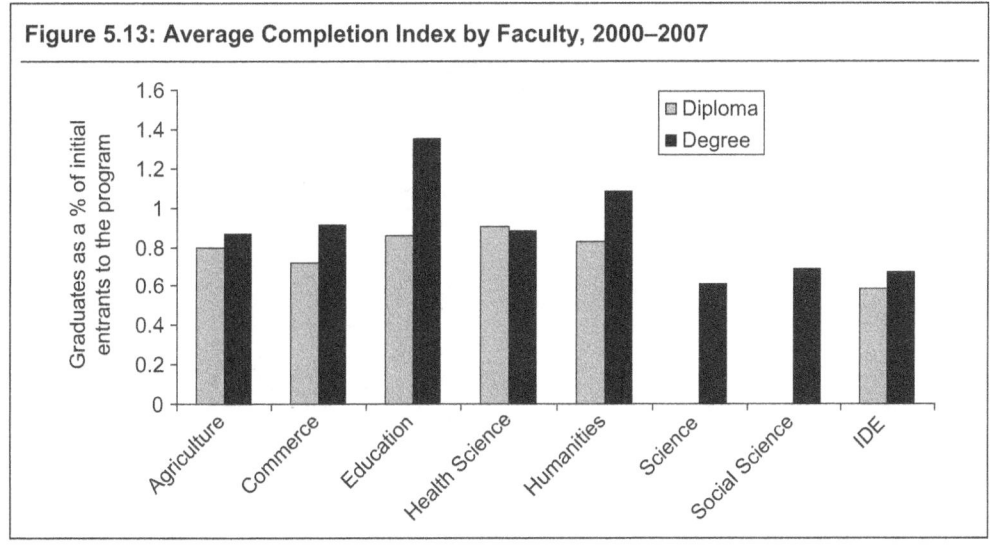

Figure 5.13: Average Completion Index by Faculty, 2000–2007

Source: University Planning Center based on data from the Registrar.

Research outputs

Research outputs are low even for a predominantly teaching university, and especially when considered against the already-noted good qualifications of the professoriate. This is regardless of the fact that research is one of the promotion criteria. This also in spite of the institution-level effort to set up structures and funding mechanisms to support research. Key structures that ought to be stimulating research are the University Research Board, the Research and Consultancy Center, and Faculty specific research committees.

As in most of Africa's universities, research funding is low, constituting only 3 percent of the UNISWA's annual budget. However, quite unique to Swaziland, the low research funding does not seem to be an explanatory factor behind the poor research output. Each year, the university allocates research grants, but many academic staff members do not apply for them. Research grants peaked in 2006/7 to over SZ1 million but declined to SZ600,000 the following year in accordance with the general GoS cutback on higher education allocation (table 5.4). The low uptake of research grants does not provide grounds for increased funding.

Table 5.4: Research Allocations in SZL Million

Year	Allocation to Research Center	Total Budget for University	% Allocated to Univ. Research	Actual and % Allocated for Research Grants	Actual and % Allocated for Operations
2003/04	480.5	32.1	1.4	(384.4) 80.0	(96.1) 20.0
2004/05	733.8	34.7	2.1	(608.3) 82.9	(125.5) 17.1
2005/06	1,008.7	51.1	1.9	(858.4) 85.1	(150.3) 14.9
2006/07	1,280.8	53.1	2.4	(1,125.8) 87.9	(155.0) 12.1
2007/08	793.3	30.2	2.6	(595.0) 75.0	(198.3) 25.0

Source: UNISWA Research Center.

University-funded research projects vary across faculties, with the faculty of Agriculture making the best input (figure 5.14).

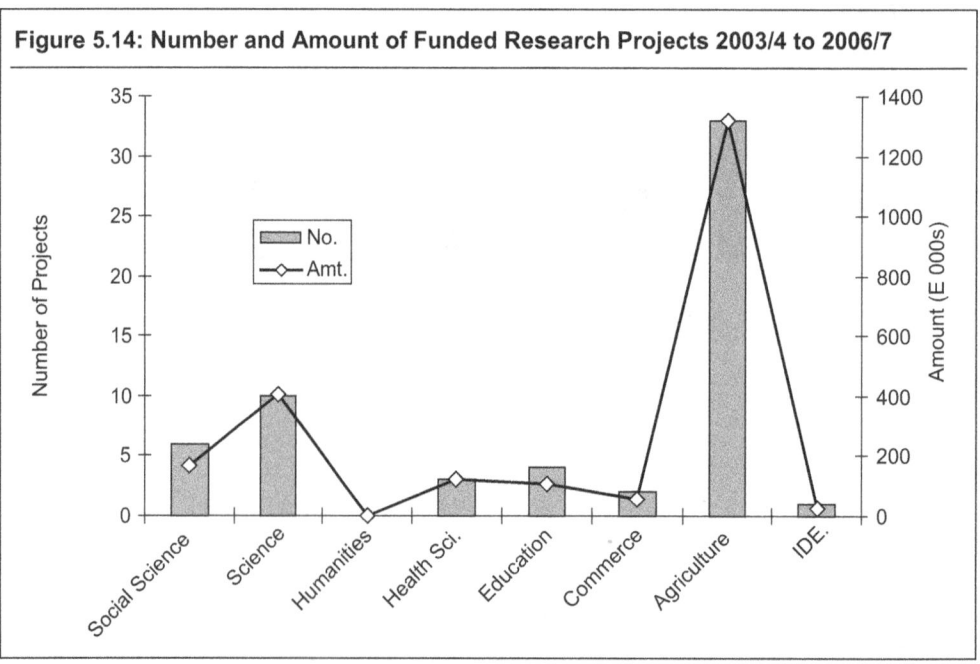

Figure 5.14: Number and Amount of Funded Research Projects 2003/4 to 2006/7

Source: University Planning Center (UPC).

Reportedly, there are more research projects that do not use the university grant funding (table 5.5). What remains unclear is why such research does not exploit the available funding, how it is funded, and the quality of its outputs. Ordinarily, grant-funded research goes through a competitive review process that should enhance its quality. The predominance of nonfunded research projects may therefore be worrisome. It is possible that these types of research projects, by avoiding competitive funding, are of lower rigor and quality. Without clear quality controls of research outputs the qualitative implications of these projects will remain unclear.

Table 5.5: Research Activities Not Financed by UNISWA Research Board, 2006/07

Faculty/Center	2004/05	2005/06	2006/07	Total
Agriculture	17	15	17	49
Commerce	1	0	7	8
Education	10	11	7	28
Health Science	14	16	14	44
Humanities	10	10	7	27
Science	16	17	32	65
Social Science	8	10	6	24
IDE	2	3	3	8
Post-Graduate Studies	0	0	0	0
Health Information and Counseling Center	1	0	1	2
Swaziland Institute for Research in Traditional Medicine, Medicinal and Indigenous Food Plants	2	5	7	14
University Research Center	0	3	0	3
TOTAL	81	90	101	272

Source: UPC.

The UNISWA research community has remained insular, and this may adversely affect the quality and development relevance of its research outputs. Mechanisms for stakeholder participation in setting the research agenda are unclear. Research tends to be conducted without much stakeholder participation. Instances of university/industry collaborative research are few and far in between. Mechanisms for the repackaging, brokerage and advocacy for the application of research-generated knowledge by potential domestic users are unclear at best.

Dissemination avenues are limited. For instance, The UNISWA Research Journal for Agriculture, Science and Technology—published twice a year—and the UNISWA Research Journal—published once a year—do not have wide circulation. They are primarily read by UNISWA staff members, but hardly outside the country. The use of internet to disseminate research outputs also tends to be limited. Combined, these factors deny UNISWA the external review and critiques that are invaluable for improving the quality, currency and development relevance of research outputs. Moreover, poor dissemination reduces chances for the application of knowledge produced by UNISWA, thus reducing the relevance of the institution to Swaziland's quest for knowledge-driven productivity growth.

The only notable constraints to research outputs are the limited infrastructure, in terms of specialized science laboratories and modern equipment, and high teaching obligations for the faculties of Commerce and Humanities.

UNISWA's international ranking

UNISWA is ranked relatively low internationally, and among African universities. This could, partly be because most international rankings emphasize research. The "World Universities Rankings on the Web" by the Laboratorio de Internet ranked UNISWA number 6,624 among world universities and 68 among universities in Africa. The "Webometrics Ranking of World Universities" for July 2007 placed UNISWA number 7,321 among world universities, and 84 among African universities. The ranking may be adversely affected by the fact that UNISWA research outputs are commonly not available on the Internet. However, other African universities that rank better than UNISWA would probably suffer the same limitation.

Relevance

As previously noted, the limited engagement of critical stakeholders—especially employers and industry—from the UC, significantly contributes to the doubtful relevance of teaching and research programs. Further, there seems to be no formal processes for placing the university at the center of the national development dialogue. Other cited factors that limit the development and market responsiveness of programs include a lack of: (i) a human resources development strategy; (ii) informative labor surveys; (iii) graduate tracer studies; and (iv) a sub-regional labor market observatory.

Perhaps due to these combined constraints, UNISWA enrollments tend to be lower in fields where there is high labor market demand, such as Engineering and Health (figure 5.15). On the other hand some fields with low demand and less likelihood of giving graduates tangible employment opportunities dominate enrollments—Humanities for instance. This also means that the limited GoS scholarships are spent on areas where there may be a high risk of graduates not repaying the loan part of their scholarships—50%—because of unemployment. Anecdotal evidence speaks to the phenomenon of unemployed humanities graduates.

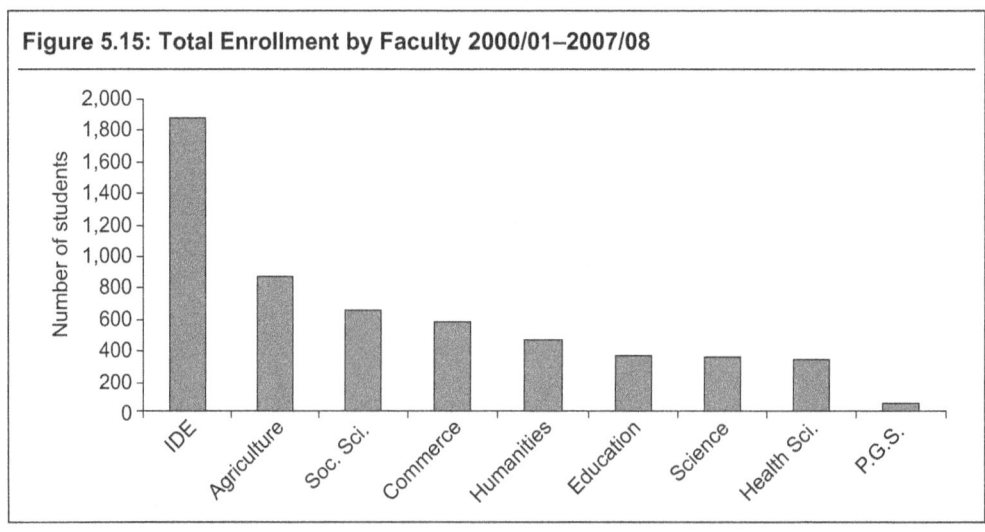

Figure 5.15: Total Enrollment by Faculty 2000/01–2007/08

Source: Vice Chancellor's annual report.

IDE enrollments follow the same pattern of concentration in humanities, and social science, especially the diploma of law and commerce (figure 5.16). This is ironic because IDE could be serving to re-tool Swazis, including the educated unemployed for areas where there are better employment opportunities.

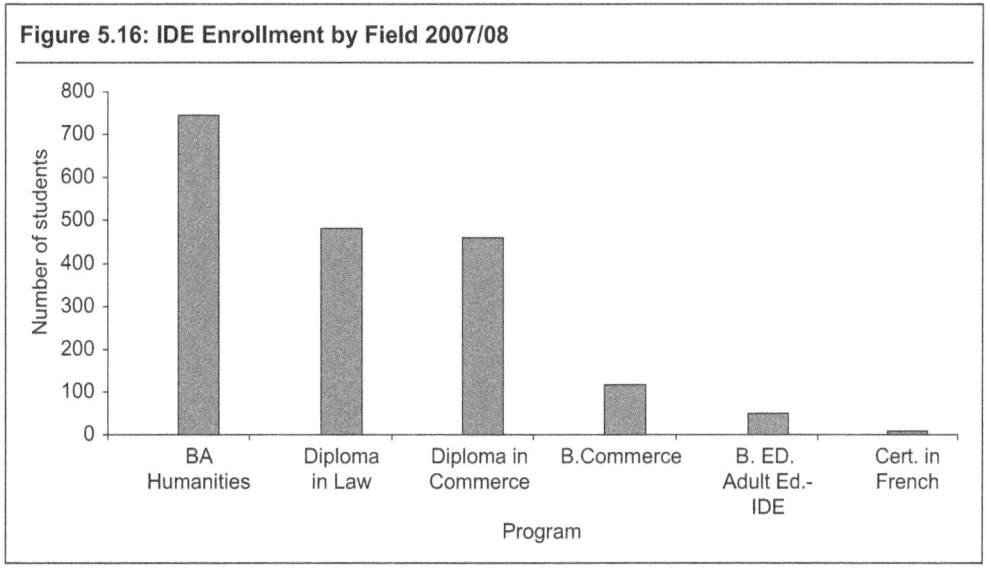

Figure 5.16: IDE Enrollment by Field 2007/08

Source: Registrar's office.

UNISWA programs also seem to not be responding to regional labor market demands outlined in Chapter 4. As another example, IDE could have exploited regional employment opportunities for the unemployed humanities graduates by mounting Portuguese crash courses for them, and exporting them to neighboring Lusophone countries—Mozambique and Angola—which have shortage of English teachers and perhaps other public servants with a good grasp of English. The use of SADC protocols on education and training and on the free movement of people could be other unexplored potentials.

Swaziland ranks very low internationally with respect to the production of scientists and engineers. Only 6 percent of university students specialize in science and engineering, relative to 50 percent in China, 34 percent for Finland and about 12 percent in Africa. It may be added that, several countries, including Finland and Australia, have decided to control enrollment in their universities based on labor market expectations for different specializations. In particular, the Finnish model seems to work well.[5]

Research programs that specifically target community, national development challenges and industry needs are rare. At times, it is even questionable to what extent research activities serve the university's own teaching needs. The use of research to facilitate teaching and learning could be highly constructive, since research has the potential of creating interest, even excitement, among students, and since students may make considerable contributions to the outcome of the research.

On the positive side, the Faculty of Commerce offers a course in Entrepreneurship. The Faculty of Agriculture also uses student projects for similar purposes. The predominance of lectures may not support these initiatives well, but they are a good start. Consideration should be given to the piloting of a range of modern pedagogies, such as Problem Based Learning (PBL), with a focus on immediate communities. Such initiatives could begin to sensitize students to the need for their work to respond to Swazi's real and felt needs.

Research and teaching programs that target stakeholder needs may attract external funding and contribute to revenues. A recent example is the electric Power Company of Swaziland, which needs more and better electrical engineers, and is therefore ready to support the strengthening of Electrical Engineering at UNISWA.

Efficiency

Probably owing to tight selection processes and the resultant student readiness at entry, UNISWA has modest repetition rates, averaging 7 percent in 2006. Repetition rates range from 4 percent in Health Sciences to 11 percent in Science/Engineering (figure 5.17). The relatively high repetition rate in Science is most likely due to the weak teaching of mathematics and science at the secondary level as outlined in Chapter 3, combined with weak academic counseling and weak remedial teaching at the university.

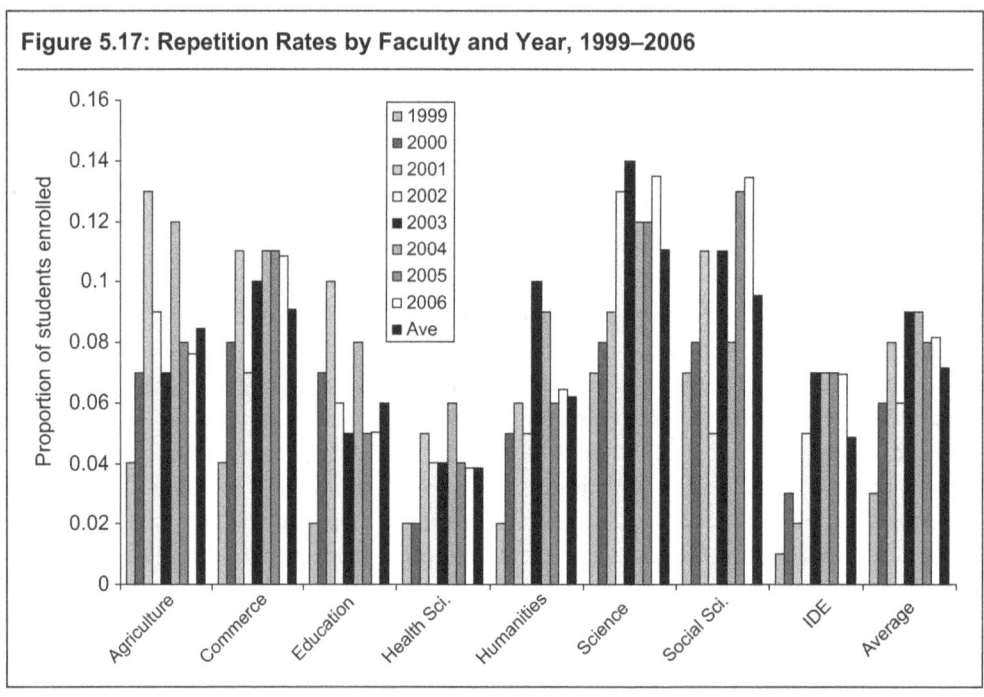

Figure 5.17: Repetition Rates by Faculty and Year, 1999–2006

Source: UNISWA University Planning Center, calculated from data from the Registrar's Office.

The current average full-time-equivalent student/staff ratio of 17:1 is reasonable for a university, but could be reconsidered against Swaziland's limited access to higher education. (table 5.6). Notably, this ratio is within the range of neighboring countries, but it is higher than the 12 hours per week recommended by UNISWA. The student/staff ratio ranges from a low 7.3:1 in the Faculty of Science and Engineering, to 40.3:1 in the Faculty of Commerce. The low number for Science and Engineering clearly relates to the time-consuming instruction in laboratory sessions. However, the same explanation hardly holds for the Faculty of Education with a ratio of only about 10:1. Part of the explanation for the low ratio is the range of subject specialists employed to training teachers for the wide range of subjects noted in Chapter 3.

Table 5.6: Students per Staff by Faculty, 2002/03 to 2007/08

	2002–03	2003–04	2004–05	2005–06	2006–07	2007–08
Agriculture	12.1	15.0	15.1	14.9	16.6	15.5
Commerce	37.6	52.6	40.9	42.6	48.4	40.3
Education	9.6	10.1	9.7	10.5	10.8	10.5
Health Science	10.6	12.7	11.4	11.3	10.4	12.5
Humanities	17.3	20.5	19.2	17.5	18.1	14.5
Science/Eng.	6.2	6.7	7.1	8.3	7.6	7.3
Social Science	17.6	19.7	19.1	19.5	19.6	21.4

Source: Calculated from the annual Vice Chancellor's reports. Note that the numbers do not include staff in administration, IDE, library and part time staff.

For a large number of courses, class sizes tend to be small, specifically at the Kwaluseni Campus (figure 5.18). Twenty percent of all classes have fewer than 5 students, 30 percent have fewer than 10 students and over 60 percent have fewer than 25 students. Only 10 percent of the classes had a "normal" size, of 25 to 45 students. Remarkably, about 10 percent (106) of the classes had been allocated space, but had no students enrolled. This confirms the already-noted adequacy of teaching spaces.

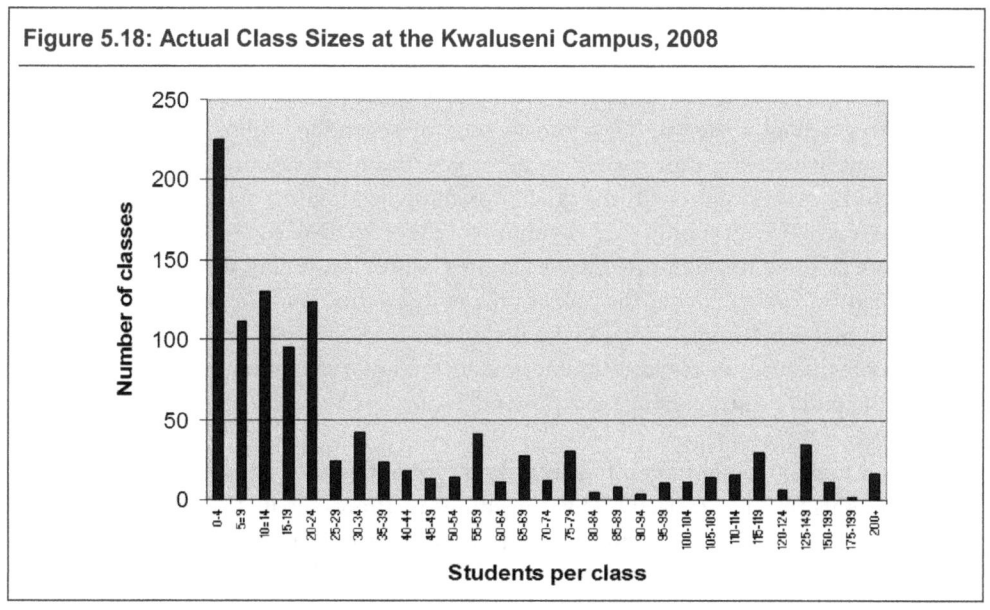

Figure 5.18: Actual Class Sizes at the Kwaluseni Campus, 2008

Source: UNISWA Planning Center (UPC).

The ratio of nonacademic[6] to academic staff at UNISWA is reasonable. Figure 5.19 below shows that Swaziland has a 2:1 ratio of nonacademic to academic staff. This is near the average for other African universities.

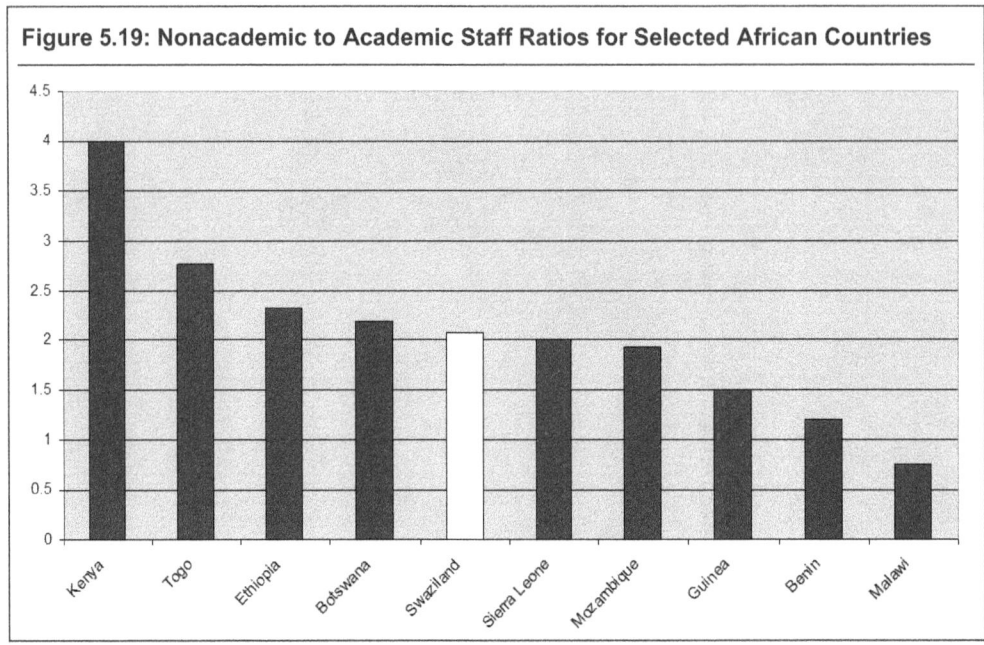

Figure 5.19: Nonacademic to Academic Staff Ratios for Selected African Countries

Source: Darvas, 2007.

Course overlaps are a key source of resource inefficiency. Many courses overlap or are given for a very small number of students. This is costly in terms of physical space and in terms of teacher time and salaries. A rationalization of the course system at UNISWA might lead to improved efficiency and considerable savings.

The duration of programs is another source of resource wastage. Many degree programs are 5 years in duration, with the first year dominated by repetition of secondary school material. This transference of secondary school education to the university, where the unit cost is so high, is a drain on resources. Moreover, there seems to be no concerns with the quality of students at entry, except for mathematics and science. The upgrading of secondary school graduates in these subjects can therefore be done through pre-entry programs, whose providers should be selected on a competitive basis to avoid the risk of university capture and the reinstatement of the problem that was being avoided in the first place.

Another source of resource inefficiency is the low repayment rate of the loan part (50%) of students' scholarships. As presented later in Chapter 6, the repayment rate is estimated at 8 percent.

Due mainly to shortage of scholarships, the university is operating at about 60 percent of its physical capacity. This consittutes unaffordable ineficiencies in the use of the teaching staff, physical facilities, plant, equipment and furniture.

The university is also over-dependent on government funding. Raising the proportion of own-source revenues from the current 2 percent to 10 percent would save substantial government resources.

Conclusion

As in other countries, Swaziland's higher education systems could facilitate the country's transition to knowledge-driven growth. However, a set of factors substantially limits this potential. The policy framework that guides the development of higher education is dated and out of sync with the current development dialogue. It is therefore highly unlikely that this aged policy will guide the transformation of higher education into a key lever of Swaziland's development reform. The legal framework that enacts the subsector development is even older, dating back to 1983.

The potential role of higher education is further inhibited by its limited and even declining access. Access is too low to supply Swaziland the threshold of high-level skills required to lead knowledge-driven growth. Access is also inequitable by gender, rural locations and low SES. Combined, these inequities limit the potential to use higher education as a key lever for social equity. In fact, higher education is distinctly pro-rich in virtually all aspects, and this defies all efforts toward shared growth.

As with GET and TVETSD, Swaziland's HE is of reasonable quality. However, the down side of this achievement is that the observed quality may be substantially aided by the system's stringent selectivity and exclusivity. Regrettably, the exclusivity compounds academic and social advantage, thus forcing children of the poor out of the higher education system. The resilience of the quality is yet to be tested by the wide range of student ability that normally accompanies broad access.

For its teaching and research programs, higher education has low outputs. For teaching programs, this is attributable to the shortage of government scholarships. For research, it seems to be low expertise which, strangely, co-exists with high qualifications of the professoriate. Other sources of inefficiencies are the under-utilization of physical capacity, low class sizes, poor curricula articulation, long duration of programs and course overlaps.

The university has tended to be insular and this has substantially reduced the development responsiveness of its programs and outputs. Other constraints are the lack of clear mechanisms for centering the university in the national development dialogue, poor information on the labor market, lack of strategic guidance in terms of the sector policies and strategic plans and lack of a national human resource development strategy. Moreover, the university has lacked initiative to create a strategic future outlook and to connect to the global development dialogue.

All the same, UNISWA presents a good base from which to build a high quality, efficient and development-responsive higher education system.

Notes

[1] See: *Accelerating Catch-up. Tertiary Education for Growth in Sub-Saharan Africa.* The World Bank, 2009.

[2] Ibid.
[3] UNESCO. 2006. *Global Education Digest*.
[4] Due to unresolved data inaccuracies, the IDE completion rate reported in the overall university records is more than double what comes out of IDE records and this difference could not be resolved.
[5] J. Davies, T. Weko, L. Kim and E.W. Thulstrup, "Thematic Review of Tertiary Education: Finland". OECD, Paris, 2006.
[6] For Swaziland: nonacademics include 52 administrative staff

CHAPTER 6

Cost and Financing of Education, Training, and Skills Development

Introduction

Through Vision 2022 and the PRSAP, Swaziland has undertaken to strengthen its human capital base within a context of low growth and fiscal stress. The country therefore faces a dual challenge to increase investment in the sector while tightening resource efficiency. The latter challenge is even the harder because the sector is located within a broader context of growing government expenditure.

Government Finances

Tables 6.1 and 6.2 show government revenues and expenditure over recent years. Between 2000/2001 and 2008/2009, the share of revenues as a percentage of GDP rose from 27 percent to 34 percent, helped mainly by SACU receipts. The 9-year average for SACU receipts accounted for 56 percent of the GDP. While a critical resource, SACU receipts fluctuate much more than other sources of revenue. Therefore, they are a source of instability and unpredictability in the government's revenues. Other key contributors to the revenues are personal income tax (14%), sales tax (12%), and company taxes (8%).

Table 6.1: Government Revenue 2000/01 to 2009/10

| Year | Total Revenue | | | SACU receipts | SACU receipts as % of total revenue | Grants | Grants as % of total revenue |
	Emalangeni (millions)	As % of GDP	Index 2000=100				
2000/01	2,825	26.9	100	1,407	49.8	112	1.8
2001/02	3,111	27.5	110	1,504	48.3	127	1.6
2002/03	3,426	27.4	121	1,619	47.2	163	1.4
2003/04	3,908	28.4	138	1,878	48.1	138	1.2
2004/05	4,842	31.5	171	2,773	57.3	116	1.2
2005/06	5,499	33.1	195	3,137	57.0	172	1.0
2006/07	6,557	34.8	232	4,017	61.3	90	0.9
2007/08	8,998	43.4	318	6,291	69.9	100	0.8
2008/09	8,007	35.1	283	5,000	62.4	98	0.8
2009/10	8,240	33.5	292	5,000	60.7	96	0.7

Source: Ministry of Finance; IMF (2008).

Table 6.2: Total Government Expenditure 2000/01 to 2009/10

Year	Total expenditure				Current expenditure		Interest on all public debt		Interest on external debt	
	Emalangeni (million)	As a % of GDP %	Index	As a ratio of total govt. revenue	As a % of total expenditure	As a % of GDP	As a % of total expenditure	As % of GDP	As a % of total debt interest	As a % of GDP
2000/01	2,968	28.2	100	1.05	77.5	23.8	2.1	0.6	91.1	0.6
2001/02	3,455	30.5	116	1.11	70.6	22.5	3.0	0.9	94.4	0.9
2002/03	4,018	32.1	135	1.17	71.6	23.4	4.2	1.3	100.0	1.3
2003/04	4,315	31.3	145	1.10	75.6	23.1	3.1	1.0	78.7	0.9
2004/05	5,557	36.2	187	1.15	74.3	27.9	3.0	1.1	70.8	0.8
2005/06	5,826	35.1	196	1.06	60.5	21.2	4.4	1.6	61.9	0.7
2006/07	6,876	36.5	232	1.05	84.5	30.8	4.9	1.8	n.a.	n.a.
2007/08	8,446	40.8	285	0.94	87.0	35.5	2.2	0.9	n.a.	n.a.
2008/09	8,493	37.2	286	1.06	n.a.	n.a.	n.a.	n.a.	n.a.	n.a.
2009/10	8,600	34.9	290	1.04	n.a.	n.a.	n.a.	n.a.	n.a.	n.a.

Source: Ministry of Finance; IMF (2008).
n.a. Not applicable.

Grants are a fairly insignificant portion of the government revenues. Moreover, their contribution declined from 1.8 percent in 2000/01 to 0.7 percent in 2009/10. The government's nonreliance on external grants is healthy, and signals potential sustainability of programs. However, the sustained slow growth, fiscal stress and increasing demand for investment, especially in social sectors, may necessitate an increase in the proportion of grants.

In recent years, government expenditure has increased substantially more than increases in revenues.[1] Total expenditures increased from 28 percent of the GDP in 2000/01, and may reach 35 percent in 2009/10 (table 6.2). As a consequence, the budget deficit rose to more than 5 percent of the GDP in 2006/07, from a strong budget surplus in 1997/08 while fiscal prospects show no signs of long-term improvement. The fiscal stress has its origins in the combined slowing tax revenue growth and increased upward pressure on spending. Fiscal stress is also evident in budget overruns and even in a large shortfall in the public pension fund.

Public Spending on the ETSDS

Swaziland's level of investment in the sector is higher than what UNESCO generally uses as a desirable target for developing countries—6 percent. The share of sector expenditure as a percentage of the GDP increased from 6 percent in 2000 to 7.7 percent in 2004, but began to decline reaching an estimated 6.7 percent in 2009. For most of the decade investment kept close to 7 percent of the GDP with a peak of nearly 8 percent in 2004.

Education spending as a percentage of total government expenditure (TGE) declined from 21 percent in 2000 to 17.6 percent in 2007, and is projected to increase to 19.2 percent in 2009 (table 6.3).

Table 6.3: Public Spending on Education as a Share of GDP and TGE (2000–2009)

	2000	2001	2002	2003	2004	2005	2006	2007	2008	2009
Current prices (SZLm)										
GDP (A)	10,509	11,334	12,519	13,775	15,353	16,617	18,854	20,710	22,808	24,609
Total govt. exp. (B)	2,968	3,455	4,018	4,315	5,557	5,826	6,876	8,446	8,493	8,600
Total educ. Exp. (C)	629	661	802	946	1,180	1,219	1,230	1,485	1,570	1,649
Govt exp. share (B/A)	28.2	30.5	32.1	31.3	36.2	35.1	36.5	40.8	37.2	34.9
Educ. share of GDP (C/A)	6.0	5.8	6.4	6.9	7.7	7.3	6.5	7.2	6.9	6.7
Educ. share of govt. exp. (C/B)	21.2	19.1	20.0	21.9	21.2	20.9	17.9	17.6	18.5	19.2
Constant 2007 prices										
GDP	17,575	17,753	18,077	18,777	19,251	19,673	20,231	20,710	21,122	21,552
Growth rate of real GDP		1.0	1.8	3.9	2.5	2.2	2.8	2.4	2.0	2.0
Total govt. Expenditure	4,964	5,412	5,802	5,882	6,968	6,898	7,379	8,446	7,865	7,531
Total educ. Expenditure	1,052	1,035	1,158	1,290	1,480	1,443	1,320	1,485	1,454	1,444

Source: Ministry of Finance; IMF, 2008 (for GDP and GDP deflator figures).
Note: Government spending figures are confirmed actuals for years up to 2005, reportedly reliable estimates of actuals for 2006, and approved budget figures for 2007 to 2009. Year 2000 refers to financial year 2000/01, and so on.

Trends in public spending presented in figure 6.1 were due to changes in the economic size of the government as a whole and not so much to changes in sector priorities. Despite the decline between 2000 and 2007 education's share of government expenditure, public spending on education in real terms, increased by about 40 percentage points. However, the 2007 medium-term expenditure framework (MTEF) projected a decline in education spending in real terms between 2007 and 2009, due mainly to declining growth.

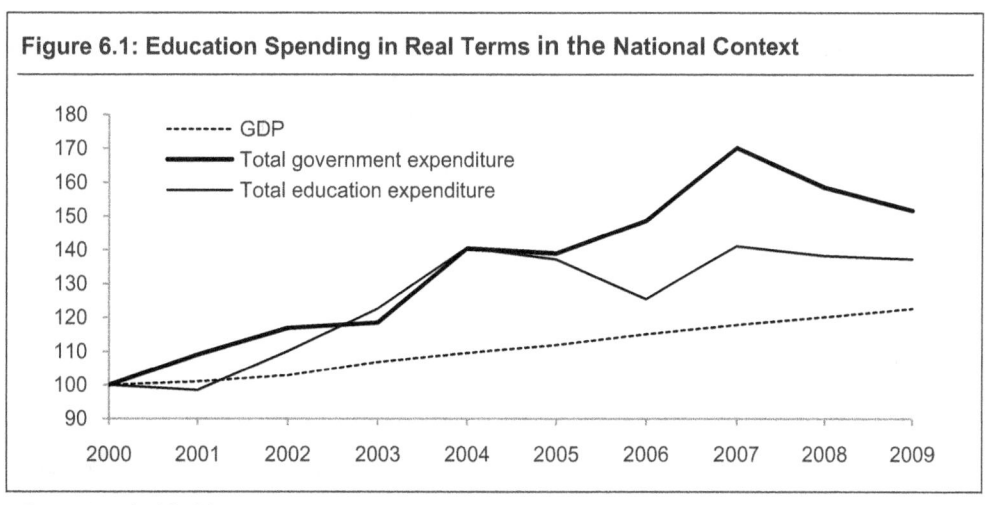

Figure 6.1: Education Spending in Real Terms in the National Context

Source: As of table 6.2.
Note: 2000 values are indexed at 100.

Observed sharp increases in public spending have been due to the rise in the civil service wage bill particularly in 2004. The temporary dip in 2006 was due to a one-year freeze of nominal increases in the sector.

Driven mainly by an unsustainable wage bill,[2] recurrent expenditure dominates overall public expenditure. In 2005, for instance, recurrent spending accounted for 78 percent of total government expenditure leaving only 22 percent for capital expenditure.[3] Capital spending in the ETSDS is much lower than for the overall government level. The percentage devoted to capital spending has never exceeded 8 percent. The average for the 2000 to 2009 period is 4.5 percent (table 6.4).

Table 6.4: Capital Spending on ETSDS (2000–2009)

	2000	2001	2002	2003	2004	2005	2006	2007	2008	2009
Total educ. Expenditure	629	661	802	946	1,180	1,219	1,230	1,485	1,570	1,649
Educ. capital spending	46	34	46	24	34	67	61	56	59	62
Capital/Total	7.3	5.1	5.7	2.5	2.9	5.5	5.0	3.8	3.8	3.8

Source: Ministry of Finance.

The overall picture is one of serious budgetary constraints in the coming years, linked largely to stagnant economic growth and a possible deterioration due to the deepening global financial crisis. It seems likely that total public spending on education will decrease in real terms. This underlines the importance of focusing on policy choices that promote efficiency gains, and on budgetary trade-offs between education subsectors.

Public Spending on the Sector in a Subregional Perspective

Relative to its GDP per capita PPP, the proportion of the GDP that Swaziland allocates to the sector is far less than for Botswana and Namibia. However, it is the fifth highest in the immediate sub-region[4] and seems fairly within the norm (figure 6.2).

Except for the investment reforms proposed in this report, there seems to be no immediately apparent reason for Swaziland to either increase or decrease its overall spending. It is noteworthy that the worldwide pattern where spending on education tends to increase with increases in GDP per capita[5] is only faintly visible in the sub-region.

Private Spending on ETSDS

Swazi households contribute to the education of their children far more than in other SACU countries with higher average household incomes—South Africa, Botswana, and Namibia. Table 6.5 shows that private financing accounts for 19 percent of total spending. In schools (public and private), fees paid by households account for 99.8 percent of overall spending on ECCD, 14 percent of primary education spending and 30 percent of secondary education spending.[6] In comparison to South Africa, the proportions of private financing of primary and secondary education were 5 and 10 percent respectively and, this was in 2005 before substantial fee reductions that followed the introduction of 'no fee schools'. Perhaps, one would expect the figures to be higher in South Africa,[7] given the higher levels of household income. The fact that

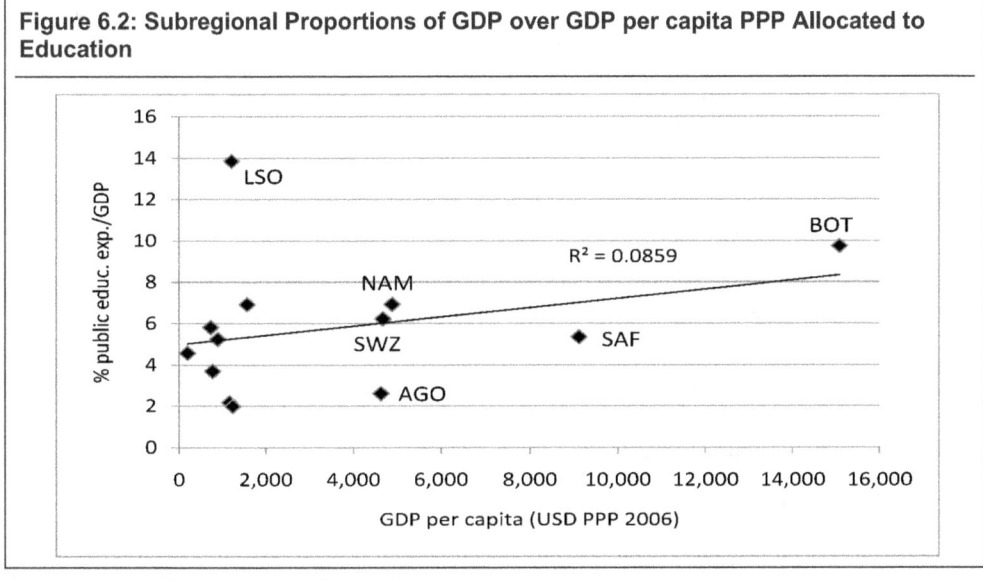

Figure 6.2: Subregional Proportions of GDP over GDP per capita PPP Allocated to Education

Source: UNESCO: UIS (2008) and IMF (2008).
Note: The most recent UIS value was used, and the 2006 IMF financial figures.

the opposite is the case suggests that school fees in Swaziland are too high (table 6.5). We estimate that Swaziland's low-income households spend, on average, 22 percent of their income on primary education. This is neither just nor sustainable.

Table 6.5: Public and Private Financing of ETSDS (2007)

	Public		Private		Total
	SZLm	% of total spending	SZLm	% of total spending	SZLm
ECCD	0.1	0.2	26.0	99.8	26.1
Primary schools	526.2	85.9	86.0	14.1	612.3
Secondary schools	513.2	69.6	224.7	30.4	737.8
TVETSD (formal)	28.5	91.4	2.7	8.6	31.1
ABET/TVETSD	7.3	100.0	0.0	0.0	7.3
Teacher education	32.8	100.0	0.0	0.0	32.8
University	243.8	98.1	4.7	1.9	248.5
Other*	132.7	100.0	0.0	0.0	132.7
Total	1,484.5	81.2	344.1	18.8	1,828.6

Source: Ministry of Finance, Ministry of Education.
* Mainly administration and support services.

The remarkably low private contribution to tertiary education and training stands out in stark contrast to the very high private contributions at the GET and ECCD levels (table 6.5). For most countries, the common pattern is for post-secondary education to attract more private funding than primary and secondary education. In South Africa, for instance, households pay for about half of the cost of post-secondary education, either through upfront fee payments, or through public or private loans. This is done in view of the high private returns to post-secondary education and the common underrepresentation of the poor at this level. This justifies structuring public financing in such a way that households pay more at the post-secondary level. The reverse pattern of private financing of education in Swaziland points to a system that is inefficient and not sufficiently pro-poor.

External Financing of the Sector

External funds comprise an insignificant proportion of sector funding and are not currently listed in the MoE's budget book. However, a few agencies are prominently contributing to sector development. Examples are UNICEF's provision of school grants in certain districts in support of OVCs, the World Food Program (WFP) contributions to school feeding programs, and the European Commission (EC) sector grants amounting to SZ25 million between 2006 and 2010.

Share of Public Spending by Subsector

Table 6.6 presents enrollment and spending patterns across levels of the sector; using International Standard Classification of Education (ISCED) levels. Enrollments and total spending are expressed as percentages of the total, and expenditure per student is expressed as multiples of unit cost for primary education.

Table 6.6: Public Recurrent Unit Cost by Level of ETSDS (2007)

ISCED level		Public spending (SZLm)	% of public spending	Enrollment	% of total enrollment	Per pupil spending	Ratio of primary
0	ECCD	0.1	0.0	46,000	10.6	1	0.0
1	Primary	526.2	35.4	224,000	51.8	2,349	1.0
	Secondary	513.2	34.6	74,429	17.2	6,895	2.9
2	Lower secondary	374.9	25.3	53,210	12.3	7,045	3.0
3	Upper secondary	138.3	9.3	21,144	4.9	6,541	2.8
4C/5B	TVETSD (formal)	28.5	1.9	672	0.2	42,376	18.0
4C	ABET/TVETSD	7.3	0.5	1,399	0.3	5,184	2.2
5B	Teacher education	32.8	2.2	632	0.1	51,963	22.1
	University	243.8	16.4	5,445	1.3	44,769	19.1
5A	Under-graduate	241.1	16.2	5,385	1.2	44,769	19.1
6	Post-graduate	2.7	0.2	60	0.0	44,769	19.1
	Other*	132.7	8.9				
	Total	1,484.5	100.0	432,377	100.0	3,433	

Source: Ministry of Finance, Ministry of Education.
* Mainly administration and support services.

From a financing perspective, it can be safely concluded that ECCD is not a priority for the GoS. Funding is grossly inadequate and has declined from 0.08 percent of the 2000/2001 sector budget to 0.05 percent in 2006/2007. This can hardly support the broadening of access to quality ECCD services proposed in this report. Public funding amounts to an average of SZ4 per child per year, which inadequately covers teaching and learning materials.

Without public support, ECCD centers rely on fees for their survival. The estimated average annual fees are SZL765 per term.[8] An exception is NCPs that receive donor funding, and therefore charge nominal fees. Fees vary widely based on the SES of children catered-for in the centers (figure 6.3). They range from SZ30 to E7,800 per year. Apart from private and government contributions, several other actors modestly contribute towards ECCD services. Examples include UNICEF, WFP, Save the Children, NERCHA, international nongovernmental organizations (INGOs), local NGOs, and faith-based groups.

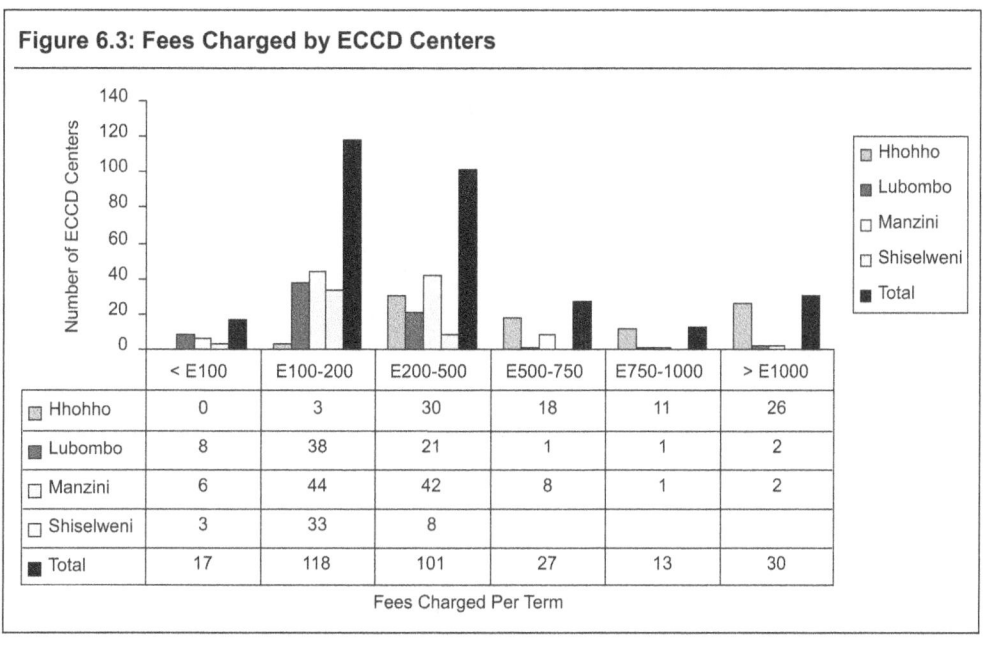

Figure 6.3: Fees Charged by ECCD Centers

Fees Charged Per Term	< E100	E100-200	E200-500	E500-750	E750-1000	> E1000
Hhohho	0	3	30	18	11	26
Lubombo	8	38	21	1	1	2
Manzini	6	44	42	8	1	2
Shiselweni	3	33	8			
Total	17	118	101	27	13	30

Source: 2006 ECCD survey.

The proportions of public recurrent spending allocated to primary and to secondary education have increased over time, but not adequately to facilitate broad-based access to quality GET. For primary education, the proportion increased from 31 percent in 1991 to 35 percent in 2007. Arguably, this is still very low by world standards. On the other hand, the secondary education share rose from 27 percent in 1999 to 35 percent in 2007. However, a breakdown of these proportions shows that 25 percent is allocated to junior secondary education while less than 10 percent is allocated to senior secondary education. These figures will need to be substantially increased if Swaziland is to expand access to secondary education. As reflected in table 6.5, Teacher Education, TVETSD, and ABET account for negligible proportions of the sector's recurrent expenditure. In contrast, a significant 16 percent is allocated to higher education, against less than 2 percent of the total student population. Even when considering the high cost of services at this level, this seems disproportionately high.

Spending on administration has displayed a worrying upward trend in recent years, even after nonadministration items, such as OVC grants, are removed from the administration category (this irregular categorization in the official budgets is itself problematic). The proportion allocated to administration rose from 3.6 percent of total education spending in 2005, to 5.1 percent in 2009. Given the serious constraints in the government budget as a whole, this trend should be reversed. A further 2.0 percent of this allocation is accounted for by support services like curriculum development, library services and psychological services. Around 1.7 percent (around SZ25 million in 2008) is allocated to post-secondary scholarships for students who study abroad, mainly in South Africa.

Unit Cost

The unit costs presented in table 6.6 indicate that the sector has a skewed cost structure in favor of tertiary education and training. Moreover, the emerging cost structure points to unaffordably high costs of post-secondary education and training. The secondary education unit cost is 3 times that of primary education, when considering only public funding, and around 4 times that, when considering both public and private spending. By any standards, these differentials are too high. A rough estimate—due to data problems—is that per pupil spending on junior secondary schooling is 8 percentage points higher than at the upper secondary level. This is a bit uncommon since in most contexts, spending on senior secondary is higher than for junior secondary. As multiples of primary education, the unit cost for tertiary education levels are 18 for TVETSD, 22 for teacher education and 19 for higher education. Again these are disproportionately high by any comparison.

Intra-Subsector Allocation and Unit Cost

Early childhood care and development

ECCD in Swaziland is almost exclusively privately funded, yet as presented in Chapter 2, there are many compelling reasons for public investment at this level. At present, the government provides SZ4 per child per year, relative to an estimated SZ500 per child that is currently invested in ECCD privately. The arguments for increased investment in this level of the subsector are presented in Chapter 2.

Public spending on primary education

The government invests modestly in primary education, relative to its GDP per capita. Public revenue accounts for 87 percent of the total subsector revenue (see table 6.8). Government funding of staff and materials for primary schools comes to 84 percent, whilst the remaining 3 percent is made up of financial transfers paid directly to schools, the so-called OVC grants.

The "nonpersonnel recurrent" spending in table 6.7 includes free textbooks, exercise books and stationary for learners in all grades 1 to 7. This program started in 2002 and reached full coverage by 2007. The unit cost for these resources is about E189 per pupil, leaving a further E439 for spending on other nonpersonnel recurrent items. The latter almost exclusively comes out of the school fund. MoE records indicate that the single largest item covered by this E439 tends to be school lunches, which, in absence of a centrally-run school feeding program, are managed by schools.

Table 6.7: Financing Details for Primary Education (2007)

Financing per pupil by source	E	% of total
Public spending	2,349	87.2
Private spending (fees)	344	12.8
Total	2,693	100.0
Teacher cost details		
Teacher count (A)	6,741	
Average teacher pay (B)	67,547	
Enrollment (C)	224,000	
P/T ratio (D=C/A)	33.2	
Financing per pupil by category		
Teachers (B/D)	2,033	75.5
Nonteaching staff	0	0.0
Nonpersonnel recurrent	625	23.2
Capital expenditure	35	1.3
Public expenditure on pupil subsistence	0	0.0
Total	2,693	100.0

Source: Ministry of Finance, Ministry of Education.

Distinguishing features of the primary subsector financing include: a reasonable proportion of teacher costs (75 percent), no expenditure in nonteaching staff, and substantial private contributions to the revenues. All these features are rare in the subregion. Another distinguishing feature is the close to nonexistent-capital expenditure, which needs urgent attention.

Private spending on primary education

Private spending, derived mainly from fees, accounts for 13 to 14 percent[9] of the subsector revenue. The practice of allowing public institutions to charge fees, and then using public funds to substitute some or all of the fees charged—not necessarily for the poorest pupils, as will be seen in the post-secondary sectors—is a key feature of education financing in Swaziland.

Primary education unit cost

The combined private and public revenues translate into a unit cost of E2,693 which is much lower than in neighboring countries, but correlates with Swaziland's GDP per capita (figure 6.4). In general, public spending per primary pupil tends to be a fixed percentage of GDP per capita—around 15 to 20 percent. Swaziland is on the trendline, suggesting that spending per pupil is more or less what it should be given the level of GDP per capita.

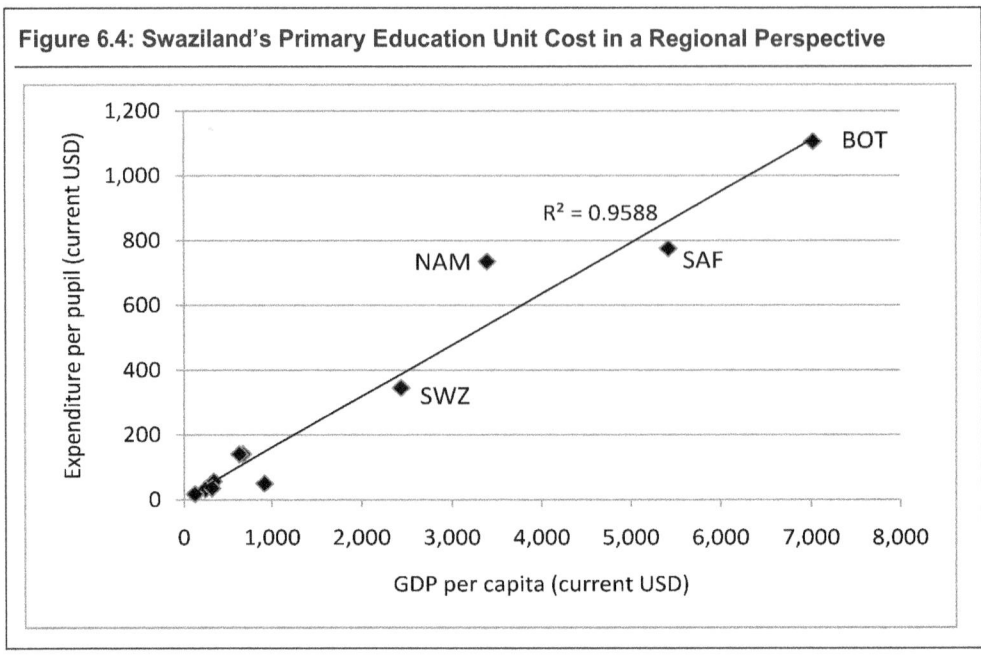

Figure 6.4: Swaziland's Primary Education Unit Cost in a Regional Perspective

Source: UNESCO: UIS, 2008. IMF, 2008.

Key issues in the financing of primary education

Primary education school fees are intolerably high, especially given the level of poverty in the country. Fees are higher than for neighbouring countries—Botswana, Namibia and South Africa—which have a larger middle-class base.[10] The average primary school fee is estimated to be SZ550 per year. Though it is difficult to obtain recent figures on household income, reportedly the lowest monthly wage in the formal sector is around SZ2,000 per month, and in the informal sector it could be as low as SZ300. Assuming one wage earner per pupil—most certainly far less than this for most households—the average fee, which is around E550 per year,[11] comes to around 22 percent of the annual earnings of the informal sector wage earner.

The high level of fees suggests that schools do not implement the policy on setting fees. The policy states that parents should have a deciding vote on the level of fees. However, in practice, head teachers are said to have considerable influence in setting the level of fees, especially in poor communities and where parents have low levels of education.

Recent GoS initiatives that ought to have lowered fees seem to not have had the desired impact. For many years, school fees were meant to cover all the nonpersonnel recurrent costs of the school. However, in recent years, the free textbooks scheme substantially increased public funding of nonpersonnel items. Between 2005 and 2007, the real or inflation-adjusted increase in the budget allocation for primary schools' 'consumable materials and supplies' was 22 percent. This should have resulted in a corresponding reduction in school fees, but generally this did not occur. The SZ344 and SZ625 values in table 6.8 indicate that currently, fees account for just under half of nonpersonnel recurrent spending in public primary schools.

The provision of OVC grants also seems to not have lowered fees. If anything, nonOVC children are subsidizing OVC. In 2007, the government contributed E250 per OVC pupil. There were around 70,000 OVCs pupils, which means that 30 percent of all enrolled learners were recipients of this funding. However, the grant was just under half of the average school fee charged, though this is at an aggregate level.[12] It is tacitly accepted that schools should not charge OVCs any fees. Thus, the effect in most schools is that non-OVC pupils subsidize OVC pupils. On average, E129 of the E550 school fee per non-OVC goes towards subsidizing OVC pupils.

Anecdotal evidence points to significant and common irregularities with the management and use of school fees and the OVCs grants—the latter paid directly into the school bank account. Parents are often not aware of how money is spent. The MoE does not regularly audit school accounts and finances, supposedly because of a shortage of auditors to perform this task on an annual basis. In some schools, proper auditing only occurs when the head teacher retires. Policy allows the employer to deduct money from the head teacher's pension account to compensate for missing funds, and it is common for the head teacher's retirement to be accompanied by an audit. This is clearly inadequate.

Public contribution to the capital expenditure on primary education is remarkably low, accounting for 1 percent of total spending. Communities are expected to raise funds for new construction and for maintenance. Therefore, households could contribute more than the fees reflected in table 6.7. Data on these contributions are scant. Most schools earmark a portion of the fees to a special capital investment fund. From the school budget details collected by the MoE, this allocation ranges between E50 and E100 per pupil. The MoE's approach has been to prioritize increasing public funding for nonpersonnel recurrent items, as opposed to capital items. Arguably, this practice exacerbates the financial burden for education on households.

Public spending on secondary education

As a proportion of the subsector revenues, the public spends less on secondary than on primary education (table 6.8). Public spending accounts for 74 percent of total revenue. Public subsidies for the poor account for 7 percent of total revenue. Around 40 percent of students (approximately 30,000) receive an average subsidy of E1,500.

Highlights of spending patterns on secondary education

Teacher salaries account for a remarkably low 59 percent of total spending and equally remarkable is that nonpersonnel costs amount to 34 percent of total spending. The high expenditure on nonpersonnel items is made possible by high fees. For instance, nonpersonnel spending exceeds fee income by a small margin, which reflects some MoE spending on items such as office stationery for schools (see table 6.8). These are rare proportions by any comparison.

As with primary education, capital spending is very low—6 percent. Even further, the 6 percent was exceptional for 2007. For most years, the allocation has been between 1 and 2 percent.

Table 6.8: Financing Details for Secondary Schools (2007)

	E	% of total
Financing per pupil by source		
Public spending	6,895	74.4
Private spending (fees)	2,376	25.6
Total	9,271	100.0
Teacher cost details		
Teacher count (A)	4,146	
Average teacher pay (B)	97,471	
Enrollment (C)	74,429	
P/T ratio (D=C/A)	18.0	
Financing per pupil by category		
Teachers (B/D)	5,430	58.6
Nonteaching staff	86	0.9
Nonpersonnel recurrent	3,155	34.0
Capital expenditure	600	6.5
Public expenditure on pupil subsistence	0	0.0
Total	9,271	100.0

Source: Ministry of Finance, Ministry of Education.

Private spending on secondary education

Private spending on public secondary education is not only very high, but it also accounts for a high proportion of overall secondary school revenue (ext. 26 to 30%).

Secondary education unit cost

Due mainly to low STR, public spending on junior secondary education is higher (E7,045) than for the senior level (E6,541). However, changes in STR proposed in Chapter 3 should help drive down these unit costs. Due to data limitations, it is difficult to gauge exactly how secondary school teachers are deployed across the two levels. Therefore our cost estimates assumed that teacher utilization was more or less the same for junior and senior secondary schools.

As with primary education, the secondary education unit cost seems to be in line with Swaziland's GDP per capita (figure 6.5).[13] However, it is likely that a regional comparison that included both public and private funding of public schools would place Swaziland at an exceptionally high spending level.

Figure 6.5: Secondary Education Unit Cost in a Regional Context

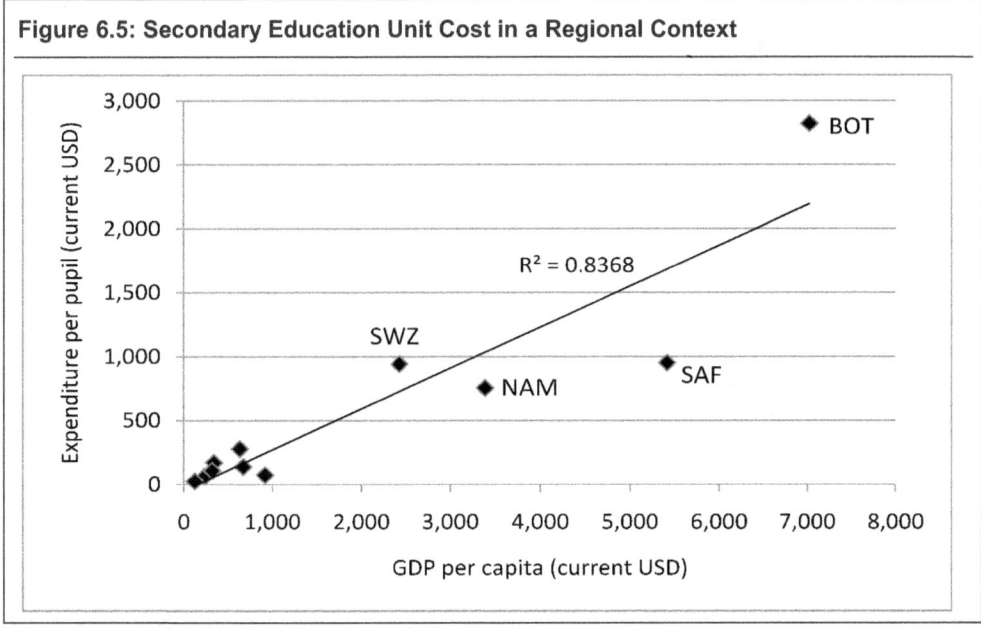

Source: UNESCO: UIS (2008) and IMF (2008).

Key issues in the financing of secondary education

The average fee for a public secondary school is estimated to be a total of E3,300, and E2,270 when excluding OVC grants. Again, this is exceedingly high for Swazis. Even many nonpoor households would find secondary school fees, which can reach E8,000 in urban areas, high. In South Africa, for instance, the average fees are about R820 (2006 est.). Even students who are eligible for subsidies must pay fees because the subsidy is inadequate to cover the full fee amount. Therefore, unlike in primary education the principle that subsidization of OVC students is taken as an adequate substitute for such fees, does not apply. The low STR distorts the unit cost with the lower secondary cost being higher than for senior secondary.

For the huge levels of private contributions, it was not possible to obtain details on what fee income in secondary schools is spent on—at least not to the degree that was possible for primary schools. Poor school financial management practices are blamed. Moreover, there are suspicions that a substantial amount of funding simply disappears.

Surprisingly, given the high level of nonpersonnel spending, the general impression is that secondary schools are less than modestly resourced. This is evident in physical facilities, maintenance, media centers, stationery and so on.

Capital investment is similarly as low as in primary education and therefore similar consequences would accrue to this level as well.

Public spending on tertiary education and training

This section deals exclusively with public tertiary education and training as provided in TVETSD institutions, VOCTIM, SCOT, and two teacher training colleges.[14] The four public institutions treated below account for about 18 percent of public post-secondary spending (see table 6.9).

Table 6.9: Financing Details for TVETSD—SCOT and VOCTIM (2007)

	E	% of total
Financing per pupil by source		
Public spending	42,376	91.4
Private spending (fees)	3,963	8.6
Total	46,338	100.0
Teacher cost details		
Teacher count (A)	100	
Average teacher pay (B)	116,240	
Enrollment (C)	672	
P/T ratio (D=C/A)	6.7	
Financing per pupil by category		
Teachers (B/D)	17,298	37.3
Nonteaching staff	6,331	13.7
Nonpersonnel recurrent	15,508	33.5
Capital expenditure	0	0.0
Public expenditure on pupil subsistence	7,203	15.5
Total	46,338	100.0

Source: Ministry of Finance, Ministry of Education.

Vocational and Commercial Training Institute Matsapa (VOCTIM)

VOCTIM fits Swaziland's overall pattern of exceedingly high fees. Average annual tuition is about E7,000, and E16,000 when inclusive of subsistence items and boarding. Trainees do not receive public subsidies. About a third of the trainees who had not completed grade 12 provide for their subsistence privately[15] and this makes the analysis of real costs and allocations difficult. Unit cost is also high. Regular state funding is five times what it is in secondary schools—on a per capita basis—and fees are three times as high. High-expenditure unit cost is evidenced in very high nonpersonnel recurrent spending of E9,116 per student, and an extremely low STR of 5.9:1. As presented in Chapter 4, this pattern is partly the result of the fact that enrollment declined by about a third between 2002 and 2007, whilst funding remained more or less unchanged. In its current state, VOCTIM seems unsustainable. To become sustainable, unit cost must be driven down by a combination of increased enrollment and STR.

Swaziland College of Technology (SCOT)

Unlike VOCTIM, SCOT trainees receive a 50 percent subsidy and they are to compliment it with a 50 percent government loan offered at a 5 percent fixed interest rate. The combined package is referred to as a scholarship. Scholarships apply to the rest of post-secondary institutions, including the private teacher training college. It would, therefore, appear that scholarships are used as an incentive for learners to complete senior secondary school. Recipients of scholarships get about 15 percent of the money as a cash subsistence allowance. Across all institutions, revenues from repayments accounted for only about 8 percent of the total spending. Given the negligible repayment levels, the tables in this report reflect the whole amount of the scholarship and, therefore, ignore the repayment rate.

The average scholarship for SCOT is E12,664 per year. However this differs across trainees. About 30 percent are part-time students, and do not receive the part of the scholarship corresponding to subsistence. About 10 percent have not completed Grade 12 and are studying for qualifications below a diploma level. They too do not receive scholarships. In addition to note receiving the subsistence allowance, they pay full fees.

In real terms, SCOT may regularly receive less revenue than reflected in the official figures due to a reported "top-slicing" of funds officially earmarked for SCOT by the MoE. This phenomenon is not said to be corrupt or illegal, but is rather administrative. It was not possible to ascertain the exact extent of this, but it appears to be limited to nonpersonnel funding. However, even if a large portion of funds do not reach SCOT, this would not change the conclusion that per student funding at SCOT is remarkably high.

Table 6.10 presents statistics for the two public teacher training colleges whose profile is similar to that of SCOT.

Table 6.10: Financing Details for Public Teacher Education (2007)

	E	% of total
Financing per pupil by source		
Public spending*	44,667	100.0
Private spending (fees)	0	0.0
Total	44,667	100.0
Teacher cost details		
Teacher count (A)	95	
Average teacher pay (B)	106,012	
Enrollment (C)	632	
P/T ratio (D=C/A)	6.7	
Financing per pupil by category		
Teachers (B/D)	15,935	35.7
Nonteaching staff	6,051	13.5
Nonpersonnel recurrent	14,545	32.6
Capital expenditure	0	0.0
Public expenditure on pupil subsistence	8,135	18.2
Total	44,667	100.0

Source: Ministry of Finance, Ministry of Education.
* This table covers the funding of the two public teacher training colleges only, so figures here would differ slightly from those covering all three colleges.

Key issues in the financing of tertiary education and training

This subsector equally reflects excessive fees and high unit cost. In addition, scholarships or lack thereof are set at the same level regardless of students' SES. This unduly benefits the rich who happen to dominate at this level. The loan repayment scheme is not enforced, perhaps staying true to its label of "scholarship." Despite their advantaged backgrounds, students are not expected to pay upfront fees through private means. This is an inequitable use of public resources, especially against the generally high private returns of post-secondary education and training. The punitive approach to students who have not completed grade 12 is unjustifiable especially in a country that could use more skills than it produces. Financial management of public institutions is highly centralized. This has become a serious disincentive for institutions that could have raised their own revenues.

Financing higher education

Overall, the average unit cost of UNISWA is E44,769—but without taking into account the 8 percent loan repayment. For the nearly 4,000 full-time students the unit cost is estimated at E53,000. For the approximately 1,600 part-time students it is around E25,000. Students enrolled at the IDE therefore cost half the full time student. Their lower cost is mainly attributable to their reduced usage of institutional resources and to the fact that they do not receive subsistence allowances.

By virtue of the tuition charged, IDE student subsidize full-time students. The average tuition fees for IDE students are around E5,500, against E8,500 for full-time students. Therefore, IDE students pay 0.65 what full-time students pay even though they cost 0.50 of a full time student's cost. Yet the cost of educating an IDE student is about half of the cost of educating a full-time student. Thus the widespread perception that IDE students are subsidizing full-time students is not unfounded—though ultimately almost all the funding comes from the government.

Table 6.11 provides an overview of the allocation of resources in UNISWA.

Table 6.11: Financing Details for the University (2007)

	E	% of total
Financing per pupil by source		
Public spending	44,769	98.1
Private funding	872	1.9
Total	**45,641**	**100.0**
Teacher cost details		
Teacher count (A)	335	
Average teacher pay (B)	333,567	
Enrollment (C)	5,445	
P/T ratio (D=C/A)	16.3	
Financing per pupil by category		
Teachers (B/D)	20,502	44.9
Nonteaching staff	9,204	20.2
Nonpersonnel recurrent	5,216	11.4
Capital expenditure	521	1.1
Public expenditure on pupil subsistence	10,198	22.3
Total	**45,641**	**100.0**

Source: Ministry of Finance, Ministry of Education.

Regardless of which figure one uses, total annual spending per university student in Swaziland appears to be high. In South Africa, total public higher education funding, including the net public cost of the country's student loan system is around E20,000. Figure 6.6 shows the unit cost in selected SACU countries.

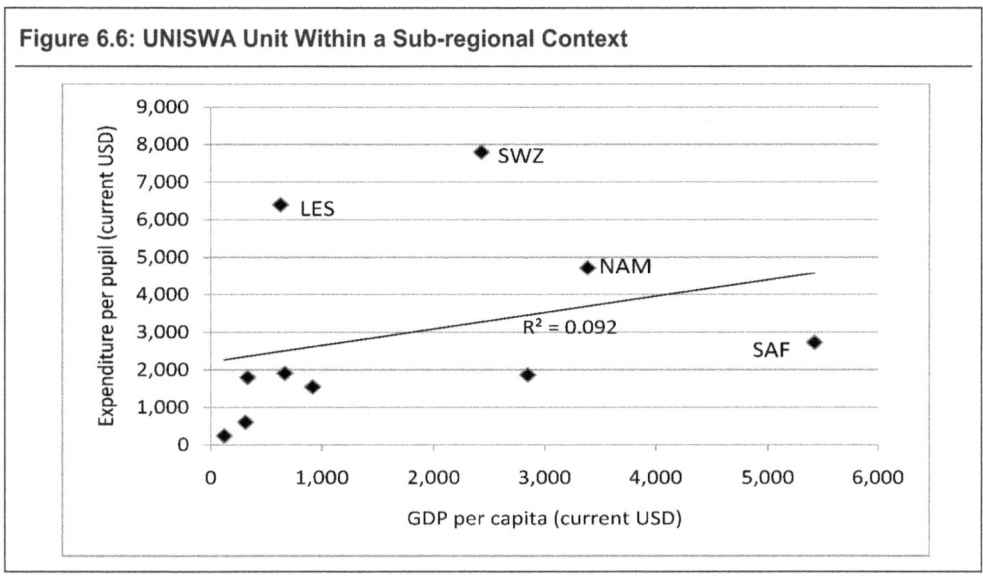

Figure 6.6: UNISWA Unit Within a Sub-regional Context

Source: UNESCO: UIS (2008) and IMF (2008).
Note: Botswana was left out as its expenditure per pupil value, at around US$30,000, seems to be incorrect.

The fact that Swaziland is a small country raises the possibility that diseconomies of scale could explain the exceptionally high unit cost. However, this explanation does not hold when Swaziland is compared to Lesotho and Namibia. In addition, the correlation between per student funding at the university level and population, for countries with a population of less than 15 million, is effectively zero, whereas a negative correlation would have been expected if economies of scale had existed (figure 6.7).

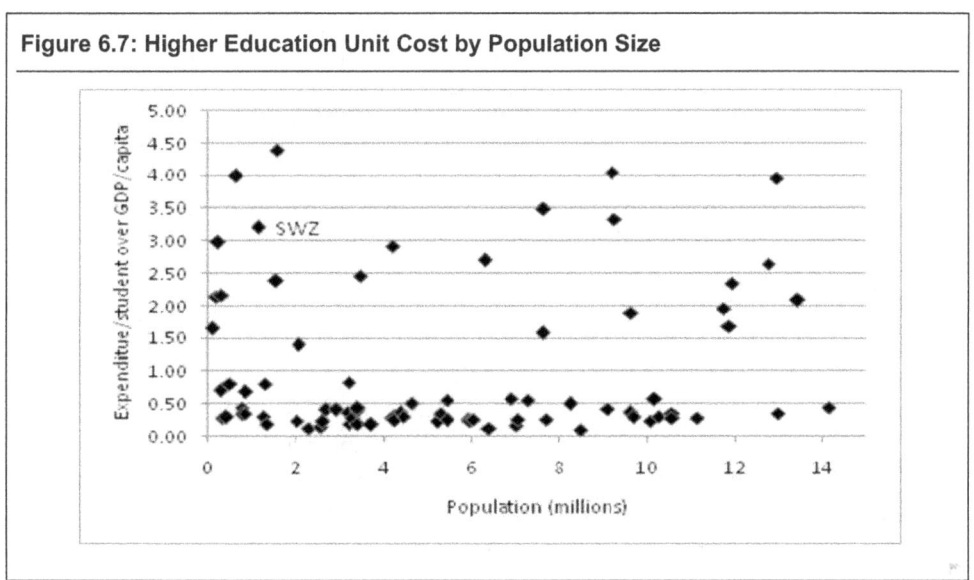

Figure 6.7: Higher Education Unit Cost by Population Size

Source: UNESCO: UIS (2008) and IMF (2008).

Key issues in the financing of higher education

Relative to the proportion of students (less than 2 percent) university education accounts for a disproportionately high percentage of the sector budget (16 percent).

Furthermore, student subsistence allowances for accommodation and meals are a critical cost driver, accounting for nearly 23 percent of public spending (table 6.11). Given that the bulk of university students come from affluent households, a full public subsidy for their subsistence over and above the technically full subsidy for their tuition hardly seems consistent with the equity and shared growth principles of Vision 2022 and the PRSAP. This is more so in a country where nearly 80 percent of the population lives on less than US$2 per day, where many children do not have access to basic education, let alone the benefit of school feeding programs.

The unit cost is too high and needs to be aligned with those of countries of comparable income and population size. Diverse mechanisms should be used to drive down the unit cost including the introduction of competition through private universities.

Private funding of higher education accounts for a low 2 percent of total revenues even when taking corporate donations into account (table 6.11). This is very low, particularly when juxtaposed with the substantial private financing of GET. There seems to be much room for improvement. In South Africa universities' income from 'private gifts and grants' has historically come to around 4 percent of total revenue.[16]

The nonpersonnel recurrent spending amount which appears low—in absolute per student terms—is lower than for any of the colleges.

Average staff costs appear high in comparison to South Africa, which effectively shares the same labor market. Given that staff unit costs are difficult to reduce without losing qualified staff, reductions in the total cost would need to occur through raising STRs. In Chapter 5, we showed that there are small subject offerings whose resource-intensity is not justified by their labor market relevance or importance to the country's development strategy.

The cost per graduate is too high partly because of the long duration of programs and the lack of vertical articulation of programs. Given the quality of students at entry, most of the university 4 and 5 year programs could be reduced by a year. Because of poor articulation of programs people with certificate and/or diplomas have to re-start their studies from year 1 if they should want to acquire degrees. This works out to an unjustifiable 7 to 8 years of an undergraduate degree program—refer to Chapter 5.

Equity of Public Spending

Resources allocated to the sector disproportionately benefit the rich except at the primary level (see figure 6.8). Given the high private returns to post-basic education and training, this pattern runs contrary to the goals of the PRSAP to reduce social inequalities and to empower the poor to gain sustainable income.

Overall, the poorest 40 percent of the population receive only 31 percent of public spending on education, while the richest 20 percent receives 32 percent. The spending ratio per member of the population for these two groups is thus more than 2 to 1 in favor of the richer group. The richest 20 percent of the population receives 16 percent of spending on primary education and this is progressive. In contrast, they receive 28 percent of spending on secondary education which is well above their share and an enormous 68 percent of spending on tertiary education and training (figure 6.8) where close to 70 percent of students come from the richest quintile.

Ironically, the proportion of public spending is lower precisely at the lower levels of the system where the poor have most access.

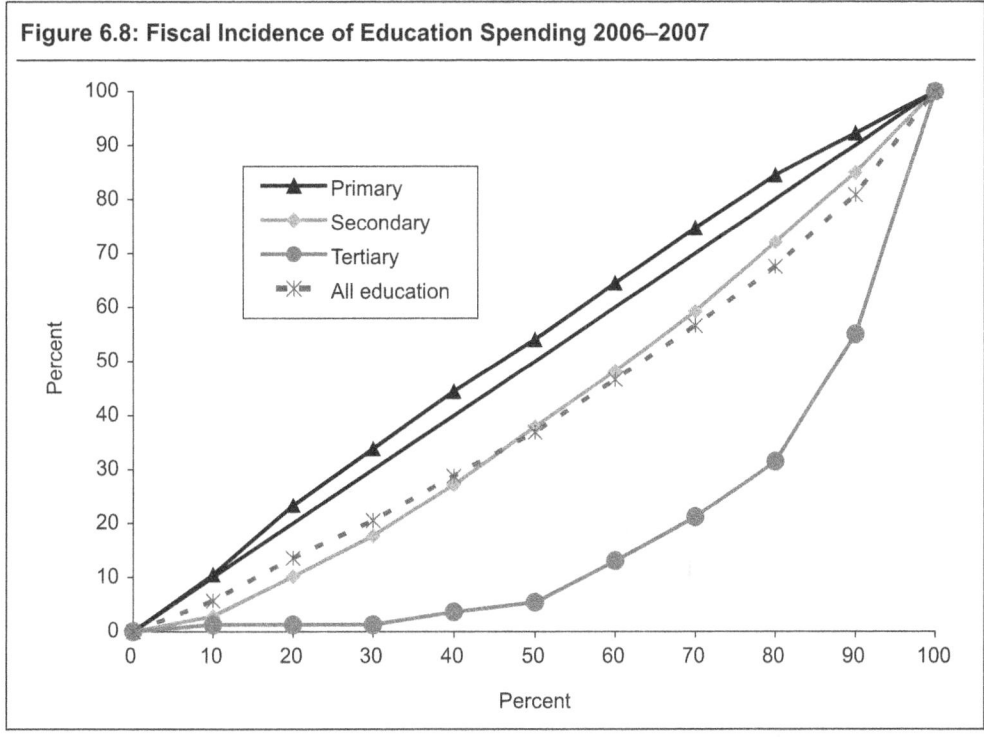

Source: Own calculations from MoE data and CSO (2008).

Despite the unfavorable benefit incidence picture, it is noteworthy that within the primary schooling level, the only level for which we have internationally comparable educational performance data, Swaziland has been relatively successful in containing inequality in educational quality. Though poorer pupils perform worse than richer pupils in reading and mathematics, the gap is smaller than in many other countries within the region. Therefore, young Swazis do not experience an exceptionally unequal education system, at least not at the primary level. However, as one moves up the levels of the system, it becomes increasingly unequal, largely due to unequal access to public education. This results in an overall picture of inequality that is worse in Swaziland than in comparable countries. Clearly policies to bring about greater equity need to concentrate on the secondary and tertiary levels.

Conclusion

Overall Swaziland invests just slightly little above the UNESCO norm for a developing country. About 7 percent of GDP and 20 percent of the TGE are allocated to the sector. This level of investment is adequate for the current ETSDS. However, the proposed sector reforms will, at least in the immediate to medium term, demand more resources than currently invested. Given the already high proportion of government investment in the sector, required additional resources would have to come from a combination of efficiency and external grant financing.

Public spending almost totally excludes ECCD. Though increased over time, the shares of primary and secondary education are too low to facilitate broad based access to quality GET. Public spending disproportionately favors the tertiary level of the system which is dominated by the rich. At the same time, the tertiary level is resource inefficient. The overall cost and the unit cost of tertiary education is unjustifiably high. The latter is due mainly to the decline in enrollment and the consequent low STRs. Stringent efficiency measures are required to release the funds much required to open pro-poor access to tertiary education and training.

Private contributions to ECCD and to GET are unsustainably and unjustifiably high. In contrast, there is little to no private contribution to tertiary education and training, except for students who enter without having completed grade 12. The punitive approach to entrants who have not completed grade 12 is inexplicable and hardly just.

Despite their potential to raise funds, tertiary education and training institutions are over-dependent on the government for their financing. For TVETSD institutions some of the disincentive to raise part of their revenue is their over-centralized management, including the management of their finances. The Government seems to not have endorsed a payroll levy that could have helped to finance TVETSD. In addition, the Government seems to have terminated or suspended tax breaks that enterprises used to receive for training their employees.

Relative to countries of comparable income and of comparable governance ratings, Swaziland has a striking dearth of international partners for sector development. All these factors put the burden for financing the sector almost solely on the government.

Public funding of education disproportionately benefits the rich, except at the primary level.

All said, Swaziland will need substantial resources to finance sector reforms that will enable it to strengthen its human capital development as proposed in this report and in line with the PRSAP. Diversification of funding sources and improved resource efficiency will be critical for implementing proposed sector reforms.

Notes

[1] Ministry of Economic Planning and Development. 2006.
[2] Other sources of pressure come from growing needs in the social sectors (health, education, social welfare) exacerbated by poverty and HIV/AIDS.
[3] Ministry of Economic Planning and Development. 2006.
[4] The countries are: Swaziland, South Africa, Lesotho, Botswana, Namibia, Angola, Mozambique, Zimbabwe, Zambia, Malawi, Tanzania, Kenya and Uganda. These are the continental SACMEQ countries, with the addition of Angola. Moreover, the group includes all continental SADC countries with the exception of the Democratic Republic of Congo (for which education statistics are particularly unreliable).
[5] See for instance Mingat and Tan (1998).
[6] Due to inconsistencies in data sources, these estimates vary in other parts of this report. Data reconciliation is still ongoing.

[7] Analysis of South Africa's 2005 Income and Expenditure Survey.
2006 ECCD survey. NB: The average fee is likely to be skewed because of the inclusion of a few schools which charge high fees.
[9] The exact percentage could not be estimated due to data inconsistencies that are still being investigated.
[10] In 2006, South Africa instituted a policy of no-fee-schools that effectively covers schools serving the poorest 40 percent of learners. This is an instructive policy that Swaziland may want to consider. Even before the policy, in 2005, the mean primary school fee per pupil in South Africa came to R477, but the median came to only R50 (own analysis of South Africa, 2006). Given that high fees in middle class schools in South Africa push the mean up, and given that the South African middle class is proportionally larger than the Swaziland one, the relevant comparison to the Swaziland mean would be somewhere between the R477 and R50 values. Fees at the primary level are therefore undoubtedly higher than they are (or were up to 2006) in South Africa.
[11] The difference between the E550 amount and the E344 figure in table 6.7 is due to the fact that fees are generally not collected from OVC grant recipients.
[12] There are considerable differences between schools with regard to the fee charged, and reliable statistics are not available.
[13] NB: The USD figure of just less than 1,000 obtained for Swaziland from UIS data tallies well with the E6895 public revenue per pupil value in table 6.9.
[14] The private teacher training college—Nazarene—was however included in the overall sector financing (table 6.7).
[15] As a matter of practice all tertiary education and training students who have not completed grade 12 do not receive government scholarships.
[16] See http://www.education.gov.za/dynamic/imgshow.aspx?id=1149 for details.

CHAPTER 7

Conclusions and Recommendations

Introduction

This chapter summarizes key findings and recommendations from the above presented analysis of the adequacy of Swaziland's ETSDS to effectively support growth acceleration, social equity, and global competitiveness as envisaged in Vision 2022, NDS, and the PRSAP. For its broad framework, the analysis was guided by modern economic growth theory which identifies human capital/skills, technology absorptive capacity/innovation, and investment climate to be equally as important determinants of growth as labor and capital. Therefore, a key question addressed in the analysis was whether the current ETSDS can effectively supply the human capital/skills required to complement the current technology and investment climate in facilitating self-sustaining growth. Human capital here is narrowly conceived to mean educated, trained and skilled labor.

For an answer to the reverse question of whether Swaziland's investment climate and its technology readiness can adequately complement skills in spurring growth acceleration, we relied on findings of recent World Bank supported ICA (2007), the results from the WBI's 2009 Knowledge Assessment Methodology (KAM), and the 2009 WEF's ranking of countries' global competitiveness.

The analysis covered all levels of the ETSDS from ECCD to HE and also included cross-sectoral issues of cost and financing, HIV/AIDS and ICTs. It also covered the formal and nonformal sectors. The informal sector was only marginally covered in terms of the recognition of prior learning (RPL) through TVETSD trade tests. For a more specific analytical framework, each subsector was analyzed for the adequacy of its access, quality, equity, relevance, efficiency, and delivery capacity.

Strategic Orientation

Other than key national development reform documents—Vision 2022, NDS and the PRSAP—the analysis was strategically oriented by two key premises. The first is that Swaziland's growth acceleration is most likely to be knowledge driven not only because globally, knowledge is a key driver of growth, but also because Swaziland has limited natural resources. Its critical resource is therefore its human capital. Therefore, for Swaziland, an effective growth strategy has to necessarily entail intensive human capital development.

The second premise is that because of limited internal sources of growth, Swaziland's growth strategy has to entail a deliberate harvesting of opportunities provided by its immediate sub-region—mostly but not exclusively SADC countries. From the point of view of human capital, a key sub-regional opportunity that could play to Swaziland's advantage is that it is immediately surrounded by fast growing— safe for the current global economic downturn—natural resource-rich countries with acute skills shortage. Therefore, Swaziland may consider strategically orienting its ETSDS toward the export of skills. The short-term benefits will be remittances and the deepening of the capacities of exported skills. Long-term benefits will the brain circulation required to lead the country's transformation into a knowledge and technology-driven economy.

Conclusions

Weak policy and strategic direction

The development of the sector is guided by a dated policy (1999,) which no longer reflects current development thinking in Swaziland or globally. Though it has notable areas of strength and currency, the policy is no longer sufficient to guide the transformation of the sector into an effective tool that supports the national development reform agenda.

Key sector challenges and/or emerging issues have also been managed without much policy guidance and this has in most cases led to inadequate responses to the issues. Examples are ICTs in education, HIV/AIDS, and education, the provision of books and instructional materials and subsectors like ECCD, HE, TVETSD, and ABET.

The legal framework for the sector is even more dated; going back to 1983 and generally weak. Emerging legal issues in the public sector have tended to be handled through incoherent instruments such as office circulars. Private provision of ETSDS services is almost completely unregulated, especially for ECCD, GET, and TVETSD.

Other than the dated policy, the sector has been operated without a strategic framework that is well-anchored in the overall national development reform strategy and that is periodically updated as development challenges change. Without a well articulated and nationally-owned sector strategy, the sector has often been left without a clear direction on the key development challenges it ought to be responding to. The sector has also been left vulnerable to convenient criticism of not being responsive, when the 'context' to which it should respond has remained undefined.

The weak sector policy and lack of strategic plan has led to ad hoc sector development with little to no estimates of long-term cost implications, affordability, and sustainability of evolving developments. The lack of strategy has also left the sector at risk of contradictory tacit policies and unbalanced development.

The sector has also operated without a national human resources development strategy that, in the immediate term, could have guided the types and number of expected outputs. The human resources development strategy (HRDS) which is currently under development by MoPSI should be finalized and applied as part of the strategic direction for the sector.

Fragmented management

The management of the sector has mostly been fragmented with subsectors, and even parts of single subsectors operating as 'loosely coupled' entities rather than a system. The un-systemic approach to the management of the sector is best manifest in the lack of vertical articulation across subsectors and, the weak horizontal articulation within and across subsectors. Poor articulation has translated into limited pathways and excessively expensive upward movement within the sector. The fragmentation is also evident in the lack of coordination across diverse stakeholders and service providers, even public service providers with TVETSD and ECCD being the worst of the cases.

Weak capacity for information management

Swaziland's education information management is just too inaccurate, unreliable, untimely, and too limited in coverage to support sector analysis, planning for sector development, monitoring, evaluation and impact assessments. In addition, there is limited analytical capacity required to transform data and information into core inputs for policy decisions, strategic planning, effective monitoring and evaluation, and impact assessment.

Limited external financing base for the sector

Swaziland seems to have limited capacity to mobilize external resources for sector development. The dearth of international development partners in the sector is striking, especially when compared to countries of more resources and/or comparable governance issues.

Tertiary institutions that should be able to raise their own funds and alleviate the financing burden on the government are not fully exploiting their potential. For instance, own source revenues account for 2 percent of the university revenues. The current financing of higher education does not enable the university to collect up-front fees from students who are able to pay. In addition, the repayment of tertiary student loans is a low 8 percent. Because of the low interest rate of the student loans (5%) and clear prospects of nonpayment, families that could afford commercial loans for their children's tertiary education have no incentive to secure such loans. Due to over-centralized management and control, including financial control, SCOT and VOCTIM seem to have lost the incentive to raise funds. The end result is that the Government has to almost solely bare the financing burden of TVETSD and of tertiary education.

The government does not seem to have exploited opportunities for external financing of the sector. A payroll levy that could have been applied to reduce the government's financing burden for TVETSD has not been endorsed. Tax breaks that employers used to receive for training their employees seem to be 'suspended or terminated.' Employers have cited this as a disincentive for training. This further reduces external financing sources for the sector.

Weak sector budget structure

The current budget structure cannot support effective monitoring of spending. Spending categories are not always clear. Examples include the integration of OVC grants into the administration costs, the merging of ABET and TVETSD budgets, and the separation of scholarships from their respective subsectors. For instance, university scholarships are not itemized under university-related budget items. The budget structure is also skewed toward tertiary levels of the sector.

Mixed and pro-rich quality

Relative to SACU countries, Swaziland stands out as having a much better quality of GET as evident in its performance on SACMEQ II. Swazi learners also perform very well on national primary school leaving examinations, international end- of-secondary school examinations, international TVETSD examinations such as Pittman, City and Guilds, and the UK-ACCA examinations. Pass rates at tertiary institutions are also impressively high. However, we strongly hold that high pass rates at the secondary and tertiary levels are helped by the stringent selectivity and exclusivity of the system that does not effectively support children of the poor as they try to climb the ETSD ladder. By the university level, 70 percent of those retained in the system come from the highest income quintile. Even at the lower levels, learners of high SES fair better than their counterparts. If resource inputs are anything to go by, ECCD services are of better quality for high income children. As shown in Chapter 3, SES is significantly associated with performance on SACMEQ tests. Beyond the overall pass rates, learning outcomes for mathematics, science and siSwati are very low. The high repetition rates within GET cast further doubts on the teaching and learning effectiveness and therefore the quality of education. The lack of standards for both GET and TVETSD also makes it difficult to assert the level of quality as well as to absolutely and relatively benchmark it. All the same, Swaziland has built a formal ETSD system of a quality that provides a solid base for future sector improvements. This cannot be said for SACU MICs.

Limited access

Current levels of access are severely inadequate to supply Swaziland with the skills required to complement the current technology and investment climate in spurring self-sustaining and knowledge driven growth. Access is limited at all levels of the sector and is most severely so for ECCD, secondary education, TVETSD and HE. Only 35 percent of children of eligible ECCD age are enrolled in centers. Even then, most of these centers offer partial aspects of what ought to be a full ECCD program. Sixteen percent of children of primary school age are not enrolled in primary education. A staggering 74 percent and 88 percent of children of eligible age are not enrolled in junior secondary and senior secondary schools respectively. As shown in Chapter 3, the nonformal sector enrolls a limited numbers of children who are out of formal schools. In 2007, an estimated 480 were enrolled in NUPE. In 2008, about 320 and 380 were enrolled in junior secondary and senior secondary nonformal programs respectively. About 7 percent of school leavers gain access TVETSD. A range of platforms offer TVETSD to youth and adults but these are without standards and are unregulated. In 2006, about 560 were in nonformal TVETSD. An additional 600 to 800 were involved in some form of informal training and presented themselves for RPL through trade tests. Enterprises trained 27 percent of their unskilled workers. About 2501 trainees were enrolled in unregulated private training institutions mostly focusing on commercial training for which there is limited market demand. HE NER is estimated at 2.6 percent. GER is about 4 percent and about 5 percent when considering study abroad (2007 est.).

For households, and for the government, the cost of education, training and skills development services is a primary constraint to broadening access. Primary school fees alone account for nearly 22 percent of the income of poor households. About 14 percent of primary education expenditures and 30 percent of secondary education expenditure are contributed by households. These are unprecedented proportions, especially for a country where 80 percent of the population lives on less than US$2 per day! High fees are among the key determinants for children dropping out of school and further reducing access. For the government, the unit cost for all forms of tertiary education and training are too high and these limit the number of scholarships the Government can afford to give. For secondary education, the limited physical capacity of the system translates into low access. Limited capacity also translates into unbearably long distances that GET learners have to walk to school, some averaging 17 kilometers. Such long distance may encourage learner tardiness, truancy and dropping out. Access is also limited for learners with disabilities.

Resource inefficiency

For different reasons and along different dimensions, all levels of the ETSDS are resource-inefficient and this limits the resources the Government could use to broaden access and deepen quality. For ECCD, TVETSD and HE, the underutilization of existing physical capacity is a key source of resource inefficiency. For the latter two levels, underutilization results from the limited government scholarships, which translate into low intake, underutilization of all physical resources, low STR, high unit cost and the consequent resource inefficiency. The extended duration of most university programs and the consequent resource implications seem unjustified given the student quality at entry. Poor vertical articulation of curricula/programs across the ETSDS overextends the duration of upgrading programs, further draining scarce resources. This easily costs the Government and households 75 percent more to produce each upgrading graduate. The current 8 percent repayment of tertiary student loans adds to the cost of the system and resource wastage. For GET, high repetition rates, high year-input per graduate and broad curricula—including prevocational and practical subjects—are a drain in resources.

It is worth noting that some internal efficiency indicators at the tertiary level are very good. Repetition and dropout rates are remarkably low, especially when compared to South Africa and Namibia for instance. Equally impressive are progression and completion rates. Maintaining these good aspects of the system while opening access for those who are currently excluded, would be a laudable achievement for Swaziland.

Inequity of access, inputs, and outcomes

On diverse fronts, the system is chronically inequitable and this renders it an ineffective tool for redistributing income and facilitating social equity as intended in the PRSAP. If anything, the current system reproduces and cements current social inequalities.

People of high SES have a better chance of access to quality ETSD. They have better ECCD and GET services, better access to TVETSD, and they dominate participation in HE.

Rural dwellers have limited access to ETSD. Children of urban and more affluent families have better access to virtually all levels of the ETSDS but more so for ECCD and HE. All formal TVETSD institutions are in urban centers and this gives urban dwellers easier access than their rural counterparts. UNISWA's campuses are also mostly in urban and/or peri-urban centers. The nonformal second chance opportunities for GET cater mainly to urban dwellers by virtue of their location. Rural dwellers tend to have access to lower levels of TVETSD. This situation does not bode well for the PRSAP efforts to bridge income and social inequalities between urban and rural areas.

Adult learners have limited pathways to GET, to upgrade their skills, and to re-tool themselves for emerging opportunities. Adults may not use the nonformal pathway to attain a primary school certificate. Without this certificate, it is difficult for them to progress through the GET levels. TVETSD programs mainly target pre-employment trainees and thus leave out adults who could have benefited from them. The programs are mainly of long duration and this constitutes a disincentive for adults to up-skill or to gain new skills. Similarly, tertiary institutions have very limited short-term courses that would benefit adults. The limited opportunities for just-in-time short-term courses restrict Swaziland's agility to respond to unexpected opportunities such as those provided by FDIs and by labor market changes.

Learning outcomes are also better for learners of high SES. Logically, they have better levels of educational attainment. This is most evident in the distribution of GET learning outcomes and in the predominance of high SES learners in the higher levels of the system.

Quality-enhancing resource inputs are concentrated in urban centers where a larger proportion of children are from more affluent families. This is most evident in the resourcing of ECCD centers and in the deployment of qualified GET teachers.

Public spending disproportionately benefits the rich except at the primary level. The top quintile receives 28 percent of public subsidies to secondary education and 68 percent of subsidies to higher education. These inequities are even more stark when considering that 70 percent of university students come from the richest quintile.

Private or households contributions to the sector are highest at the GET where the bulk of the poor participate and virtually nonexistent at the tertiary level which is dominated by the rich.

Doubtful relevance

Due mainly to poor vertical articulation, the system has low internal relevance. Lower levels seem to not be able to effectively prepare learners for subsequent levels. High GET repetition rates suggest that learners enter this level without the requisite readiness to learn. This is due mainly to the poor access to "quality" ECCD programs even for the 35 percent of children who are enrolled. This is also evident when tertiary institutions insist that upgrading students re-start programs of studies from scratch. It is also clear in the limited pathways within and across subsectors and between the formal and the nonformal systems.

The combined lack of national and sub-regional labor market information, tracer studies, and national human resources development strategy leaves the system with limited cues on the types of outputs it must supply. Tertiary-level courses seem to be determined by the availability of resources such as teachers and facilities rather than by the market demand. The tertiary system seems to not have established mechanisms for staying in tune with and responding to the needs of their immediate communities, industry and to the overall national development challenges. Mechanisms for involving stakeholders in determining programs of study and research programs are weak and most key stakeholders have little opportunity for inputs.

TVETSD programs are yet to mainstream HIV/AIDS. In addition, all levels of the ETSD have weak to no pastoral counseling programs for learners/students.

Table 7.1: Key Recommendations in Sequential Order

Immediate (2009/2010)	Medium-term (2011/2015)	Long-term (2016/2020)
Strengthen policy and strategic direction for future sector development		
• Revise the 1999 sector policy with emphasis on translating the sector into a national and seamless LLL system with real pathways and equal opportunities for all. The policy should respond to the current national development reform agenda. It should also be cognizant of current global thinking on the role of ETSD in supporting knowledge-driven growth and social equity. • Develop a long-term sector strategy that operationalizes the national sector policy and that promotes a balanced development of the sector. • Develop a simulation model to estimate the cost of proposed sector reforms, affordability and sustainability of the strategy and to guide policy debates and decisions on trade-offs between investments in the sector. • Finalize the draft TVETSD policy in line with the national sector policy. • Finalize the draft ECCD policy and align it to the sector policy.	• Develop an ABET policy. • Develop a sector-specific ICTs policy that is anchored in the national ICTs policy. • Develop a sector-specific HIV/AIDS policy. • Develop a GET textbook policy to guide provision, distribution, management and utilization. • Develop a higher-education policy which emphasizes the subsector's leadership in knowledge and innovation, national development and Swaziland's global competitiveness. • Update the 1983 Education Act to better enable the implementation of new policies. • Update subsector specific Bills and Acts in alignment with the new Education Act. • [MoPSI to finalize the HRDS]	• Periodically update the sector policy, and strategy to reflect new development challenges.

(Table continues on next page)

Table 7.1 (continued)

Immediate (2009/2010)	Medium-term (2011/2015)	Long-term (2016/2020)
\multicolumn{3}{c}{**Adopt a balanced expansion of access to ETSD**}		
• Apply the above mentioned simulation model to guide an appropriate balance in expansion of access, staying cognizant of the national development imperatives. • From 2010, implement the universal free primary education policy (UFPE). • Extend the primary school entry to 8 years in order to fast track UFPE. • Where demand warrants it, extend Sebenta programs to select primary schools and provide NUPE programs to all children of primary school-going age. • Benchmark NUPE levels to those of formal primary education and allow for primary school re-entry at grade/age appropriate levels. • Make provision for adult learners who complete NUPE to write primary school leaving examinations. • Adopt a policy to dissociate the intake of SCOT and UNISWA from the number of available Government scholarships. The policy should also allow for fee-paying students to be admitted by these institutions.	• Expand pro-poor ECD access to reach 60 percent NER and expand pro-poor pre-primary access to reach 80 percent NER. • Expand formal and nonformal primary education access to enable a '100 percent' NER. • Sustain the extended primary school entry age until 2012, and then revert to the 6-year entry. • Expand physical capacity for a 100 percent progression from primary to junior secondary education. • Expand senior secondary education access to 50 percent NER. • Re-register all "illegal schools" based on their compliance with the BMP (below). • Expand physical capacity for 15 percent progression from junior secondary school to VET. • Upgrade 4 RECs into VTC and introduce Level III training for secondary school learners. • Attain full operational capacity for SCOT and UNISWA.	• Expand pro-poor ECD access to reach 80 percent NER and pro-poor pre-primary access to reach 100 percent NER. • Expand senior secondary education access to reach a 60 percent NER. • Upgrade 4 RECs into VTCs and sustain the provision of Level III training for secondary school learners. • Expand physical capacity for a 30 percent progression from junior secondary to VET • Expand physical capacity for 80 percent progression rate from senior secondary to tertiary education and training comprising: • 40 percent TVETSD, including nursing education and health sciences; • 20 percent HE; • 20 percent educator training.

(Table continues on next page)

Table 7.1 (continued)

Immediate (2009/2010)	Medium-term (2011/2015)	Long-term (2016/2020)
Eradicate sources of inequalities of ETSD opportunities		

• Adopt a per capita financing framework for GET and TVETSD to enable fiscal resources to follow students rather than follow nonfiscal resources.
• Eradicate financial barriers to primary education by abolishing direct and indirect costs for all primary education pupils within the formal and nonformal system.
• Sustain grants for OVC.
• Develop an inclusive education policy.
• Articulate a quota system for admitting children from rural and poorly resourced schools to grade 8 and grade 11 and develop academic support programs to enable them to catch up with their counterparts.
• Design an incentive package including salary increments and promotion criterion and redeploy qualified teachers to rural schools.
	• Create physical capacity for a 60 percent NER for ECD.
	• Adopt a per capita financing formula for ECD and pre-primary education.
	• Sustain grants for OVC and make them conditional on successful completion.
	• Eradicate physical barriers to access to GET by:
	  o implementing the inclusive education policy;
	  o articulating, adopting and implementing a catchment area policy that enables all GET learners to be within a 3 kilometer radius of their school or within a 30 minute walking distance from their school;
	  o developing a learner transport policy and implementing it;
	  o developing an operational plan for mitigating socio-cultural barriers to GET learners such as HIV/AIDS stigma, cultural discrimination and class discrimination;
	• Implement the grade 8 and grade 11 admission quota system.
		• Create physical capacity for an 80 percent NER for ECD.
		• Sustain conditional grants for OVCs.
		• Articulate and formally adopt a GET funding formula that allows for a household-to-Government contribution ratio of 10:90 for junior secondary education and 20:80 for senior secondary education.
		• Eradicate physical barriers to GET by:
		  o creating capacity for 80 percent progression rate from primary to secondary education;
		  o developing and implementing a hostel policy where the catchment area and learner transport are not effective solutions;
		  o implementing the operational plan for mitigating socio-cultural barriers to GET access.

(Table continues on next page)

Table 7.1 (continued)

Immediate (2009/2010)	Medium-term (2011/2015)	Long-term (2016/2022)
Improve and consolidate the quality of ETSD		
• Formally adopt a competency based GET and TVETSD. • Adopt a policy to introduce a time bound teacher/instructor licensee. • Adopt a policy to import qualified mathematics, science and ICTs teachers. • Articulate a localization plan for mathematics, science and ICTs expatriate teachers. • Adopt a policy to introduce tertiary pre-entry programs for mathematics, science and ICTs. The service provider for these programs should be selected on a competitive basis.	• Define competencies to be acquired at each GET and TVETSD level. • Define competencies that teachers/instructors need to teach at each level of the ETSDS. • Revise GET and TVETSD curricula in line with competency-based education and training (CBET). • Revise assessment tools to reflect agreed GET and TVETSD competencies. • Revise student report cards to communicate acquisition of agreed competencies. • Develop standards for GET and TVETSD. • Develop input norms for GET/VET institutions and articulate a BMP for each level of these institutions. • Develop and adopt the national qualification framework (NQF) based on the standards for students and educators/instructors. • Revise teacher education and instructor curricula to prepare educators for CBET. • Develop a time bound teacher/instructor license system. • Define competencies for GET and TVETSD school/institution heads • Develop a modularized school/institution head training program and integrate financial management in the training program. • Implement tertiary pre-entry programs.	• Implement a time bound teacher/instructor licensee system. • Localize all mathematics, science and ICTs teachers. • Train all school/institution heads, develop their performance standards and place them on performance contracts. • Re-register all GET/VET institutions in compliance with the NQF and the BMP. • Once all GET/VET institutions are in compliance with the BMP, articulate the optimum package for all institutions to comply with.

(Table continues on next page)

Table 7.1 (continued)

Immediate (2009/2010)	Medium-term (2011/2015)	Long-term (2016/2020)
Improve resource efficiency and diversify the financing base		
• Optimize the use of current physical capacity for ECCD, TVETSD and HE capacity. • Implement the current repetition policy. • Adopt the policy to increase STR at all levels of the system. • Appoint a private entity to manage the tertiary student loan scheme, and charge it to optimize repayment rates to 30 percent. • Redesign the scholarship scheme into a fully-recoverable loan scheme, and delegate its management to the private entity. • Decentralize the management of SCOT and VOCTIM and allow them to manage their own source revenues. • Institute the payroll levy. • Articulate and implement an operational plan for re-attracting international development partners to the sector.	• Rationalize the GET curriculum into 4 core subjects and 3 electives. • Transfer prevocational subjects from GET schools to VET institutions and replace them with a level III qualification. • Increase STR to 40:1 for primary education, 35:1 for secondary education, and 15:1 for tertiary institutions. • Reduce tertiary unit cost by expanding enrollments (refer to recommendation on access) and thus increasing the STR as outlined above. • Reduce the duration of UNISWA courses by 1 year. • Implement the new student loan scheme. • Optimize the tertiary loans repayment rate to 60 percent. • Streamline and improve the sector budget structure to enable effective monitoring of spending. This should include cleared separation of spending items line, unbundling OVCs grants from "administration," clear delineation of ABET and TVETSD expenditure, and the inclusion of scholarships under the budgets of respective recipient institution.	• SCOT and UNISWA should contribute 10 percent of their expenditure from their own source revenues. • Optimize tertiary repayment rates to no less than 80 percent.

(Table continues on next page)

Table 7.1 (continued)

Immediate (2009/2010)	Medium-term (2011/2015)	Long-term (2016/2020)
Improve relevance		
• Establish the NTA with employer majority and employee representation in the board of directors. • Expand industry representation on the University Council.	• Commence a phased implementation of CBET. • Implement the NQF. • Regularize student tracer studies exploiting the potential for web-based self-tracer. • Regularize periodic review of TVETSD programs. • [MoEE to regularize labor surveys.]	
Strengthen management capacity		

• Against an adopted sector strategy, undertake a full audit for the MoE's delivery capacity, and develop a capacity development program. However, immediately:
• expand the EMIS by seconding two qualified personnel from the CSO to the MoE to re-establish the EMIS unit at the MoE;
  ○ redesign the EMIS and its yearly publication to facilitate effective monitoring of sector programs;
  ○ strengthen the capacity of the planning unit of the MoE by appointing an additional policy research and planning specialist;
  ○ elaborate the mandate of the planning unit to include the monitoring and evaluation of the sector programs;
  ○ train at least two staff of the planning unit on budgeting.
	• Develop a capacity development program and integrate it into the first medium-term sector program.
	• Implement the capacity development program.	

References

ADEA. 2008. 2008 Biennale on Education in Africa. *The Challenge of TVETSD Reform in Mozambique: Goals, Options and Constraints*. ADEA.

AIDS Information Center. 2000. Kampala. Uganda.

Allen, Irma A. 1985. *The Development of a National Core Curriculum for Pre-School Staff Development in Swaziland*. Report presented to Ministry of Education and UNICEF, Swaziland.

Altman, M. and Mayer, M. 2003. "Overview of Industrial Policy," in Human Sciences Research Council (2003), Human Resource Development Review 2003: Education, Employment and Skills in South Africa, HSRC Press, Cape Town.

Atchoarena, David and Paul Esquieu, eds. 2002. *Private Technical and Vocational Education in Sub-Saharan Africa: Provision, Patterns and Policy Issues*. IIEP, UNESCO, Paris.

Batra, G. and Andrew Stone. 2004. "World Business Environment Survey," in *Global Competitiveness Report 2004/05*; and *Investment Climate, Capabilities and Firm Performance: Evidence from the World Business Environment Survey*. Washington, D.C., World Bank.

Banerjee, A., Galiani S., Levinsohn, J. and Woolard, I. 2006. "Why is Unemployment So High in South Africa?" CID South Africa Project Report, Harvard University, July.

Bell, B, Devarajan, S., Gersbach, H. 2003. "The Long-Run Economic Costs of AIDS: Theory and an Application to South Africa."World Bank, Washington, DC.

Bennell, Paul. 1999. "Learning to Change: Skills Development Among the Economically Vulnerable and Socially Excluded in Developing Countries." ILO, Employment and Training Working Paper No. 43, ILO: Geneva.

Bloom, David E., Ajay Mahal, and River Path Associates. 2002. "HIV/AIDS and the Private Sector – A Literature Review."

Bloom D., Canning D. and Chan K. 2006. "Higher education and development in Africa." Africa Region Human Development Working Paper. 102. World Bank. Washington D.C.

Bhorat, H. Lundall, P. Rospabe, S. 2002. "The South African Labor Market in a Globalizing World: Economic and Legislative Considerations." International Labor Organization. ISBN 92-2-113057-6.

Bhorat, H. and Lundall, P. 2002: "Employment, wages and skills development: Firm specific effects – Evidence from two firm surveys in South Africa." Development Policy Research Unit: Working Paper No. 02/68, Cape Town.

Burger, R. and Yu, D., 2007. "Wage Trends in Post-Apartheid South Africa: Constructing an Earnings Series from Household Survey Data." Working Papers 9609, University of Cape Town, Development Policy Research Unit.

Central Statistical Office 2008. *Swaziland demographic and health survey 2006-07.* Mbabane (report and dataset). Available from: <http://www.measuredhs.com> [Accessed July 2008].

Chaturvedi, E., B.C. Srivastava, J.V. Singh, and M. Prasad. 1987. "Impact of Six Years' Exposure to the ICDS Scheme on Psychosocial Development." Indian Pediatrics 24:153-64.

Chisholm L., Makawti, G., Marope, M. and Safuli, S. 1998. SADC initiatives in education policy development, planning and management: Report of a needs assessment study. Harare: UNESCO and Mbabane: SADC Human Resources Development Sector.

DANIDA. 2002. "Evaluation Report: Danish Assistance to Vocational Education and Training." Ministry of Foreign Affairs, Copenhagen.

Dahlman, C., Zeng, D. and Wang. S. 2007. Enhancing China's competitiveness through life-long learning. The World Bank, Washington D.C.

Dias, R. and Posel, D. 2007. "Unemployment, Education and Skills Constraints in Post-Apartheid South Africa." DPRU Working Paper 07/120, March. http://www.commerce.uct.ac.za/research_units/dpru/WorkingPapers/PDF_Files/WP_07-120.pdf

Draft Action Program for the Reduction of Poverty (2005–2015), PRSAP Volume 2. Poverty Reduction Task Force, Ministry of Economic Planning and Development, March 2005, Swaziland.

Earthtrends Country Profiles. Economic Indicators—Swaziland. Http://earthtrends.wri.org/pdf_library/country_profiles/eco_cou_748.pdf.

Edwards, L. 2003. "A firm-level analysis of trade, technology and employment in South Africa," Discussion Paper 5, Globalization and Poverty Program, Department of Economics, University of Cape Town, Cape Town.

Edwards, L. and R. Lawrence. 2006. "South African Trade Policy Matters: Trade Performance and Trade Policy." National Bureau of Economic Research Working Paper No. 12760.

Fasih T. 2008. "Linking education policy to labor market outcomes." Washington, DC, World Bank.

Flethcher, Frances Gail. 1993. "The Tender Years: A Guide and Reference for Pre-School Teachers in Swaziland." National Spiritual Assembly of Baha'is of Swaziland, P.O. Box 298, Mbabane.

Food & Beverage SETA. 2005. "Sectoral Skills Plan: 2005-2010." Draft Document: October 2005, Food & Beverage SETA, Pretoria.

Forsythe 2002. Whalley, Amy and Alan Whiteside. 2007 "Reviewing Emergencies-Shifting the Paradigm for a New Era," National Emergency Council on HIV/AIDS (NERCHA), September.

Gerein, N., Green, B, and Pearson, S. 2006. "The Implications of Shortages of Health Professionals for Maternal Health in Sub-Saharan Africa." *Reproductive Health Matters* 14(27): 40–50.

Glewwe, P., H.G. Jacoby, and E.M. King. 2001. "Early Childhood Nutrition and Academic Achievement: A Longitudinal Analysis." *Journal of Public Economics* 81(3): 345–368.

Glewwe P., E. Maiga, and H. Zheng 2007. "The contribution of education to economic growth in sub-Saharan Africa: Review of evidence." Department of Applied Economics. University of Minnesota.

Goldberg, Itzhak, Lee Branstetter, John Gabriel Goddard, and Smita Kuriakose. 2008. "Globalization and Technology Absorption in Europe and Central Asia: The Role of Trade, FDI, and Cross-border Knowledge Flows." Working Paper No. 150. World Bank, Washington, DC.

Government of the Kingdom of Swaziland. *The Industrial and Vocational Training Act, 1982. Act No. 16 of 1982.* Ministry of Enterprise and Employment.

———. 1984. *National Education Review Commission (NERCOM).*

———. 2003. *The Human Resources Planning and Development Bill, 2003.* Draft working document.

Grantham-McGregor, S.M., C.A. Powell, S.P. Walker, and J.H. Himes. 1991. "Nutritional Supplementation, Psychosocial Stimulation, and Mental Development of Stunted Children: The Jamaica Study." Lancet 338:1-5.

Gustafsson, M. and van der Berg, S. *Economic and financial aspects of education in Swaziland: Input into World Bank Review of Education and Training in Swaziland*

Hanushek E. and Kimko D. 2000. "Schooling, labor-force quality and the growth of nations." *American Economic Review.* 90:1184-1208.

Hanushek E. and Wößmann. 2007. Education quality and economic growth. Washington DC. The World Bank. De Ferranti et al. 2003. Closing the gap in education and technology. Washington DC, The World Bank.

IIEP: SACMEQ (2004). SACMEQ II 2000 dataset. Harare.

International Monetary Fund. 2008. Staff Report for the 2007 Article IV Consultations. IMF.

———. 2006. *Staff Report for the 2005 Article IV Consultations.* IMF.

———. 2008. World Economic Outlook Database.

International Organization for Migration. 2008. *World Migration Report 2008,* p. 411.

Davies, J., T. Weko, L. Kim and E.W. Thulstrup, "Thematic Review of Tertiary Education: Finland." OECD, Paris, 2006.

Johanson, Richard. 2004. "Implications of Globalization and Economic Restructuring for Skills Development in Sub-Sahara Africa," ILO Geneva, June 2004.

Johanson, Richard, and Arvil Van Adams. 2004. *Skills Development in Sub-Saharan Africa.* World Bank, Washington, D. C.

King, Kenneth and Robert Palmer. 2006. "Skills Development and Poverty Reduction." *The Post-basic Education and Training Working Paper Series No. 9.* Edinburgh: Centre for African Studies, and "Skills, Poverty Reduction, Growth and Equity: The Lessons."

Kitaev, Igor. 2002. "Synthesis of Main Findings from Two Studies on Private Technical-Vocational Education and Training in Ghana and Zambia. (Phase II)", draft ILO International Training Center, Turin.

Krueger, A. and Lindhal M. 2001. "Education and Growth: Why and for Whom? *Journal of Economic Literature* 39 (4): 1101-36

Litchfield, Daphne O. 2007. *An investigation of problems faced by the preschool program in the Manzini region*. Thesis submitted in partial fulfillment of the requirement for the degree of Bachelor of Education Faculty of Education, University of Swaziland

Lokshin, Michael M., Elena Glinskaya, and Marito Garcia. 2000. "The effect of early childhood development programs on women's labor force participation and older children's schooling in Kenya". Policy Research Working Paper no. WPS 2376. World Bank, Washington, D.C.

Lumbila. K. 2005. "What makes FDI work? A panel analysis of the growth effect of FDI in Africa." Africa Region Working Paper No. 80. World Bank, Washington D.C.

Macwele, M & Mgotiama, Z. 2002." Swaziland: Adult basic and literacy education in SADC: Towards a regional strategy." Paper presented at the Centre for Adult Education, University of Natal Pietermaritzburg, 3-6 December.

Marope. M.T. 2005. Namibia human capital and knowledge development for growth with equity. The World Bank, Washington, D.C. NB: The Higher returns in Namibia could reflect the scarcity premium.

Ministry of Education. 1999. *National Education Policy Statement*.

Ministry of Education and UNICEF, Swaziland. Caring for Our Children: Manual for Caregivers.

Ministry of Economic Planning and Development (MEPD). 2006a. Vol. 1:42.

———. 2006b. *Yingcamu: Poverty Reduction Strategy and Action Program*. Volumes 1 and 2. The Poverty Reduction Task Force.

———. 2006c. Yingcamu: Towards Shared Growth and Empowerment. Poverty Reduction Strategy and Action Program, Volume 1. Swaziland.

Ministry of Education. 1990. "Skills for the Future: The Relevance of School and Tertiary Education to the World of Work." Report of the Special Committee to Study Pre-Vocational Education, Mbabane. October.

Ministry of Finance, 2008. *Estimates for years from 1st April 2007 to 31st March 2010*. Mbabane.

Ministry of Public Service and Information (MOPSI). 2005. *National Skills Survey, Swaziland: Final Report*. UNISWA Consultancy and Training Center. February 28.

Msibi, Themba C. 1998. *Role and function of pre-school education in preparing children for the first three grades in primary school in Swaziland*. Thesis submitted in partial fulfillment of the requirement for the degree of Bachelor of Education. Faculty of Education, University of Swaziland

Mutula, S. and Van Brakel, P. 2007. "ICT skills readiness for the emerging global digital economy among small businesses in developing countries. Case Study of Botswana." February 2007.

Myers, Robert. 1995. The Twelve Who Survive: Strengthening Programs of Early Childhood Development in the Third World. 2nd Ed. Ypsilanti, Mich.: High/Scope Press.

Myers, Robert, et al. 1985. "Preschool Education as a Catalyst for Community Development." Report prepared for U.S. Agency for International Development, Lima, Peru.

National Development Strategy. 1999. *Vision 2022, Key macro and sectoral strategies*. Mbabane: Government Printer.

National Review Commission on Education (NARCOM Report), 1985. "Reform Through Dialogue," February.

NERCHA. 2008. Presentation.

Nicci Earle & Andrew NM Paterson The shape of demand for high-level agricultural skills in the South African labor market in Development Southern Africa. Vol. 24, No. 4, October 2007.

NORRAG News No. 37. "Education and Training Out of Poverty: A Status Report." May.

OECD. 2000. "Links between Policy and Growth: Cross Country Evidence." *Economic Outlook.* 68:133-154.

———. 2005. *Education at a Glance.* Paris.

———. 2008. *African Economic Outlook 2008 – Mozambique Country Report.*

———. 2008. *African Economic Outlook 2008 – Namibia Country Report.*

Paes de Barros, R., and R. Mendonça. 1999. "Costs and Benefits of Pre-school Education in Brazil." Rio de Janeiro: Institute of Applied Economic Research.

Physicians for Human Rights. 2007. Epidemic of Inequality: Women's Rights and HIV/AIDS in Botswana and Swaziland. Cambridge, Massachusetts.

Press Release, Consulta, San Jose Costa Rica, October 25, 2007 (http://www.iadb.org/res/ConsultaSanJose/).

Reporters Without Borders. 2006 *Annual Report.*

Roberts, Jennifer. December 2003. "Vocational Education and Training in the Kingdom of Swaziland,) SADC VET Project.

School Referral Program Implementation Report (2006).

Sebenta National Institute. 2008a. *Sebenta National Institute: strategic plan, 2008-2011.* Mbabane: Lwatio Management Services.

———. 2008b. *Sebenta National Institute: Annual financial statements for the year 31 March, 2007.* Mbabane: Price water house.

———. 2008c. *Annual report 2006.* Mbabane: Sebenta National Institute.

Siaciwena, R. 2007. *A review of the Institute of Distance Education (IDE) of the University of Swaziland: A study commissioned by the Commonwealth of Learning*, Vancouver, Canada.

Simelane, T. 2008. *New AIDS figures: 26% HIV positive.* Retrieved on the 8th August, 2008 from the World Wide Web: http/www.osisa.org/node/9536.

South Africa. 2005. Income and Expenditure Survey.

Swaziland College of Technology. "2007/2008 Prospectus."

Swaziland Ministry of Education and European Development Fund. 2009. Support to Education and Training in Swaziland; Direct Decentralized Operation; Program Estimate No. 3, Operational Period from 16 November 2007 to 31 March 2009.

Telecom Namibia. 2006. Annual Report 2005/2006.

Tuck, Ron. 2007. *An Introductory Guide to National Qualification Frameworks: Conceptual and Practical Issues for Policy Makers.* ILO, Geneva.

UNDP. 2009. Human Development Report. http://hdrstats.undp.org/countries_fact_sheets/cty_fs_SWZ.html. Accessed Jan 16, 2009.

UNESCO: UIS. 2008. Education statistics (dataset). Montreal. Available from: <http://www.uis.unesco.org/ev_en.php?URL_ID=3753&URL_DO=DO_TOPIC&URL_SECTION=201> [Accessed July 2007].

UNESCO. 2006. Global Education Digest. Paris.
UNESCO BREDA. 2005. EFA paving the way for action. UNESCO, Dakar. Senegal.
UNICEF. 2001. *The State of the World's Children Report.*
UNICEF. 2006. *Report on the Assessment of Neighborhood Care Points, Swaziland.*
UNISWA Consultancy and Training Center, *National Skills survey, Swaziland: Final Report.* February 28, 2005
Verspoor A. M. with SEIA Team. 2008. "At the Crossroads. Choices for Secondary Education in Sub-Saharan Africa." The World Bank. Washington DC.
Vilakazi, Lineo. 2000. *Situation Assessment Report: Early Childhood Care and Development in Swaziland.* Ministry of Education and UNICEF.
VOCTIM. 2007. Annual Report to the MoE.
Xaba, Mildred. 2006. *School Health Program Report, 2006.* Ministry of Health and Social Welfare, 2006, Swaziland.
Young, Mary E., and Linda M. Richardson. 2007. "Early Childhood Development: From Measurement to Action." Children and Youth Unit, Human Development Network. World Bank, Washington, DC.
Young, Michael. 2005. "National qualifications frameworks: Their feasibility for effective implementation in developing countries." Skills Working Paper No. 22. ILO, Geneva.
World Bank. 2000. *Can Africa Claim the 21st Century?* Washington, D.C.
World Bank. 2006. "Swaziland: Achieving Education for All Challenges and Policy Directions." Washington, DC, World Bank.
———. June 2007. "An Assessment of the Investment Climate in Swaziland," Regional Enterprise Development Program, Pretoria. Draft. (Hereinafter referred to as "ICA" report). Washington DC. World Bank.
———. 2008a. *Kingdom of Swaziland Interim Strategy Note.* Washington DC: World Bank.
———. 2008b. *World Development Indicators.* Washington DC. World Bank.
———. 2009a. *Accelerating Catch-up. Tertiary Education for Growth in Sub-Saharan Africa.* Washington DC. World Bank.
———. 2009b. Public Expenditure Review: Fiscal Sustainability and the Management of Swaziland's SACU Revenue Windfall. Washington, DC, World Bank.
———. Early Childhood Development Website. http://web.worldbank.org/WBSITE/EXTERNAL/TOPICS/EXTCY/EXTECD/0,,contentMDK:20260272~menuPK:521671~pagePK:210058~piPK:210062~theSitePK:344939,00.html
World Economic Forum. 2009. *Global Competitiveness Report.*

APPENDIX

Applicable Practices and Lessons from the Republic of Korea and Singapore

Strong and focused government leadership backed by robust growth enabled the implementation of substantial sector reforms within a reasonably short period of time. Between 1965 and 1999, Singapore's GDP multiplied by a factor of 7, while that of the Republic of Korea increased by a factor of 7.8. Korea's GDP per capita increased from US$100 in the 1960s to US$15,000 in 2005, with exports leaping from US$1 billion in the 1970s to US$250 billion in 2005. This level of growth enabled the governments to afford the reforms and to reduce private costs to ETSD.

Clear strategic orientation and prioritization of development reforms: Singapore deliberately planned development reforms with three distinct phases: (i) a third tier rapid and labor absorbing industrializing economy from the early 1960s, (ii) a second tier capital intensive economy starting in the early 1980s and (iii) a knowledge-based economy starting in the early 1990s. Korea progressed through four planned development phases: (i) economic disruption and recovery 1945-1960, (ii) export oriented high-growth 1961-1979, (iii) structural adjustment and stabilized growth 1980-2000, and (iv) transition to a KBE 2001-to date.

Aligning sector reforms with overall national development reform agenda: Across the two cases, major sector reforms were impelled by the need to respond to the human capital needs emerging from the national development reform agenda. Singapore's development reforms impelled three waves of sector reforms: starting with a technically-oriented system where emphasis was placed on exposing learners to technical skills, followed by an efficiency-driven education, then an ability-driven phase. Korea's sector reforms responded to its four stages of development and followed these four phases: (i) reconstruction and the expansion of access with emphasis on attaining UPE; (ii) expansion of secondary education access and the development of TVETSD including technical high schools; (iii) improving the quality of general education and training, coupled with the expansion of access to higher education, with the latter emphasizing relevance and competitiveness; and (iv) human resources development with emphasis on relevance, acquisition of core competencies, and the promotion of LLL among others.

Emphasis on labor market responsiveness: With clear signals from the overall development reform, Singapore's sector programs were consistently adapted to the emerging labor market demands. In 1964 Singapore established vocational secondary schools to meet market demands of the intended rapid labor-absorbing industrialization. By 1968, all male students were to have a two-year exposure to technical subjects, while female students were given an option to register for home economics and one technical subject. Within two decades, 20 percent of secondary students were taking technical education. In the early 1980s they emphasized science and technology to create a labor force that would support its overall strategy to attract high-tech FDIs and to promote R&D. The second phase of development, therefore, entailed the expansion of access to higher education with an emphasis on science and engineering graduates. The 1990s saw a shift from the efficiency-based education of the 1980s to ability-driven education. The move to KBE also implied the need for continuous learning.

Sustained, aggressive, and sequenced expansion of access starting at the lower levels: within 2 decades Singapore attained UPE and universal lower secondary education, allowing for attention to be focused on quality. In the late 1940s, Korea had 53 percent adult illiteracy, and 12.6 percent of its population had secondary education or higher. Within 5 decades, it had reached 90 percent NER for primary, middle school, and high school by 1957, 1990, and 1999, respectively. More than 50 percent of high school graduates entered higher education.

The massification of quality education backed by labor-absorbing growth and effective demand for skills enabled shared growth.

Emphasis on quality: Within 40 years—1965 to 2005—Singapore developed an education system from a state that was comparable to that of most current developing countries, to one that is comparable to OECD countries, and even better in some respects. Some of the quality enhancing strategies were: differentiated curricula, streaming of primary school learners from grade 2 (in 1979) and of secondary learners from Form 2 (in 1980), emphasis on higher order thinking and the understanding of concepts, regular student assessment, enhanced use of ICTs as a management tool and to facilitate learner-centered instruction, and collaborative learning. In addition, schools were given autonomy over the curriculum and could customize it to their students' perceived abilities and expressed interests. Enrichment programs for 6 to 16 year olds were developed, including a foreign country visit program. Attractive incentive packages were developed to retain quality teachers. They were offered higher remuneration than medical doctors, civil servants, and entry point lawyers, and a fully subsidized 100 hours of in-service professional training per year.

Emphasis on equity: Well-structured sector plans enabled Singapore to improve education standards with equal treatment for all learners. Early on the system emphasized mathematics and science. Korea abolished entrance examinations for primary and secondary schools, and replaced them with a lottery assignment. They replaced specific higher education institution entrance examinations with a national one, instituted and enforced a catchment area system, allocated more resources to schools in a poor condition, reduced costs by providing free textbooks, and declared private tutoring illegal and replaced it with school broadcast programs.

Clear priority setting and appropriate budgeting: In 1965, Singapore's education budget accounted for nearly 29 percent of the total government budget, 59 percent of which was allocated to primary education, 27 percent to secondary education, and 14 percent to higher education.

Resource efficiency: During the early efforts to universalize access, Singapore instituted a range of cost saving measures such as double and even triple shifting of physical facilities, managing teachers' salaries, high Stirs, and low cost but high quality books and instructional materials. Korea also adopted resource-efficient measures in the early stages, including large classes and double to triple shifts.

Capable institutions with capacity to implement reforms: Capably-led institutions and unwavering commitment to implement reforms were also key to Singapore's successful reforms.

Eco-Audit

Environmental Benefits Statement

The World Bank is committed to preserving Endangered Forests and natural resources. We print World Bank Working Papers and Country Studies on postconsumer recycled paper, processed chlorine free. The World Bank has formally agreed to follow the recommended standards for paper usage set by Green Press Initiative—a nonprofit program supporting publishers in using fiber that is not sourced from Endangered Forests. For more information, visit www.greenpressinitiative.org.

In 2008, the printing of these books on recycled paper saved the following:

Trees*	Solid Waste	Water	Net Greenhouse Gases	Total Energy
289	8,011	131,944	27,396	92 mil.
*40 feet in height and 6–8 inches in diameter	Pounds	Gallons	Pounds CO_2 Equivalent	BTUs